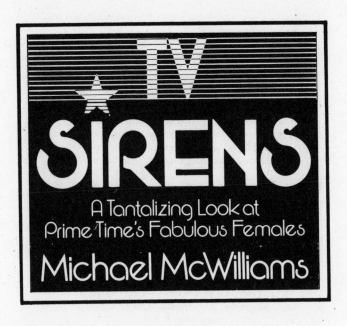

★ TV SIRENS

A Tantalizing Look at Prime Time's Fabulous Females

Michael McWilliams

A Perigee Book

Perigee Books
are published by
The Putnam Publishing Group
200 Madison Avenue
New York, NY 10016

Portions of this book originally appeared in *The Village Voice*.

Designed by Oksana Kushnir

Library of Congress Cataloging-in-Publication Data

McWilliams, Michael.
TV sirens.

1. Television personalities—United States
—Biography. 2. Actresses—United States—
Biography. I. Title.
PN1992.4.A2M46   1986   86-15113
791.45′028′0922
ISBN 0-399-51292-6

Printed in the United States of America
3   4   5   6   7   8   9   10

I'd like to thank Jim Vesely and Cliff Ridley of the *Detroit News* and Jim Forkan of *Advertising Age* for their indispensable generosity; Stephen Harvey and Jim Baker for their kindness and intelligence; Richard Goldstein and Karen Durbin for helping me find my voice at *The Voice*; Gene Brissie of Putnam for his uncommon patience; Mary McWilliams Fadden for loving her children without treating them as children, and her mother, Santa Toarmina, who once, while raising six kids during the Depression, wrestled a social worker to the ground and bit her on the leg.

For the photos in this book, I'd like to thank CBS-TV, NBC-TV, ABC-TV, PBS, Warner Bros. Television, Aaron Spelling Productions, Columbia Pictures Television, Lorimar-Telepictures Corp., United Artists Television, Embassy Television, Universal Television, Viacom International, MTM Enterprises, Filmways, Paramount Television, MGM Television, Twentieth Century Fox Television, and Metromedia.

For Stuart, Peter, and Denis

It's not the men in your life that count—it's the life in your men.

—Mae West

Contents

Introduction

Forget the pyrotechnics of MTV, the proliferation of buddy-buddy cop shows, the ascendance of family-oriented sitcoms. *The* prime-time phenomenon of the '80s is the Revenge of the TV Diva. Television has revived the halcyon days of Hollywood by becoming a veritable diva dumping ground.

Joan Collins, always a poor man's Taylor until *Dynasty,* is the Queen Bee, but it doesn't stop there. There's Diahann Carroll and Ali MacGraw keeping Alexis company, Barbara Stanwyck and Katharine Ross spicing up *The Colbys,* Ava Gardner and Ruth Roman gracing *Knots Landing,* and Barbara Bel Geddes holding down the fort on *Dallas.* There's Jane Wyman on *Falcon Crest,* with limited appearances by Lana Turner, Gina Lollobrigida, and Celeste Holm. There's Kim Novak and Tippi Hedren resurrecting Hitchcock, Elizabeth Taylor and Jean Simmons sprucing up *North and South,* and Dorothy Malone and Ruth Warrick returning to *Peyton Place.* There's Joan Fontaine replacing Loretta Young on *Dark Mansions,* Angela Lansbury carrying a Top-10 show, and Doris Day primping for pet care. There are TV movies with Katharine Hepburn, Bette Davis, Sylvia Sidney, and Lucille Ball. There are guest shots by Ginger Rogers on *Glitter,* Jane Russell on *The Yellow Rose,* Gwen Verdon on *Magnum, P.I.,* Debbie Reynolds on *Hotel,* and Yvonne De Carlo on *Murder, She Wrote.* There are more guest shots by Dorothy McGuire on *St. Elsewhere,* June Allyson on *Airwolf,* Dorothy Lamour on *Crazy Like a Fox,* and Olivia De Havilland, Luise Rainer, and Spelling-knows-who-else on the unsinkable *Love Boat.* And need we point out that Stanwyck, Simmons, and Ingrid Bergman all won Emmys since a marginal Warners player was elected President?

If Nancy is the power behind that throne, the diva is the force behind the predominant genre of '80s television: the soap opera. This form belongs to the diva because it allows her to squeeze irony out of emotional excess (unlike the sitcom queen, the diva is a comedienne by proxy). It's telling that the diva and her genre were resurrected simultaneously. She may seem emblematic of a reactionary time, an age obsessed with the trappings of wealth and power, but her actual impulse is revolutionary. Unlike the male action hero, who subscribes to a code of honor, the soap-opera diva revises her life according to her feelings. She's a self-made woman. Her genre is a pretext, a means of projecting her image. The image is survivalist and inevitably nostalgic. That's the paradox of the diva: she's her own creation and her own institution, at once subversive and traditional. In the anti-inventive '80s, she thrives.

The other great period for TV divas was the '50s. Wyman, Young, and Ida Lupino ruled the airwaves when virgins (Doris Day, Audrey Hepburn) and whores (Marilyn Monroe, Ava Gardner) dominated Hollywood. Even then, the pioneers were faced with an array of supporting players from the '30s and '40s who'd become comedy stars through television: Lucille Ball, Eve Arden, Ann Sothern. By the '60s, the pioneers had to tangle with blockbuster westerns (*Bonanza, Gunsmoke, Wagon Train),* though Stanwyck, never one to be undone, donned spurs for *The Big Valley*. By the '70s, old genres had become camp—except the sitcom, sustained through the inventiveness of MTM and Norman Lear. The TV divas lay in wait, lipstick at the ready, until the social climate shifted in their favor.

There are divas, and there are divas. There are has-been divas (Young, Lollobrigida, Rainer), never-were divas (Holm, Bel Geddes, Allyson), and never-will-be divas (MacGraw, Ross, Linda Evans). There are divas who are great actresses (Stanwyck), good actresses (Wyman), and bad actresses (Turner). There are more divas, in fact, than there are stars in heaven, but the true diva boasts a past as rich as the women she plays. A diva's work is not merely inseparable from her life, it often *is* her life. It seems no accident that Davis's (first) comeback as Margo Channing centered on a middle-aged legend trying to hold onto a younger Gary Merrill. Or that Taylor gave her paramount performance in *X, Y and Zee* (1972) as a brazen wife who'll try anything to keep her burned-out mate from straying. Or that Sophia Loren got to play her own mother in a TV movie. Davis's Emmy-winning role in *Strangers: The Story of a Mother and Daughter* anticipated her offspring's "Bette Dearest" memoir by six years. The importance of television to a diva is that it allows her to maintain the tradition of autobiography.

If autobiography is the content of divahood, self-debasement is its style. Margaret Thatcher's life may parallel her work, but she's far from a diva. A true diva is willing to humiliate herself for a greater glory. Norma Shearer, Greer Garson, Meryl Streep—all are too dignified to qualify. Stanwyck's entire post-'40s career is a case in point. From her embittered adulteress in Fritz Lang's *Clash by Night* to her lascivious matron in TV's *The Thorn Birds,* Stanwyck has virtually defined divahood. She never looked down her nose at television, winning Emmys for three different series over a twenty-three-year period. A true diva risks appearing on television because she's accustomed to being disreputable in order to be adorable.

A diva deliberately exaggerates the masculine and feminine sides of her personality. But unlike Boy George or Annie Lennox, who ape the mannerisms of the opposite gender, the diva absorbs the characteristics of both genders and glorifies them. She is, to quote Antonio Fargas in *Car Wash,* "more man than you'll ever be and more woman than you'll ever get." Dressed to kill, she outfoxes Woman and overpowers Man, but remains remote, singular, perverse. In network television, where any sort of gender bending is anathema, the diva has a field day. Where else can she topple a dynasty wearing a $10,000 gown?

Television has become a camping ground because it's the last stop in a diva's journey toward immortality (there's simply no place for a freelance diva to go *except* television, given the demise of the studio system and the skyrocketing expense of Broadway). Yet camp, in its purest form, barely exists anymore: *Dynasty* is too knowing to be camp, too self-reflexive to be a soap opera. It's *The Joan Collins Story* told in a post-camp style. It can't be turned into a joke, because it already gets the joke. Its popularity rests upon the fact that everybody laughs at (with) it, together.

Malice in Wonderland, the ostensible biography of Louella Parsons and Hedda Hopper that aired in 1985, exists to tell us all about its divas. When Elizabeth Taylor (Louella) glowers at Jane Alexander (Hedda) and snarls, "Honey, I was at the top when you were a has-been practicing to be a never-was," she's telling more about herself than about her character. When Alexander slaps her ass and bellows, "That's prime-grade rump roast and nobody owns it but me," she's showing us how a "serious" actress can work against type and have a good time. The first is saying, "Divahood is my life." The second is saying, "Divahood is fun." Both are saying, "Thank God for television."

The contrast of Alexander (Henry Fonda's favorite Actress) and Taylor (everybody's favorite Movie Star) points up a final fact: TV divahood extends beyond Hollywood legends slumming on television. They may be the Grandes Dames of the medium, but they're far from the whole story. In a sense, every actress gets her "revenge" simply by getting work. It's now respectable for Glenn Close to appear in a TV movie and acceptable for Farrah Fawcett to star in an off-Broadway play. As divisions among media blur, acting gets sharper. Sylvia Sidney fills the small screen with her larger-than-life eyes, while Kathleen Turner brings to the big screen her daytime-soap chutzpah. Hollywood may be dead, but there's a TV diva born every minute.

Note From the Underground

Restricting *TV Sirens* to 200 personalities was no mean feat: prime time has produced more goddesses than the ancient Greeks. I've focused on those stars who best exemplify their respective categories. Still, there are actresses who are difficult to peg to a single slot. Patty Duke is a Miniseries Maven, an Assorted Sitcom Queen, a Harris Harridan, a Mother Figure, a Distinguished Guest & Dramatic Do-Gooder, a Kitchen-Sink Chameleon, an aspiring Grande Dame, and the real-life president of the Screen Actors Guild. But in my heart, she'll always be a Little Darling. Just as the number of TV divas is limited, so are their individual programs. There's not much to say about Ava Gardner in *The Long Hot Summer* except to mention she was wasted in her role. By sticking to pivotal performances, I'm better able to express the essence of a TV diva. Even so, there are heart-breaking omissions. I've tended to concentrate on those women whose careers extend into our present age. This excludes a number of Grande Dame runners-up, who either enjoyed an early success and then vanished or never gained a strong enough foothold in television: Ida Lupino, Sylvia Sidney, Myrna Loy, Alexis Smith, Loretta Young, Joan Bennett, Susan Hayward, Jean Arthur, Eleanor Parker, Claudette Colbert, Teresa Wright, and the ever-elusive Audrey Hepburn. I could have expanded the Glamorous Strangers category to include them all, but some intrepid researcher would undoubtedly have uncovered evidence of an aged Pola Negri in an episode of *Search for Tomorrow*. The contents of this book are but a beginning. I salute all TV divas—wherever they are, have been, or will be.

1
PRIMA DONNA

Barbara Stanwyck

"Does it sound sordid? All right. It sounds sordid."

—Barbara Stanwyck, *Clash by Night*

There are three things you can say to kill a conversation: (1) "I left my wallet at home"; (2) "My malaria is flaring up again"; and (3) "Barbara Stanwyck is the greatest actress of the twentieth century." In his autobiography, *The Name Above the Title,* Frank Capra wrote that when Stanwyck began her film career, she gave everything she had on the first take. So he'd shoot her scenes with multiple cameras to insure the freshness of her performance. "Underneath her sullen shyness smoldered the emotional fires of a young Duse or Bernhardt. Naïve, unsophisticated, caring nothing about makeup, clothes, or hairdos, this chorus girl could grab your heart and rip it to pieces. She knew nothing about camera tricks: how to restrict her body movements in close shots. She just turned it on—and everything else stopped on the stage." Stanwyck's image as the murderous Phyllis Die-

trichson in *Double Indemnity* or the crusty Victoria Barkley in *The Big Valley* is well-earned, but the feeling that shatters her reserve has always been overlooked. When, after icily pursuing Richard Chamberlain in *The Thorn Birds* for two-and-a-half hours, Stanwyck howls through tears, "Inside this stupid body, I am still young! I still feel! I still want! I still dream!," she's taking naked naturalism to the outer limits. Her volatility made her adept at every genre: she's the only diva who has as many comedic masterworks to her credit as dramatic triumphs—half Rosalind Russell and half Ingrid Bergman. Yet the caricature of Stanwyck as a tough-talking dame from the Joan Crawford School of Dramatic Arts persists. There are good reasons for this: both Stanwyck and Crawford endured wretched childhoods; both were Broadway flappers who made good in Hollywood; both were hard, adoptive mothers who cut adrift their naughty children; both married and divorced pretty leading men; both became more mannish as they grew older; and both demanded an exaggerated sense of propriety. But while Crawford

Barbara Stanwyck in The Thorn Birds

remained mannequin-like and rather sweetly humorless, Stanwyck kept getting edgier and more ironic. When, in the late '50s, Crawford was torturing younger underlings in *The Best of Everything*, Stanwyck was rebelling against bourgeois domesticity in *Crime of Passion*—her rage directed as much at her social environment as at grabbing the audience's attention. Basically, Stanwyck combines the glamorous allure of Crawford and the full-throttled naturalism of Bette Davis. But if she's given less credit for her realism than for her artifice, it's because she never got a crack at the kind of tony projects that win Oscars. The titles of her movies alone—from *Ten Cents a Dance* to *Walk on the Wild Side*—evoke Douglas Sirk's defense of Hollywood: "There is a very short distance between high art and trash, and trash that contains the element of craziness is by this very quality nearer to art." As movies grew respectable, TV became the new trash receptacle. In her first TV appearance—live—Stanwyck did a riotous send-up of *Gaslight* on *The Jack Benny Show*. Over the next thirty-five years she racked up more than two hundred performances in series episodes, TV movies, and miniseries. Her first series, *The Barbara Stanwyck Show,* was a dramatic anthology along the lines of *The Loretta Young Show* (which Stanwyck hosted on Loretta's days off). But while Young insisted on dramas of spiritual uplift (she liked playing nuns), Stanwyck descended into gutsier genres—thrillers and soap operas. Though the show won her an Emmy, it lasted a single season. Her recurring role on *The Untouchables* as a hard-nosed government bureaucrat easily exploited her public image as a "tough broad" and a "real pro." This image be-

came the driving force behind Stanwyck's paramount series hit, *The Big Valley,* which ran for four seasons and earned her a second Emmy. But the show, as rousing as it was, miscast Stanwyck—she was never at her best as a patrician toughie upholding civilized virtue (that's Katharine Hepburn stuff). Besides, Stanwyck had already done *Big Valley* on the big screen—in *The Furies*—playing a western heiress as a feisty, vicious colt. The problem is that as Stanwyck got older, the parts to match her talents weren't being written. But as Mary Carson, the lascivious matron in *The Thorn Birds,* Stanwyck constructed an edifice that could be demolished only by love (it's one of her great performances). As Constance on *The Colbys,* Stanwyck was loving, but there was no devil in her soul—she was back to being Victoria again. Ideally, she should have played Maxwell Caulfield's role—a glamorous bitch driven by lust. Also, Stanwyck's age should have been taken into account. She was trying too hard to stay in control, but she's at her best when she loses it. Scenario: Constance, suffering from memory loss, thinks she's eighteen again. She seduces dozens of servants, who are too afraid to refuse her. When she puts the make on her brother (Charlton Heston) at a Republican fund raiser, he reads her the Ten Commandments. So she stabs him to death with a knitting needle. In a tearful courtroom confession, Constance shares a lifetime of rage and regret. Wronged women around the world flock to her side. As the judge reads the verdict, a close-up of Constance freezes for the season cliffhanger. The crowning glory is that Barbara Stanwyck could do it all on the first take.

2
GRANDES DAMES

Ann-Margret
Joan Collins
Angie Dickinson
Faye Dunaway
Ava Gardner

Dorothy McGuire
Agnes Moorehead
Jean Simmons
Elizabeth Taylor
Jane Wyman

The 21 Commandments of the Grande Dame

1. Never wear eye shadow that complements a younger costar's ensemble.
2. Never decline a role when you need to make a payment on the pool.
3. Never read the obituary page in makeup.
4. Never play sports in public.
5. Never accept an award and thank Jesus.
6. Never retrieve anything yourself when you can send a limo for it.
7. Never brag about affairs with other women.
8. Never kiss a leading man who's older than you are.
9. Never consent to an authorized biography.
10. Never make any public statement about any political issue under any circumstances ever.
11. Never wear a cardigan sweater unless you're playing a woman who's dying.
12. Never allow yourself to be directed by Paul Newman or Robert Redford.
13. Never resist the urge to smoke a cigarette when you damn well feel like it.
14. Never check into the Betty Ford Center just because everybody else is doing it.
15. Never accept a role that makes you feel closer to the little people.
16. Never show creases when another actor steals a scene.
17. Never speak to a camera from *Entertainment Tonight*.
18. Never say anything about children, and avoid working with them.
19. Never marry more than ten times.
20. Never tell Joan Rivers anything.
21. Never act like a Grande Dame on the set or you won't be treated like one.

Ann-Margret in Who Will Love My Children?

character that she seemed to disappear: she was neither herself nor the woman she was playing—she was the emotion that bonded them together. This is what TV, with its fanatical attention to character, has allowed Ann-Margret to do—work from her instincts and focus on the feeling. She did this in her Hollywood heyday, but in less tony pictures, which is why critics who hate *Kitten* can hail *Children.* But when the Prima Donna herself, Barbara Stanwyck, beat Ann-Margret for the Emmy, she stood at the podium, reached out her arm, and bellowed, "Ann-Margret—you were superb!" It was a tribute from one trashy lady to another, from one Oscar-less diva to another, from the Queen of Feeling to her spiritual heir.

A nn-Margret

Ever since *Carnal Knowledge,* Ann-Margret has been treated like the oldest whore on the block who suddenly opened an orphanage. The ultimate Reformed Bimbo, she's now a serious thespian who works with classy directors on respectable projects. But the truth about Ann-Margret is a little more ambiguous: she brings out the art in the trash and the trash in the art. If you don't love her early performances in *Kitten With a Whip* and *Bus Riley's Back in Town,* you can't really appreciate her TV-turns in *Who Will Love My Children?* and *A Streetcar Named Desire*—they're flip sides of the same coin. During the toss, Ann-Margret never quite capitalized on her impact in *Knowledge,* though she was the sole reason to sit through such semi-arty epics as *Tommy* and *Magic.* She was saved, as all Grandes Dames are, by TV. As the dying, backwoods mother in *Children,* Ann-Margret reached so deeply into the anguish of her

J oan Collins

A poor man's Elizabeth Taylor until *Dynasty,* Joan Collins is the Queen Bee of prime-time soaps and a miraculous survivor. Of all the Grandes Dames, Collins's stature rests almost entirely on a single role. No, not the scheming empress in *Land of the Pharaohs,* though that comes close. It's Alexis Carrington Colby Dexter, TV's second-greatest transvestite (next to Irene Ryan in *The Beverly Hillbillies*). Collins's coup is that she doesn't play the part absentmindedly: she calculates every effect. When she bites into a strawberry while delivering a line, she knows precisely at what point to raise her eyes to catch the key light. Her preposterous drag outfits—saucer hats, furry collars, leather vests—remind you of Thelma Ritter in *All About Eve* eyeing a bedful of mink coats: "Looks like a dead-animal act." But if you're tempted to laugh at Collins, forget it. Here's a woman who already gets the joke about herself. Not only does she get it, she revels in it. Her utter narcissism feeds her perverse wit as she devours every actor who stands in her way. On a show that depends on the strength of its imagery, Collins is a riveting

Joan Collins in Dynasty

self-reflection, turning *Dynasty* into *The Joan Collins Story*. It's the story of a woman who claws her way to the top and cherishes the creature comforts she finds there. For a while, she's even bigger news than Taylor, who becomes a target of Joan Rivers's fat jokes. But now that Taylor has shaped up, Collins is looking a bit worried. She can handle Linda Evans with both gloves tied behind her back, but there's a new/old girl in town. The town is Hollywood, not Denver, and as a new/old girl herself, Collins must have a few tricks tucked in her bodice. *Sins* was the first, but there are six more deadly ones to go. Stay tuned.

Angie Dickinson

When Angie Dickinson won the Golden Globe as Best Actress in a Drama Series for her role in *Police Woman,* she giggled, "I'm not used to being referred to as an actress." The line brought down the house because everybody knows what Dickinson shrewdly refuses to acknowledge: she's better than just about any project—movies or TV— she's ever been connected with. Yes, Howard Hawks's *Rio Bravo* and Samuel Fuller's *China Gate* are auteur triumphs, but without Angie, they'd be little more than *Rambo* rumbas. Her self-effacement and candor have always obscured the fact that she can do more with a raised eyebrow and melancholy grin than most of her leading men— Troy Donahue, Gregory Peck, Ronald Reagan— can do in a lifetime of histrionics (she even gave heart to a Brian De Palma movie). Unlike the equally glorious Ann-Margret, whose *Carnal Knowledge* catapulted her into respectable parts, Dickinson has remained a material girl. *Police Woman* features her as Pepper Anderson, undercover temptress. A typical episode has Dickinson in a Day-Glo miniskirt and fishnet stockings luring an urban sleazoid into the pen. The plots are from hunger, the direction by rote, but Dickinson never flinches—she plays it as if she were doing *Hedda*

Gabler at Circle in the Square. She's at her best when reflected in the eyes of likable character actors: Tom Skerritt, Earl Holliman, Peter Finch. Her presence has enlivened many a miniseries, from *Pearl* to *Hollywood Wives.* Her TV movies have ranged from the smart *(A Touch of Scandal)* to the soulful *(A Sensitive, Passionate Man).* She guested in the '50s *(Perry Mason)* and fizzled in a series *(Cassie & Company).* She's never stopped working, but we don't see her enough.

Faye Dunaway

If history didn't exist, Faye Dunaway would've invented it. Her myth-ridden TV career is split between her post–Bonnie Parker roles in the '70s (the Duchess of Windsor, Aimee Semple McPherson) and her Joan Crawford–period parts in the '80s (Evita Perón, Queen Isabella). The difference between the two is that of the Stone Age and the Industrial Revolution: Dunaway may never shake the specter of *Mommie Dearest.* Not since *Mildred Pierce* cemented Crawford's image for the ages has a movie so transformed an actress's career. It's not for nothing that Crawford's favorite contemporary actress was Dunaway. Playing Crawford, Dunaway topped them both—she was more Crawford than Crawford and more Dunaway than Dunaway. Eyebrows arched in terror, mouth quivering with rage, Dunaway was a monument to fury: a Method diva impersonating a movie diva on her way to becoming a TV diva. After *Mommie* Dunaway had nowhere to go but TV. Where else could her haunting mannerisms and outsized emotions be contained? Surely not in movies like *Chinatown* and *Network,* where her personality would be shaped by artsy male egos. She's too big to be anybody's muse, which is why she plays historical legends so brilliantly—she needs to reflect an image as imposing as her own. Her towering, ferocious performance in *Evita Perón*

Faye Dunaway in Christopher Columbus

not only told us All About Evita, it evoked all the splendor and horror of an entire epoch. Lately Dunaway has been saying she wants to do more comedy. But why lighten up when you can carry the weight of the world? Faye Dunaway is the most thoroughly self-created actress of her generation—a TV star filtered through a '40s movie queen. She's the most majestic Grande Dame.

Ava Gardner

If Ava Gardner did more television, she'd rival Barbara Stanwyck as Prima Donna. She achieves more effect with less effort than any Grande Dame.

With just three of her recent TV roles—the murderous Agrippina in the miniseries *A.D.,* the scheming Ruth Galveston on *Knots Landing,* and the furious sheik's wife in *Harem*—Gardner takes her place among TV's greats. Squeezing more scathing irony out of a simple line reading than just about any actress alive, Gardner wraps her tongue around every syllable and tilts her head back to savor the flavor. On *Knots Landing* she makes the innocent question, "Doesn't anybody carry cigarettes anymore?," sound like the most insinuating of inquiries. More than most Grandes Dames, Gardner is an example of a TV diva's art reflecting her life. In an industry of make-believe, this sharecropper's daughter from North Carolina forged an image of down-to-earth intelligence and self-effacing humor that's been fodder for the gossip columns from the beginning of her career. Even as an anonymous starlet at MGM, Gardner got Hollywood's attention by marrying Mickey Rooney and divorcing him a year later. By all accounts, Gardner expressed a traditionally male libido—she went after what she wanted and didn't care what anybody thought. She married and divorced both Artie Shaw and Frank Sinatra, and made no secret of her taste for bullfighters. She now lives in London and says she does TV "for the dough, honey." One can only hope that her bank balance always stays low.

Dorothy McGuire

A beacon of sanity in the dark world of the Grande Dame, Dorothy McGuire has always been one of the most misused actresses of her generation. As early as *Gentleman's Agreement,* McGuire was cast as a sweet-souled witness to social horrors—a '40s Mary Tyler Moore. But underneath that clear-eyed intelligence and determined decency lay an actress of greater complexity. Her best movie role, as the troubled war widow in *Till the End of Time*

(the year before *Agreement*), allowed her to be tender, yes, but also showed her falling into bed drunk after a long night on the town. Coming to TV in the early '70s, McGuire starred in a couple of movies before landing her paramount role as the matriarch in the miniseries *Rich Man, Poor Man.* Waiting all her career to play a part of such depth and range, McGuire ruthlessly exposed the two sides of her character over a twenty-year period: an impoverished hausfrau who seems justified in her bitterness and a rich-bitch matron who falls prey to petty prejudices. She redeems both women with the most wrenching deathbed scene in TV history. Gasping for air through plastic tubes, begging to be held by the son she slighted all her life, McGuire leaned her head back, let a single tear slip from her right eye, and achieved transcendence. If McGuire handled this role so beautifully, it may be because she herself is a woman with two sides: the sensible adult and the stingingly candid diva. Her recent stints on *Highway to Heaven* and *St. Elsewhere* tended to tap only the sweet strains in her nature. But as the persecuted nursing-home patient in *Amos,* McGuire has a love affair against the house rules. So long as McGuire keeps breaking the rules, she'll be a lady to reckon with.

Agnes Moorehead

If Agnes Moorehead had been born beautiful, she'd have been the greatest star of the twentieth century. As it was, she had to settle for being one of its greatest actresses. Fierce, intense, bitterly severe, she gave new meaning to the term histrionic hysteria: she was avant before her costars were en garde. As the old-maid aunt in *The Magnificent Ambersons,* Moorehead went over the top so many times, she actually induced vertigo. Just when you thought she surpassed herself in a scene, she'd do something you never saw before. After a series of

Ava Gardner in A.D.

Dorothy McGuire in She Waits

Agnes Moorehead in Bewitched

unrewarding roles in the '50s, Moorehead made an easy transition to television, where her pointy features, police-siren voice, and brazen acting style matched the kinkiness of '60s genres. She played a raving crone battling an alien spaceship in an episode of *The Twilight Zone* and won an Emmy for her wicked portrait of Emma Valentine in *The Wild, Wild West.* But it was as Endora, Elizabeth Montgomery's malicious mother on *Bewitched,* that Moorehead staked her claim to Grande Damehood. An intergalactic Auntie Mame, Moorehead fought for dominance in a bright orange wig, fluorescent silk muumuu, and enough blue eye shadow to put Max Factor in the Fortune 500. Hissing every line, craning her neck like a demented pelican, thrusting her painted nails into Kabuki-like positions, Moorehead created a visual style that corresponded to her colorful technique. She never topped this spectacle after *Bewitched,* but short of replacing Tallulah Bankhead, she couldn't be expected to. Her gifts were too otherworldly for this mortal world. Whatever dimension she inhabits today, she's undoubtedly the reigning Grande Dame.

Jean Simmons

If Deborah Kerr had gone into another profession, Jean Simmons would be a bigger star today. There was only so much room in Hollywood for two English ladies who began their careers at roughly the same time. While Kerr racked up six Oscar nominations, Simmons was peddled as a poor man's Audrey Hepburn. But there's a delicious irony at the heart of this rivalry: Simmons's career looks better in retrospect, not because she got the plum roles, but because she's a better actress. Her career is a triumph over inferior material. Only a diva could make *Hilda Crane* and *Home Before Dark* such mesmerizing experiences (and only a saint could have stayed married to

Stewart Granger for ten years). This transcendent quality made Simmons an ideal candidate for TV divahood, and in the classic miniseries *The Thorn Birds* she delivered. As a well-bred woman who marries beneath her, Simmons conveyed heartbreak with the dignity of a queen, enduring poverty out of respect for its destructive power. But her character was complex: she loved her husband and felt indebted to him. This is, of course, *The Jean Simmons Story:* she loves her work too much to let an unappreciative industry wear her down. Her more recent role as a movie actress suffering from Alzheimer's disease in an episode of *Hotel* drove the point home—she's in complete command of her craft no matter what the obstacle. Her performance not only made mincemeat of Joanne Woodward's Emmy-winning weepfest as an Alzheimer's victim in *Do You Remember Love,* it made sense in terms of an entire career.

Elizabeth Taylor

When Barbra Streisand sang, "I'm the greatest star/I am by far," in *Funny Girl,* I kept looking around the screen for Elizabeth Taylor. Even those unschooled in the politics of Diva know that Taylor is The Greatest Star By Far precisely because her work reflects her life. Yes, she's The Most Beautiful Woman Who Ever Lived, but without her marriages, divorces, Oscars, personal setbacks, and dramatic comebacks, she'd be just another movie star. Her arrival at TV divahood was the longest journey since Marco Polo's discovery of China: a thirty-year movie career that collapsed with the studio system, a Broadway career that began in triumph with *The Little Foxes* and ended two years later with *Private Lives,* and a stay at the Betty Ford Center that cleaned up her act. When she took her act on the road again, she stunned the world—she looked better than ever. She also

Jean Simmons in The Thorn Birds

Elizabeth Taylor in Malice in Wonderland

took to TV with a renewed vigor. Her previous TV roles had stuck her in lachrymose situations opposite far lesser mortals: *Divorce His/Divorce Hers* (Richard Burton), *Return Engagement* (Joseph Bottoms), and *Between Friends* (Carol Burnett). But as Louella Parsons in *Malice in Wonderland*, Taylor dug her still-sharp claws into her best role in years. Playing a threatened Hollywood survivor, Taylor brought out the wit in her character's ridiculous predicament. What few people understand about Taylor is that she's a great comedienne—a feisty farceur with a true gift for mimicry. Her riotous turn on *Here's Lucy* was the single best episode of that series, while her greatest movie performance, in the outrageously funny *X, Y and Zee*, tapped her talents in the same way *Malice* did. She's a sly Dame with a Grande past.

Jane Wyman

Jane Wyman puts the Grande in Dame, though part of that Grandeness is in her own head. As Angela Channing on *Falcon Crest*, Wyman etches the most acid portrait of divahood ever to reach prime time: she makes Joan Collins look like Greer Garson. Dried up, bitter, furious at life and herself, Wyman's Angela is an irredeemable bitch—a high-fashion harridan. Though she plays the part with a single-minded emotion (pissed-off), Wyman brings a scathing irony to her line readings, speaking for the sheer pleasure of crunching words between her teeth. The underlying joke of her portrayal is that she looks and sounds almost exactly like Nancy Reagan—close-cropped auburn mane, immaculate suits in shades of red, sharp vocal tones (Angela even lives near Ron's gubernatorial stamping ground in Northern California). This spectacle is curious for Wyman. She is, after all, the woman who snatched Ray Milland from a pit of despair in *The Lost Weekend,* endured social persecution for the love of Rock Hudson in *All That Heaven Allows,* and won an Oscar as a deaf-mute rape victim in *Johnny Belinda.* Even as a pioneer TV diva in the '50s, Wyman brought a warm dignity to the *Fireside Theatre,* later renamed *Jane Wyman Theater.* But on *Falcon Crest* Wyman creates a chilling Theater of the Absurd—she's preposterously vicious. Maybe after being a '30s chorus girl, a '40s dramatic actress, and a '50s matinee queen, Wyman needed to bounce back in the '80s as something more— something that drew together the strands of her exceptional career. What she did was absorb and exaggerate the strength of every indomitable woman she ever played. Flushed with power, she's a credit to her ex-husband.

Jane Wyman in Falcon Crest

DISTINGUISHED GUESTS & DRAMATIC DO-GOODERS

Ingrid Bergman
Glenn Close
Bette Davis
Jane Fonda
Katharine Hepburn

Vanessa Redgrave
Gena Rowlands
Meryl Streep
Cicely Tyson
Joanne Woodward

A Distinguished Guest & Dramatic Do-Gooder is a Glamorous Stranger with "class." Her appearances on television are never viewed as the last resort of an unemployable goddess—they're special events deserving of Emmys. A born slummer, the DG/DD works to be admired—she doesn't squander her gifts on mere entertainment. She's obsessed with reality, with improving the human condition, and wears her social conscience on her sleeve. The ten actresses listed here have fifteen Oscars and fifty nominations among them; all but two have won Emmys. Much of this industry adulation is well-deserved: the DG/DD is nothing less than talented. But her talent is the sort you can't help noticing—she makes certain you sit up and applaud. Her naturalistic technique may seem the opposite of Hollywood narcissism, but her hunger for appreciation is the ultimate form of vanity. Her choice of roles is a function of her esthetic: she'd rather play Joan of Arc than the Queen of Sheba. A bit of a bore, her "genius" is skin-deep. She often begins her career as a sly vamp (she's a dish deep down), but eventually winds up an Oscar champ—she'd rather be dead than just another camp. The artifice of her early, sexy roles is stripped away by a careful selection of respectable parts. She stays around forever because the lines that inevitably crease her face are always considered emblems of "character" rather than signs of a broken-down movie star desperate for work. Unlike the Grande Dame, whose every move is reflected in the roles she plays, the DG/DD dons a fright wig and putty nose to show everybody what a serious actress she is. Incurably noble, she wants to be loved not for who she is, but for the moral eminence of the heroines she plays.

1 Ingrid Bergman

A fresh-faced Garbo with ten times the talent, and the indisputable Queen of Naturalism, Ingrid

Bergman went "from saint to whore and back to saint all in one lifetime" (sez she). But the beauty of Bergman—early on, anyway—is that she showed the whore in the saint and the saint in the whore. Her '40s Hollywood roles as nuns *(The Bells of St. Mary's)* and noble ladies *(Casablanca)* mesh nicely with her '50s European parts as neurotic wives *(Voyage to Italy)* and persecuted matrons *(Europa '51).* Bringing an electrifying eroticism to her sweet-spirited heroines and a saintly goodness to her embittered mid-lifers, Bergman made chastity seem sexy and secular humanism seem religious. But the parallels between her life and work were less ambiguous to professional bluenoses, who saw only a doctor's wife walking out on her nuclear family in America and into the arms of a continental lefty (Roberto Rossellini). When Bergman became a saint again, winning a second Oscar for *Anastasia,* she lost the tension between her "good" and "bad" sides: she became an institution. Her movie comedies were innocuous *(Indiscreet, Cactus Flower)* and her television dramas adapted from official classics *(The Turn of the Screw, Hedda Gabler).* By the time she reached her twilight years, when she knew she was dying of cancer, Bergman interpreted another Bergman (Ingmar) onscreen and another legend (Golda Meir) on the tube. Her glorification of Golda made the mistake of telling us that she, too, was a noble figure. One missed the scrappy, independent diva who so shocked the world, and who, when accepting her third Oscar, criticized the Academy for not giving the award to Valentina Cortese.

G|lenn Close

In the '30s, it was Norma Shearer and Luise Rainer. In the '40s, Greer Garson (queen) and Teresa Wright (princess). In the '50s, it was Loretta Young on the tube and Deborah Kerr at the Bijou. In the '60s, Katharine Hepburn became one. In the '70s, there was none, except Lily Tomlin, who was parodying it—the Tasteful Lady, and her twin sister, the Noble Nellie. In the '80s, we've been hit with a motherlode—Streep, Fonda, Field, Spacek, Lange—each of whom seems hell-bent on portraying the spiritual triumphs of sweetie-pie heroines. But the reigning mama of them all is Glenn Close, that moist-eyed maven of the stiff upper lip. Her sensible performances in *The World According to Garp, The Big Chill,* and *The Natural* reflect the tone of her TV turn as the distraught mother in *Something About Amelia,* the Emmy-winning saga of a girl molested by her father. When Close confronts her husband—"Amelia says you've been having sex with her"—she's disbelieving, horrified, about to explode. It's a classic Close expression: she's too pure-minded to know what's going on under her own roof. There's nothing wrong with her delivery technically—it's quite subtly effective—but the ignorance of her character is frustrating. The movie never addresses the fact that a lot of mothers in that situation know exactly what's going on and don't do anything about it. That's the most shocking truth of incest, but it would take a Kathleen Turner to put it across. In 1985 Close jazzed up her image in *Jagged Edge,* just as Lange broke out in *Sweet Dreams.* But a Tasteful Lady spends a lifetime trying to get down and dirty—properly.

B|ette Davis

If Bette Davis had never played Margo Channing in *All About Eve,* she'd be a second-rung diva today. Her image was transformed in the role the way that Crawford's was in *Mildred Pierce* or Dunaway's was in *Mommie Dearest.* She gave a few great performances earlier on, especially in *Marked Woman,* but she was often either too rough *(Of Human Bondage),* too smooth *(Jezebel),* or just

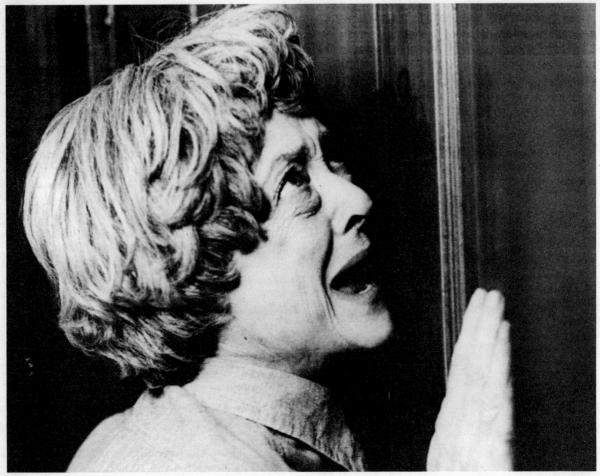

Bette Davis in Strangers: The Story of a Mother and Daughter

plain miscast *(Juarez)*. When she played Margo, she was washed up in Hollywood. Sinking her teeth into *Eve*'s epigrams, exhaling each syllable through puffs of smoke, Davis exaggerated every tic, every mannerism, every shameless upstaging tactic she had ever learned—she knew it was her last chance and she had the script to pull it off. What she couldn't know was that it was the last great role she would ever get in movies. Her second comeback, in *Whatever Happened to Baby Jane?*, was more of a comedown—the first stop on the Horror Show Express. Drifting into television, she was not at first a persuasive TV diva: *Scream, Pretty Peggy* exploited her *Baby Jane*-camp image, while *Madame Sin* showed how cemented her *Eve* mannerisms had become. But in *Strangers: The Story of a Mother and Daughter*, Davis stripped away decades of artifice to give her best performance in thirty years. Her delivery of the last line—"I love you"—is the most perfectly heart-rending reading of those words in TV history. Davis tried to recapture this intimacy in a series of sociological dramas—*White Mama, A Piano for Mrs. Cimino, Right of Way*. But for the sheer splendor of *Eve* and the total nakedness of *Strangers*, Davis must be applauded as that rare Distinguished Guest who had the guts to Do Good for herself instead of the great unwashed.

Jane Fonda

Jane Fonda used to be an actress. Her peak year—1962—yielded three great performances: the frigid widow in *The Chapman Report,* the skittish honeymooner in *Period of Adjustment,* and the garter-snapping whore in *Walk on the Wild Side.* In these roles Fonda used every ounce of her body and soul to express the yearnings of her troubled characters. She didn't care whether you liked her as a "person." By the time of *On Golden Pond,* she was a psycho-babbling tycoon publicly seeking her dying father's love (she was born a better actor than her father, but chose to be more like him as the years went by). In between, Fonda went from an underrated bimbo *(Barbarella)* to an overvalued do-gooder *(Coming Home).* Her social awareness enriched her personal life, but it ripped the guts from her art—she lost a lightness of spirit, a sense of abandon. She no longer wanted you to accept her characters on their own terms—she wanted you to respect their goodness and admire *her* for playing them. The startling candor and irony of her early work, which had made her the most promising actress of her generation, degenerated into a flag-waving weepfest. Her physical-fitness dynasty was built on two decades of self-denial and good works—'60s purity filtered through '80s smugness. Staying off screen for years after *Pond* to devote herself to politics, Fonda turned up on TV in *The Dollmaker,* a bare-bones tearjerker about a backwoods mother. Her hair pulled into a tight bun and her eyes puddling up at the drop of a corn cob, Fonda had finally become her own father's creator—Ma Joad.

Katharine Hepburn

Just because Katharine Hepburn is the Most Overrated Actress of the Twentieth Century doesn't mean she can't be a delightful diva: a Howard Hawks classic *(Bringing Up Baby),* a couple of George Cukor–Philip Barry charmers *(Holiday, The Philadelphia Story),* a pair of Ruth Gordon–Garson Kanin treats *(Adam's Rib, Pat and Mike),* one early masterpiece *(Alice Adams),* and one autumnal chef-d'oeuvre (TV's *Love Among the Ruins).* When Hepburn has a strong, witty script, she shines—her diction and cheekbones were made for smarty-pants repartee. But when she strains for tragic feeling, she has all the depth of a pancake. Her snobbish obsession with the the-uh-tah has led to trashings of Eugene O'Neill on the big screen and Tennessee Williams on the small one—she may be the only actress in history to make Mary Tyrone and Amanda Wingfield seem like the same person. When she tackles mere movie drama as opposed to Great Theater, Hepburn is attracted to some of the hoariest weepfests ever perpetrated on the American public, from *Guess Who's Coming to Dinner?* to *On Golden Pond.* But just when she seemed content to polish her Oscars, Hepburn bounced back in 1986 in *Mrs. Delafield Wants to Marry,* a lighter-than-air romantic comedy about a Waspy matron who falls for a younger Jewish doctor. Yes, Hepburn got to make her Big Speech, but she also got to be sly and merry and dryly funny. Her performance was imbued with qualities she's never really shown before: a gentle self-deprecation, a good-humored nonchalance, an unsentimental humility. At seventy-eight, Hepburn seemed to have turned a corner in her life. *Delafield* not only recalls Hollywood's heyday, it reveals an actress who's lived too long to believe that greatness can be bought with good taste.

Vanessa Redgrave

Vanessa Redgrave is a goddess and a drag. There's simply no one like her—in looks, speech, de-

Katharine Hepburn in The Corn Is Green

meanor, raw talent, or just plain chutzpah. Her Oscar acceptance speech, in which she attacked "Zionist hoodlums," was quickly followed by her casting as a Holocaust victim in TV's *Playing for Time*. The ensuing outcry was deafened only by the plaudits for Redgrave's performance: every trophy for Best Actress fell her way. The irony of the brouhaha was that no other actress on Earth could have played the part with the appropriate mix of anger and repression. Redgrave's antagonistic defense of belief in her life and work directly reflects that of her foes, both political and esthetic. Her willingness to appear ugly or naked or unappealing onscreen is a conscious political statement. She's drawn to characters who are outsiders, emotionally and socially. The more ostracized or persecuted her characters are, the freer Redgrave becomes—she seems in touch with another world. Her spectacular performance in 1985 as the wicked queen in "Snow White and the Seven Dwarfs" on Showtime's *Faerie Tale Theatre* is one of the few times I've seen an adult actress working on the same wavelength as the children who'd be watching such a show—she not only refused to condescend to her audience, she marched right into its collective head (she did the same thing for grownups in 1986's miniseries *Peter the Great*). Her most recent TV role, as transsexual tennis pro Renee Richards in *Second Serve*, took her as far as she could go. What can be next? Nothing on this planet. Maybe Redgrave can move to Venus, win the award for Best Intergalactic Actress, and criticize all those Martian hoodlums.

Gena Rowlands

The bravest and most bewitching of all Distinguished Guests & Dramatic Do-Gooders, Gena Rowlands has made a career of naked naturalism in the movies and sociological struggles on television. Her ferocious, all-out performances in *A Woman Under the Influence, Gloria,* and *Love Streams* (directed by her actor-husband, John Cassavetes) contrast nicely with her issue-oriented TV movies—*A Question of Love* (lesbianism and custody battles), *Strangers: The Story of a Mother and Daughter* (fatal diseases and generation gaps), and *An Early Frost* (homosexuality and AIDS). Rowlands seems attracted to subject above all else, but her style changes between media. Conforming to her husband's improvisational approach, Rowlands is wildly naturalistic onscreen—she explodes. But on TV, where she must meet the demands of a set script on a specific topic, Rowlands implodes, pulling all the way in and letting flickers of feeling betray her calm. Her TV characters tend to be cool and controlled on the surface, but fierce and furious underneath. When fire meets ice, the plight of the underdog melts. I'd go so far as to say Rowlands is a better TV diva than a movie actress—she needs an imposed discipline and structure to modulate her emotions. There are great moments in Rowlands's TV films:

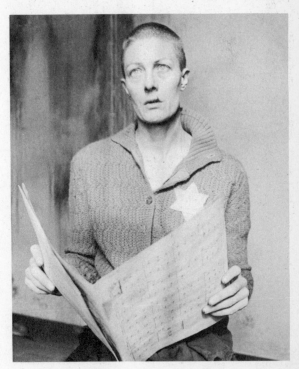

Vanessa Redgrave in Playing for Time

Gena Rowlands in Strangers: The Story of a Mother and Daughter

the catch in her voice in *An Early Frost* after her son tells her he has AIDS, or her life-story confession in *Strangers* to the mother she hasn't seen in twenty years. Rowlands is a Distinguished Guest on TV because she's a cult-movie star. But her Do-Gooding is honest. She's the only actress in this category whose heart seems connected to the issues she raises.

Meryl Streep

I first saw Meryl Streep in the Brecht-Weill musical *Happy End* on Broadway. She sang, danced, giggled, wiggled her butt, and flashed radiant smiles from the footlights. I fell in love. The next time I saw Miss Meryl, she was laying her tremulous palms on Robert De Niro's war wounds. Then she was crying up a storm in a custody battle and choosing between her children at Auschwitz and suffering from radiation in a nuclear plant and storming off into meadows with the French Resistance. Jeez, is there anything this woman can't do onscreen? Yeah, give us a good time. Never before has an actress wasted so much talent on so much pretension. Even when I caught up with her Emmy-winning role in *Holocaust,* which preceded her celebrated movie parts, Streep was still Streepy as the long-suffering wife of a concentration-camp victim. If Streep is the most lauded actress of her generation, it has less to do with her unending gifts than her perfect technique. She's replaced a full-bodied personality with the outlines of character—dyed hair, period dress, foreign accents. The result is that she plays women who bear little relation to her own sensibility. Her Oklahoma twang in *Silkwood* is as unerring as her Polish trills in *Sophie's Choice,* but what does it profit an actress to gain a mantelpiece of trophies for *Sophie* only to lose her soul? That's the one thing Streep lacks: soul. She's the coldest technician since Ethel Barrymore. Yet unlike Barrymore, Streep is tre-

mendously funny and down-to-earth in interviews. Her best performance, as the witty Southern lawyer in Alan Alda's *The Seduction of Joe Tynan,* suggests her forte may be the romantic sitcom. I can see it now: *The Meryl Streep Show.*

Cicely Tyson

On *Saturday Night Live,* Danitra Vance did a dead-on impersonation of Cicely Tyson. Arms folded, mouth immobile, head draped in white cloth, Vance insists on political discourse even when sitting next to Brooke Shields on a telethon. Surely the depth and breadth of Tyson's technical powers can't be questioned. Her towering performance in *The Autobiography of Miss Jane Pittman,* in which she aged from a young woman to a one hundred–plus matriarch, was an acting stunt that went straight to the heart. But such unyielding goodness can wear thin when it becomes a badge of courage in role after role. Tyson's Noble Nellie –drag turns as Coretta Scott King *(King),* Harriet Ross Tubman *(A Woman Called Moses),* and Marva Collins *(The Marva Collins Story)* are nothing less than scrupulous, but also predictable and a bit boring. Tyson's a classic TV diva in that she can't find a decent job in an industry obsessed with exploding spaceships and horny teenagers. But she's also a victim of TV, which feeds on sociological dramas as voraciously as the movies devour Wookies. Yes, Tyson's typecast in an insensitive business. Yes, she's wasting her technique on mundane parts. Yes, she's one of the most accomplished actresses of her generation. But she also has a humorous streak that she downplays in her self-serious roles. When she beams at her husband in *Sounder,* she makes her moments of anguish all the more effective. There's a wildness, a freedom, even a wickedness in Tyson's smile— she could play any kind of comedy. But she seems too willing a prisoner of her image—she carries

Cicely Tyson in A Woman Called Moses

the responsibility of history like sackcloth and ashes. We remember the past, Cicely. Now what about the future?

J oanne Woodward

The Queen of Social Realism, Joanne Woodward wins my vote as The Most Boring Actress Who Ever Lived. Even Luise Rainer could be delightfully preposterous in her pretensions. But Woodward is strictly business. Her two good performances—as Sally Field's psychiatrist in *Sybil* and as the jogging mid-lifer in *See How She Runs*— are both from television. When Woodward's minimalist technique is squeezed into the box, she actually looks like she's *doing* something. One of the great mysteries of divahood is why so many regard Woodward as a fine character actress capable of playing a variety of parts. Her whiny shlub from *Rachel, Rachel* isn't all that different from her weepy shlimazl from *Summer Wishes, Winter Dreams*. Even when portraying a series of identities in *The Three Faces of Eve,* Woodward relied on the outlines of character—facial tics, shrugs, jittery limbs. There's nothing going on behind her eyes except calculation for her next move. There's also little joy or free-spiritedness in her work. She makes you appreciate her art as if it were good for you, like insulin for diabetics. Her Emmy-winning performance as an Alzheimer's victim in *Do You Remember Love* oozes a self-

Joanne Woodward in See How She Runs

congratulatory bravery. If she was so convincing in *Sybil* and *See How She Runs,* it may be because she was playing characters closer to herself—not piteous victims, but fiercely proud and defiant women who know precisely what they want. Far from a saint and conscious to a fault, Joanne Woodward might consider tapping the rage and regret inside her own soul instead of banking on the decency of her characters to do the emotional work for her.

4

ASSORTED SITCOM QUEENS

Eve Arden & Ann Sothern
Doris Day
Patty Duke
Jean Hagen & Marjorie Lord
Judith Light & Shelley Long
Elizabeth Montgomery

Paula Prentiss
Inger Stevens & Gale Storm
Marlo Thomas & Barbara Feldon
Vivian Vance & Lucie Arnaz/
Penny Marshall & Cindy Williams

According to a recent poll of television critics, the Top 10 sitcoms of all time are (in order): *The Mary Tyler Moore Show, All in the Family, I Love Lucy, M*A*S*H, The Dick Van Dyke Show, The Honeymooners, Barney Miller, Cheers, The Bob Newhart Show,* and *Taxi.* This remarkably consistent list tells less about the quality of TV than the greening of yuppies. Seven of the ten shows debuted in the '70s, while the remaining three were celebrated in reruns during that time. While I heartily agree with the choices of *Mary* and *Lucy,* I can't help wondering how many of our nation's critics have given more than a passing thought to *The Beverly Hillbillies, The George Burns and Gracie Allen Show, Bewitched, Green Acres, Leave It to Beaver, The Many Loves of Dobie Gillis, The Adventures of Ozzie and Harriet,* and *The Monkees.* Even today, I prefer the larger-than-life likability of *227, Who's the Boss?, Growing Pains,* and *Perfect Strangers* to the slice-of-life prestige of *The Cosby Show, Cheers, Family Ties,* and *Kate & Allie.*

The split between slob and snob sitcoms can be seen best through their respective actresses.

From the beginning, there have been two types of Sitcom Queens: comedic stars whose series were shaped to showcase their personalities, and character actresses who played comedic types in wacky ensembles. The former tradition—Classic Sitcom Queens—can be traced from Eve Arden *(Our Miss Brooks)* and Lucille Ball in the '50s to Paula Prentiss *(He & She)* and Kaye Ballard *(The Mothers-in-Law)* in the '60s to virtually nobody in the '70s, except Penny Marshall *(Laverne & Shirley),* who tried to recreate the spirit of Lucy. The latter tradition—Kitchen-Sink Chameleons (dressed-down thespians who change genres)—extends from Jane Wyatt *(Father Knows Best)* and Vivian Vance in the '50s to Carolyn Jones *(The Addams Family)* and Cara Williams *(Pete and Gladys)* in the '60s to Norman Lear's Ladies (Jean Stapleton, Bea Arthur), Grant Tinker's Tootsies (Cloris Leachman, Suzanne Pleshette), and Susan Harris's Harridans (Lee Grant, Katherine Helmond) in the '70s. Paul Henning, the King of '60s Sitcoms, subverted the dialectic with divas who were immediately personalities *and* actresses—Gracie Allen, Irene Ryan—while Mary Tyler Moore bridged the

Kaye Ballard (left) *and Eve Arden in* The Mothers-in-Law

gap by taking a cue from Lucy: enhance your image by finding a good husband who could share an even better production company.

But the impact of Lear, Tinker, and Harris has made the CSQ all but extinct: Jane Curtin in *Kate & Allie* is about the only one left (and even she comes out of a more modern comic tradition). In the '80s, "Sitcom Queen" means one thing: KSCs showing their versatility. Shelley Long *(Cheers)*, Swoosie Kurtz *(Love, Sidney)*, Carol Kane *(Taxi)*, Eileen Brennan *(Private Benjamin)*, Audra Lindley *(The Ropers)*, Barbara Babcock *(Mr. Sunshine)*, Rita Moreno *(9 to 5)*, Barbara Barrie *(Breaking Away)*, Charlotte Rae *(The Facts of Life)*, Alfre Woodard *(Sara)*, Doris Roberts *(Angie)*—all KSCs. Even Ellen Burstyn—the Princess of KSCs—has her own sitcom. Moreover, dethroned CSQs—Marlo Thomas *(That Girl)*,

Sandy Duncan *(Funny Face)*—have gone into exile on Broadway. I don't mean to slight the talents of KSCs—Kurtz is a veritable genius—but their esthetic has become the model for younger actresses, from Justine Bateman to Rosanna Arquette. The rise of "realistic" sitcoms has turned men into stars and women into gal Fridays. We need a new category for funny ladies: Assorted Sitcom Queens.

Eve Arden & Ann Sothern

Eve Arden and Ann Sothern ought to insure their tongues with Lloyds of London. Their withering wisecracks were as responsible for the joy of '40s movies as were the heated histrionics of leading ladies (stars are replaceable, but supporting goddesses are hard to find). Their careers are remarkably similar: both made their movie debuts in 1929; both headlined popular serials—Arden as Connie Brooks on radio and Sothern as Maisie in the movies; and both starred in a series of sitcoms almost concurrently—*Our Miss Brooks* and *Private Secretary, The Eve Arden Show* and *The Ann Sothern Show, The Mothers-in-Law* and *My Mother the Car.* The overwhelming image of their dizzying credits is of a working woman who's always smarter than the man she craves. But if Arden could never resist sacrificing a bed partner for the Last Word, Sothern could never reconcile her romanticism with her repartee. Between her first and second series, Sothern went from a secretary with sexual possibilities to a hotel manager denied a promotion because a man was hired for the job—her wit and intelligence brought her the worst of both worlds. Arden never embraced extremes—she was as predictable as the sunrise, which is precisely why men took her for granted. But she got her revenge with lethal zingers (she stuck it to them before they could stick it to her). When,

Ann Sothern in The Ann Sothern Show

in *Brooks,* her obscure object of desire, Mr. Boynton, tells her to close her eyes, Arden cracks: "Not me—I wanna watch!" The splendor of Arden and Sothern is all but lost today, when every actress wants to grow up to be Meryl Streep. But for a time, these two most classic of all Sitcom Queens showed how great a diva can be with little more than a mouthful of perfectly timed put-downs.

Rose Marie (left) *and Doris Day in* The Doris Day Show

Doris Day

John Updike listed her as one of his favorite artists and Jack Lemmon said she's the best actress he ever worked with. But Groucho Marx joked that her ass is so firm you could play a game of bridge on it and Oscar Levant cracked that he knew her *before* she was a virgin. A sweetheart of pop culture vultures and a target of withering wits, Doris Day has stayed out of the public eye for more than a decade only to reemerge in *Doris Day and Friends*, a pet-care show on the Christian Broad-

casting Network. Some may argue that Day deserves to go to the dogs, but her present role strikes me as the saddest case of wasted talent since Buster Keaton fought for jobs in the heyday of the Marx Brothers. Today Day's remembered as the quintessential '50s "lady"—a campy throwback. But she never got credit for the audaciousness of her image. In nearly every one of her major movies, Day played a working woman who grapples with a male force, usually libidinous. Her capability and self-possession gave hope to girls who didn't want to put out in the back seat of a '57 Chevy just to prove their independence. But by 1968 (the last year Day made a movie), this feminist principle was under attack by the counterculture, which equated promiscuity with liberation, and by the Establishment, which denied women equal opportunity in employment. Moreover, Day's personal life reflected the demise of her career. When her manager-husband of seventeen years, Marty Melcher, died, she discovered he'd embezzled or mismanaged every penny she'd earned (she'd placed among the Top 10 box-office stars in America for eight years in a row—1958–66—and held the number-one spot for four of them). Recovering from a nervous breakdown, Day sued her ex-lawyer for $22 million—and won. But she also had to fulfill a contractual agreement made by Melcher without her consent: to star in a sitcom. For five years on *The Doris Day Show* Day played a series of Women Alone—a widowed farmer, an executive secretary, a swinging single. The show was almost unspeakably abysmal, hastily pasted together from scraps of hackneyed plots. Day seemed to express her contempt for the material by playing as many scenes as she could on her own time. She'd read her lines to a point off-camera, go home, and let the other actors do their close-ups alone (though she merrily shared scenes with Rose Marie). The irony is that two years into the show another career girl landed her own sitcom. What is Mary Richards, after all, but a continuation of Day's movie roles? I'd go so far as to say that Mary Tyler Moore wouldn't have had a career without Day's influence. But as Moore became a national treasure, Day retired to her castle in Carmel. On *Doris Day and Friends*, Day invites a guest star to her white stucco palace to talk about animals. She also makes pitches for the Pet Foundation. Although at sixty-two her looks are still spectacular, Day's attitude wavers between tearful monologues and jokey hostility. If she isn't intoning through tears, "Animals love you without condition," she's sitting at the dinner table with Les Brown and his Band of Renown, hawking memberships in the Foundation: "Listen, I put up with you guys for so many years, you owe it to me!" A lot of people owe Doris Day. Every time Shelley Long deflects Ted Danson's advances on *Cheers,* or Bess Armstrong has a hard day at the office on *All Is Forgiven,* or Judith Light is tempted by

Patty Duke in The Patty Duke Show

Tony Danza on *Who's the Boss?,* or Mary herself fights with Lou Grant, a tribute is being paid to the Queen of Modern Romantic Comedy.

Patty Duke

There are two kinds of kiddie divas: those who grow up, lose their appeal, and disappear (Shirley Temple); and those who grow up, stay seductive, and have careers (Natalie Wood). The miracle of Patty Duke is that she's been talented enough to transcend her looks and smart enough to remain a TV actress. Even before her Oscar win (at sixteen) for *The Miracle Worker,* Duke appeared on daytime soaps. Since then, she's conquered every conceivable TV genre. Her style is at once raw and controlled: she knows precisely what she's doing every time she goes over the top. Her best work has been in sitcoms, which force her to focus on tightly structured setups, and in miniseries, which allow her to go completely out of her mind. Her TV movies, from *My Sweet Charlie* to *A Time to Triumph,* tend to bring out the whiny, mush-minded brat in her. But unlike Quinn Cummings, a relentlessly obnoxious actress who played Duke's daughter on *Hail to the Chief,* Duke knows how to use her mannerisms to dramatize the anxieties of her characters. On *The Patty Duke Show,* a beautifully acted sitcom whose campy theme song inspired a hilarious *SCTV* parody ("But they're cheese hostesses/Identical cheese hostesses/And you'll find . . ."), Duke anticipated the self-conscious high-spiritedness of Cyndi Lauper while recalling the fiercely concentrated histrionics of Agnes Moorehead. She played Patty like a ten-year-old and Cathy like a forty-year-old: the unruly girl and the mature matron, the daughter and the mother—the Two Faces of Duke. Her drunken heiress in *Captain and the Kings* brought together the two sides to thrilling effect. Lately, Duke's been elected president of the Screen Actors Guild. But don't mistake her for Shirley Temple Black. She's a TV diva of exceptional force.

Marjorie Lord in The Danny Thomas Show

Jean Hagen & Marjorie Lord

When Jean Hagen left *Make Room for Daddy* after three seasons, the producers had to make room for a new Sitcom Queen, so for eight seasons on *The Danny Thomas Show* Marjorie Lord fit the bill. The difference between the two is the way in which they dealt with Thomas's rampaging ego. If Hagen, a complex character actress, chafed at

the constraints of her role, Lord, a pretty presence, let Thomas be The Star. Her Kathy Williams is the precursor to Phylicia Rashad's Clair on *The Cosby Show:* a fashion plate with a fiery temper ("Oh, you just make me so mad!"). Her function was twofold: smile sweetly while her scene-stealing kids drew laughs and coo appreciatively while her leading man did his shtick. Thomas's penchant for stopping the show cold for ten minutes at a time to do his stand-up act is almost identical to Cosby's indulgence in improvisational solos. Moreover, Thomas and Cosby prefer buddy-buddy routines with their only sons to a comedic partnership with their respective wives. Casting Hagen opposite Thomas is a little like putting Whoopi Goldberg up against Cosby. Far from a beauty but skilled at characterizational observation, Hagen had just done Lina Lamont in *Singin' in the Rain* when she starred in *Daddy.* I've never seen her look so miserable onscreen—even her skin looked bad. Given next to nothing to do, Hagen resorted to that skittish, pathetic smile she used to such devastating effect in her dramatic roles. In one humiliating episode Hagen tries to prove to her girlfriends that Thomas really loves her, which seems rather like a waste of energy. Basically, Lord made a better Mrs. Danny Williams because she happily conformed to the Thomas/Cosby ethos: a leading lady is tasty only when she's a second banana.

flaunted. On *Boss,* Light and Danza are truly liked—by their writers, by their audience, and by each other. This giddy spirit is essential to the appeal of any sitcom, and Light and Danza never seem to tire of being charming. I suspect Long will become disenchanted with romantic comedy and return to her madness-drenched roots, while Light will grow as a comedienne. Then maybe we'll know who's the boss of cheerfully sexy sitcoms.

J udith Light & Shelley Long

Judith Light and Shelley Long have become such glittering comedic presences, it's hard to remember they were once dramatic actresses. While Light won two consecutive Emmys for *One Life to Live,* Long gave an intense, freaky performance as Natalie Wood's roommate in *The Cracker Factory.* Jaunty and wisecracking on the surface, Long showed the depth of her character's derangement by hiding in the dark and cutting her wrists with her car keys. This image of appearance versus reality is the long and short of Light and Long. If Light overcame a severe weight problem to become a prime-time star, Long spruced up her scrawny, washed-out looks to become a romantic lead: both are Sitcom Queens saved by makeovers. On *Who's the Boss?* and *Cheers,* Light and Long play uptight blondes at sexual stalemates with libidinous brunettes. If I prefer Light's lightness with Tony Danza to Long's longing for Ted Danson, it's because the *Boss* lovebirds aren't continually ridiculed for their weaknesses. I think *Cheers* would be a stronger show if Diane were a genuine intellectual (a pretty Susan Sontag) and Sam were a sweet-spirited bumpkin (like Danson's fellow bartender, Woody Harrelson). Now *that* would've made for sexual tension. But it's hard to care about a pseudointellectual and a dimwitted jock whose stupidities are repeatedly

E lizabeth Montgomery

Have Elizabeth Montgomery and Jane Fonda ever had a heart-to-heart? Both kept the names of their famous fathers; both began as sexy minxes in shadowy thrillers; both married daddy-figure directors; both became light comediennes; both replaced husbands with younger partners; and both evolved into activist actresses. But while Montgomery has never won an Emmy in nine tries for five different programs after thirty-five years in television, Fonda won on her first try two years ago after having already copped two Oscars. Does this mean Fonda's a better actress? Not necessarily. What it does mean is that Emmy feels inferior to Oscar in the same way Oscar feels inferior to Tony. But Montgomery is to the tube what Garbo is to the cinema: she's as emblematic of "TV actress" as Garbo is of "movie actress." On *Bewitched* Montgomery gave her line readings increasingly fierce spins— by the time Dick (Sargent) replaced Dick (York) she hated Darrin's guts. Around this time, Samantha's evil twin, Serena, kept showing up, calling to mind Montgomery's wonderful work as Rusty Heller, the flirtatious whore on an episode of *The Untouchables* (she lost the Emmy to Judith Anderson's Lady Macbeth). Since then Montgomery's wavered between Samantha and Serena. She's tackled everything from Lizzie Borden to blind ladies, from Belle Starr to rape victims. But she's

Shelley Long in Cheers

Elizabeth Montgomery with Tabitha in Bewitched

often at her best when letting Serena show all those movie goddesses what a TV diva can do. As the doll-faced Nurse Ratched with euthanasia on her mind in 1985's *Amos,* Montgomery combined Rusty, Serena, and Lizzie in the guise of Samantha. She didn't play the part like an uptight crone—she was a lipsticked sweetie in a silk slip lasciviously eyeballing her patients. It was the performance of her career, but don't expect her to win any awards for it.

Paula Prentiss

Why isn't Paula Prentiss a bigger star today? She had everything: deft comic timing, dramatic delicacy, dynamite looks. But she's remembered for little more than her enchanting chemistry with Jim Hutton in five romantic comedies, including *Where the Boys Are.* Long, lanky, and radiantly sensible, Prentiss gave tall women hope—here was a beanstalk who lured every Jack from Woody Allen *(What's New, Pussycat?)* to Rock Hudson *(Man's Favorite Sport?).* At the height of her appeal, Prentiss starred with husband Richard Benjamin in *He & She,* a marvelously witty sitcom that recalled the marital machinations of *The Dick Van Dyke Show* and prefigured the sexual tensions in *Cheers.* Prentiss's Paula Hollister was a ditz, but she was down-to-earth, too—a working woman who couldn't quite get a grip on the craziness around her. If Mary Richards had spent a weekend in the Twilight Zone, she'd have turned out like Paula. Canceled after a single season, *He & She* became a cult classic. Prentiss meanwhile became a cult herself, meeting grisly fates in *The Parallax View* and *The Stepford Wives.* As she got older, she became thinner, more intense, wilder-looking. Her comedic work had a real lunatic edge, while her dramatic outings were seized by a kind of uncontrollable giddiness. Her pivotal performance in *Having Babies II,* as an aging model whose pregnancy prompts a suicide attempt, showed an actress walking a fine line: she was as chilling as she was heartbreaking. Even in a supporting role in the muckraking *M.A.D.D.: Mothers Against Drunk Drivers,* Prentiss undercut the program's polemic with an off-kilter emotionalism. Somewhere along the line Prentiss grew up to find a world where Hutton meant Tim instead of Jim.

Inger Stevens & Gale Storm

In between saving souls the Christian Broadcasting Network shows classic sitcoms in multihour blocks on weekday mornings, making for some very strange bedfellows. Its pairing of Inger Stevens in *The Farmer's Daughter* and Gale Storm in *My Little Margie* has so many seamy subtexts it's almost sacrilegious. If *Daughter* is downright heartbreaking in light of Stevens's tragic personal life, *Margie* is often frightening in its explicit depiction of the Electra complex. Each episode opens with photos of Storm and her daddy (Charles Farrell) springing to life and telling us all about themselves. While Farrell reminisces about how he used to have "control" over his daughter, Storm laments that her father "looks better in shorts on a tennis court than fellas of twenty-five." When Storm does date a fella of twenty-five, she usually bickers with him over Daddy: "Don't you dare agree with me when I say something against my father! *Go home!*" The ferocity of Storm's projection is both deafening and scary: she punctures your eardrums and freezes your soul. Stevens, by contrast, delivers her lines in a kind of melancholy hush: she whispers, sighs, giggles faintly. With her upswept, honey-blonde hair, deep-grooved dimples, and Cheshire-cat smile, Stevens is a shimmering image of creamy-smooth sensuality. As soon as she married her boss (William Windom), the show went color and dreamy—it became less like a sitcom and more like a late-period Bergman movie. He'd massage her feet by the fireplace while she narrowed her eyes in rapture. The horrible circumstances of Stevens's private life—from a suicide attempt to broken marriages and love affairs to a final drug overdose—adds to the allure of the most serenely beautiful woman ever to grace a sitcom.

Marlo Thomas & Barbara Feldon

In a way, Marlo Thomas and Barbara Feldon picked up where Eve Arden and Ann Sothern left off: Classic Sitcom Queens playing romantic working women. But while Arden and Sothern followed their first hits with second and third sitcoms, Thomas and Feldon deserted *That Girl* and *Get Smart* for drier terrain. Much of this was a function of the times. Thomas and Feldon came of age during

Gale Storm

Marlo Thomas in That Girl

Schlöndorff film, but her brave blockbuster, *Nobody's Child,* seemed pallid next to Sally Field's *Sybil.* Basically, Thomas may be too brainy to embody the spirits of fictional characters—she lets you know she knows what she's feeling. Feldon, meanwhile, who answered the $64,000 Question on Shakespeare, has devoted much of her time to hosting serious-minded talk shows. It seems some goddesses are just too smart to be actresses.

Vivian Vance & Lucie Arnaz/ Penny Marshall & Cindy Williams

It's a miracle Desi Arnaz never sued Garry Marshall for plagiarism. Marshall, who'd worked for Desilu as a writer on *The Lucy Show,* parlayed

Vietnam, while Arden and Sothern remembered the War to End All Wars. But Thomas and Feldon never got the praise they deserved for their earlier work. If Thomas was among TV's first single professionals, Feldon subverted masculine hierarchies with a slyly feminine force. Her Agent 99 was neither drawn as a character nor given the punch lines—she'd lean against a desk while Don Adams did his shtick. But would you believe Feldon was a delicious comedienne? The more dialogue Adams had, the more Feldon animated different parts of her body: bobbing her head, rolling her eyes, wetting her lips. She did more silent comedy than anybody since Mabel Normand. Thomas was the all-talking star of her show, but she never flaunted it. Her Ann Marie was half Jean Arthur and half Sandra Dee—a husky, frisky career girl. As she grew older, Thomas rejected this image. Her TV version of *The Lost Honor of Katharina Blum* was an improvement on the Volker

Barbara Feldon in Get Smart

Lucille Ball (left) *and Vivian Vance in* The Lucy Show

Desi's slapstick vision into a series of blockbuster '70s sitcoms: *Laverne & Shirley* revived Lucy and Ethel's escapades, *Happy Days* evoked the high school high jinks of *Our Miss Brooks,* and *The Odd Couple* recalled the same-sex mismatching of *The Mothers-in-Law.* But while Desi broke ground at the dawn of television, Marshall trod old territory in the heyday of MTM and Norman Lear. It's important to remember Desi got out of producing long before the '70s, while Marshall's work in TV was thoroughly discredited by the early '80s. This is another way of saying that the Desi/Garry tradition is a slim one at best. Without the innovations of *I Love Lucy,* it may not have survived at all. Its premise is simple: If one punch line and/or pratfall is funny, two of the same kind is twice as funny. Its actresses are exaggerated clowns, less funny for their form than fascinating for their folly. If Vivian Vance and Lucie Arnaz overcame the conventions, it's largely because they played second bananas to the paramount Desi Dame: Lucille Ball. Vance's uninhibited brilliance as Ethel Mertz rested on her physical and emotional contrast to Lucy. Required by contract to stay twenty pounds overweight to appear more dowdy than the real Lucy, Vance used her resentment to fuel her relationship with the fictional Lucy. Ethel loved Lucy—and she hated her, too: just like real Best Friends. To this day their bonding hasn't been surpassed—not by Kate and Allie, not by Cagney and Lacey. That Vance and Lucy won Emmys, while William Frawley lost five times and Arnaz was never even nominated, is a testament to the feminine fierceness of *Lucy.* It's no accident Lucy's best films—*Dance, Girl, Dance, Stage Door*—

paired her with other women. Lucy, the chorus girl, and Vance, the character actress, had kicked around backstage too long to believe in Prince Charmings. By the time of *Lucy,* both were nearly forty, and each seemed to realize that her immortality was reflected in the eyes of the other. This sense of eternity was literally embodied by Lucie Arnaz—the heir, some thought, to Lucy. But Lucie was more grown-up at twenty than her mother was at sixty. On *Here's Lucy,* Lucie exhibited extraordinary calm and poise—her wit was relaxed and gregarious (her brother, by contrast, was even more at sea than their father had been). On her recent series, *The Lucie Arnaz Show,* she showed great promise as a new-style Sitcom Queen, but the show was canceled after only a few episodes. *Laverne & Shirley* ran for seven seasons but failed to match any seven minutes of Lucy and Ethel. It was basically reactionary in its recreation of old *Lucy* skits: instead of chocolates on a conveyor belt there were bottles of beer. While Penny Marshall, a classic comedienne who was Garry's sister, maintained Desilu's tradition of nepotism, Cindy Williams, a character actress who'd worked with George Cukor and George Lucas, recalled Vance's feelings of exclusion (she eventually left the show in a huff). But their offscreen conflicts never expanded their onscreen characters—Laverne and Shirley were two shriveled peas in a pod. The combination of stale routines and personal stalemates resulted in a show that can only be called decadent. If anybody revives Desi's spirit again, he or she must find a diva who can convey what Lucy had with her Best Friend and her only daughter: unfaked feeling.

5
LEAR LADIES

Bea Arthur   Mary Kay Place
Valerie Bertinelli   Esther Rolle
Bonnie Franklin   Isabel Sanford
Marla Gibbs   Jean Stapleton
Louise Lasser   Sally Struthers

The housedress, the bathrobe, the apron—these were the accoutrements of the Lear Lady. She wouldn't be caught dead in a $10,000 gown, not just because she couldn't afford it, but because it might take food out of a starving Ethiopian's mouth. Even Louise Jefferson, after she moved on up to the East Side, favored floral-print muumuus. At first glance the list of Lear Ladies reads like a roll call at the Democratic Convention: women of all ages, classes, races, religions, and persuasions. A transsexual character spiced up *All That Glitters,* while *A.K.A. Pablo* centered on a Hispanic family. Generally, though, Lear fashioned a dialectic for Middle America: Protestant whites versus Protestant blacks, and the lower-middle class versus the upper-middle class. Yes, *All in the Family* was a ground-breaking leap, a seminal series, but it sentimentalized conflicts in a way any meathead could understand. Being issue-oriented, Lear's work is literally dated—you can tell the year of a show by its topical references. *Family,* in particular, is a stroll down memory lane ("Those Were the Days"). But like so many Jewish producers, Lear never built a masterwork based on his own background. When one considers the wealth of Jewish talent in TV comedy and the dearth of Jewish characters in hit sitcoms, one sees the dance of Hollywood liberals: boogie to mass-cult music without stepping on your own toes. But Lear's art is more confessional than it seems: a Lear Lady is a Jewish mother at heart. Loud, warm, nurturing, plump, verbal, unglamorous, and smarter than the men in her life, the Lear Lady is almost always a homebody and the bedrock of her family. She can be urban or suburban, black or white, educated or backward, but she inhabits an all-American body to express an ethnicity too many feel is not yet ready for prime time.

Bea Arthur in Maude

B ea Arthur

Bea Arthur discovered Maude long before Norman Lear did. She'd always been Maude, just as Jean Stapleton had always been Edith. Lear's gift for casting was that he hired actors who'd already developed reputations as theatrical personalities. Arthur began as a cut-rate Tallulah Bankhead—imposing, deep-voiced, dramatic. But while Bankhead, a witty beauty, commented on her art through her life, Arthur, a literal-minded actress, married Gene Saks, Neil Simon's perennial director whom she divorced decades later (yes, just like Dorothy on *The Golden Girls)*. All this is another way of saying that Bankhead drew laughs as Bankhead, while Arthur needed punch lines to lay 'em in the aisles. When Bankhead died a legend, Arthur was breaking up Broadway as Vera Charles, the Tallulahish sidekick of Angela Lansbury's Mame. By the time of *Maude,* Arthur had orchestrated Bankhead's mannerisms into a symphony of glares, frowns, smirks, winces, and truculent gestures. Whenever Maude went up against a legion of men—husband Walter, cousin-in-law Archie, neighbor Arthur—it was like watching a sitcom version of *The Little Foxes*. Arthur is like a racehorse bred on one-liners—give her a good script and she's off. In *Golden Girls,* she squeezes more venom out of a poisonous put-down than anybody this side of Maude Findlay. Unlike Stapleton, who's spent every second since *All in the Family* trying to shake the specter of Edith, Arthur seems to embrace her image—*Golden Girls* could be renamed *Miami Maude*. Created by Susan Harris, an off-Broadway Lear, *Girls* gives Arthur a golden opportunity to keep alive a theatrical tradition Tallulah herself could claim as an epitaph: self-parody is the sincerest form of artistry.

V alerie Bertinelli

Valerie Bertinelli said recently that Sally Field is her idol, which is exactly what's wrong with her career. As Barbara on *One Day at a Time,* Bertinelli had a lot going for her: smarts, looks, likability. Next to her mushy mama (Bonnie Franklin) and sullen sister (Mackenzie Phillips), she looked like the last sane person in Learland. Because she grew up on the show, Bertinelli seemed to belong to her adoring audience, as do all Little Darlings. She wanted to make the transition to adulthood, but didn't want to betray the goodwill she'd built on *One Day*. Yet Field, who used *Sybil* as a springboard to Oscar-winning roles, has become an overgrown goody-goody—a menopausal Gidget. Embracing this image, Bertinelli stars in well-meaning TV movies about war widows, wayward nuns, and friendly witnesses for rape victims. Her eagerness to prove herself as an actress *and* be loved by millions is complicated by her marriage to Eddie Van Halen. I remember seeing her a couple of years ago on *The Tonight Show,* ruthlessly grilled by Joan Rivers on how to keep a rock star on the farm after he's seen groupies. But Bertinelli shouldn't have to make excuses to Rivers or take cues from Field. She should take a hard look at how to mature as an actress without coming across as a saintly bimbette. I'd love to have seen her turn up as Fallon on *The Colbys*—instead of waltzing in as a rattled sweetie-pie (Emma Samms), she could have washed up on shore after a Van Halen yacht party. Lord knows she already looks the part. With her streaked, frizzy mane, pouty puss, and searching eyes, Bertinelli is presenting herself as one thing and claiming she wants to be another. It's time she started acting less like a New Woman and more like a Pop Princess.

(Left to right): *Bonnie Franklin, Valerie Bertinelli, and Mackenzie Phillips in* One Day at a Time

Bonnie Franklin

Bonnie Franklin's face looks like a leaky hot water bottle: rubbery and wet. Her perennial expression—beatific grin, puddling eyes, cocked head—makes the Pietà seem jolly. Her Ann Romano on *One Day at a Time* was supposed to be a daring character—a divorced mother entering the work force—but Franklin could never let a plot speak for itself. For nine years she pumped for tears. Sometimes she seemed to get turned on by her own grief—some of her reaction shots are positively orgasmic. She could be merry, too, and furious and silly and mean-spirited, but she invariably reverted to a sanctimonious grin she clearly mistook for profound. Franklin's interpretation sabotaged her talent. I remember seeing her ages ago

in the pre-Broadway run of *Applause,* stopping the show cold as she belted the title tune (she's since reprised the number on TV talk shows; it's like watching Tony Orlando sing "Tie a Yellow Ribbon 'Round the Old Oak Tree" on a Dean Martin Celebrity Roast). In *Applause,* Franklin had the promise of a bright Broadway Baby, but as the damp Earth Mother on *One Day* she allowed herself to be upstaged in the same way she bumped Lauren Bacall off the boards. Not only did the eternally deft and funny Nanette Fabray steal the spotlight, but Shelley Fabares (Nanette's real-life niece) wiped everybody off the set with her wicked impersonation of an aging prom queen let loose in the business world. Even Valerie Bertinelli, who eventually became the soul of the show, undermined Franklin's authority. Maybe the problem with *One Day* began with its creator, Whitney Blake, who'd costarred with Shirley Booth on *Hazel* and gave birth to Meredith Baxter Birney in real life. She apparently had Franklin play Hazel as a *Family Ties*–style mom. The very thought justifies matricide.

Marla Gibbs

As Florence the maid on *The Jeffersons,* Marla Gibbs marched off with every scene she was in. She didn't do it by outshouting her costars (an impossibility), but by waiting for her cues and delivering the most beautifully timed wisecracks this side of Eve Arden. She was a reminder to her employers of where they came from and a challenge to male supremacists everywhere. Gibbs has kept this image alive as producer and star of *227,* a genial sitcom that's been blasted for not being as zippy as *The Golden Girls* or as seamless as *The Cosby Show.* The show works best when it stoops to the bitchy repartee of its own golden girls instead of aping the smug perfection of *Cosby.* Indeed, the most appealing aspect of the show is its messy struggles, economic and comedic. Its characters are working-class, confused, harassed, always striving for attitude amid chaos. This vulnerability makes *227* closer in spirit to the female-dominated *Mary Tyler Moore Show:* a rattled heroine, a down-to-earth sidekick (Alaina Reed), a malicious femme fatale (Jackee Harry), a nosy neighbor (Helen Martin), and a huggable male partner (Hal Williams). But it's *MTM* filtered through Norman Lear—sweetly buffoonish. Gibbs, half elbows and half mouth, allows her lusty cohorts to steal scenes in the same way she kept *The Jeffersons* on the air for eleven years. If the show has a fatal flaw, it's that it emphasizes situation (a smashed car) at the expense of comedy (jokes arising from character). This contrasts with the strength of *Cosby,* whose humor is directly connected to human behavior. But if I prefer *227* to *Cosby,* it's because I'm more pleasantly seduced by feminine fanaticism than masculine megalomania.

Louise Lasser

Mary Hartman, Mary Hartman wasn't just a soap opera for people who didn't like soap operas, it was a TV series for people who didn't care for TV. Its star, Louise Lasser, was a perfect figurehead for the show's esthetic: deadpan smugness. Rubbing her teeth with her fingers and searching for waxy yellow buildup, Lasser reveled in a sort of detached narcissism. She wasn't playing herself or her character—she was drawing attention to her riffs as a spacey caricature. Even as a guest star on *Taxi,* playing Judd Hirsch's ex-wife, Lasser did a parody of the kind of helpmate that always refers to Lasser (*MH, MH,* too, reflected itself: a TV serial whose heroine believes TV commercials). Like her ex-husband, Woody Allen, Lasser sees the wealth of human emotion outside herself as something less important than her view of class and culture. There's "us"—the educated, the hip, the well-off—and "them"—the tacky, the vulgar, the stupid (i.e., the population of Fernwood). *Mary Hartman* was nothing less than TV's first yuppie hit—a campy celebration of cultural superiority. It filtered the cynical absurdism of Ernie Kovacs through the domestic realism of Norman Lear and came up with an extended pilot for *Late Night With David Letterman* (Letterman expunged women from the tradition and added a frat-house nastiness). The show wasn't exactly satire because its human targets were less puffed up with themselves than dragged down by their environment. Lasser never dramatized the self-absorption of her character, as Cybill Shepherd does in *Moonlighting,* or let us in on the joke of her genre, as Joan Collins does in *Dynasty.* She was like Shirley Booth on Quaaludes, which is about as apt a description of Mary Hartman as I can think of.

Esther Rolle (left) *and Ja'net DuBois in* Good Times

Mary Kay Place

There's a wonderful, wry warmth to Mary Kay Place. In *The Big Chill* she was the only character who wasn't twisted, stupid, sullen, vain, smug, obnoxious, or suicidal. All she wanted was a baby, so she merrily hopped into bed with her best friend's husband. Place doesn't make go-getting seem pushy—she's too nice. At the same time she subverts the decency of her characters with an open-eyed lustiness. Her Loretta Haggers in *Mary Hartman, Mary Hartman* is a campy cartoon—an *SCTV* send-up of a country-and-western diva—but Place gives Loretta unexpected shadings. She's almost less a Lear Lady than a Henning Honey, combining the loony logic of Gracie Allen, the corn-pone confidence of Irene Ryan, and the self-effacing sexuality of Donna Douglas. But if Place is less dynamic than any of these divas, it's because she had so few costars on *MH, MH* to charge up her feelings. I always looked forward to Loretta drop-

ping by Mary's kitchen, if only to block Louise Lasser's stares into space. Place *liked* Loretta. She admired her ambition, delighted in her defiance, even envied her sensibility. Maybe the density of Place's portrayal stems from her writing background: she won an Emmy nomination for a *M*A*S*H* episode and worked on *The Mary Tyler Moore Show*. But the struggle of her acting will be to reconcile the sharp *(MTM)* and mushy *(M*A*S*H)* sides of her personality. In 1986's *The Girl Who Spelled Freedom*, Place tearfully applauded a Cambodian refugee's spelling-bee victory. Maybe a Lear Lady lurks in her after all. But Place's aces in the hole are witty asides in lovefests *(Big Chill)* and lyrical touches in lampoons *(Mary Hartman)*. She ought to have a long talk with Loretta over a cup of coffee.

Esther Rolle

Esther Rolle can't hide her pain. A round-faced wit with deep-set eyes, Rolle can work up merriment but keeps the joy to herself. She has secrets she can't share. I don't know anything about Rolle's background or personal life, but she strikes me as the most severe black presence ever to hit sitcomland (and the most profound, too). That she wound up the heroine of a Learian series seemed to be some sort of joke: this woman hadn't had a life of *Good Times*. The show's title was intentionally ironic. Living in a Chicago project, scraping by from paycheck to paycheck, the Evans family exposed the underbelly of liberal piety. It's not for nothing that *Good Times* was a spinoff of *Maude*, in which Rolle played Bea Arthur's maid. As Arthur strained to prove her Democratic credentials, Rolle peered over a cake tin and smirked. *Good Times* itself teetered precariously between selling out (Jimmy Walker's jive-ass riffs) and talking turkey (Rolle's withering glares). When Rolle walked out on the show for a full season, she was making

Sherman Hemsley and Isabel Sanford in The Jeffersons

a statement about Lear's limitations in portraying left-wing ideals. During her exile, Rolle made a fine TV movie, *Summer of My German Soldier,* about a Jewish girl (Kristy McNichol) who falls in love with an escaped Nazi prisoner (Bruce Davison) in America's Deep South. Playing a mammytype role, less Hattie McDaniel in *Gone With the Wind* than Ethel Waters in *The Member of the Wedding,* Rolle brought out all the sorrow and wisdom of an achingly true stereotype. She won an Emmy for her performance, returned to *Good Times* for a final season, and has all but disappeared. She's probably less a victim of an insensitive industry than a prisoner of her own sensibility—a major actress with a minority viewpoint.

Isabel Sanford

You probably got your first look at Isabel Sanford in *Guess Who's Coming to Dinner?* She was the maid who bawled out Sidney Poitier for wanting to marry Katharine Houghton (you couldn't blame her—the movie was less about a bigoted society than a brain-damaged daughter). By the time of *All in the Family*—a video variation of *Dinner*—Sanford had advanced from Tracy and Hepburn's sassy domestic to Archie and Edith's next-door neighbor. And when she moved on up to the East Side in *The Jeffersons,* Sanford clipped her working-class roots and grew into a Hepburnish houseplant. The weirdness of Sanford is that the more money her character acquired, the more deafening she became as an actress—her voice vied with her muumuu-cum-wig as the loudest thing this side of a Mötley Crüe video. I don't think Sanford's tacky fashions were meant as a comment on the nouveau riche any more than Hepburn's butch outfits were supposed to suggest a double life. It's just that Sanford seemed to accept her increased responsibility with deliberate exaggeration (she even got bigger physically). Her scenes with skinny, shrimpy Sherman Hemsley were driven by a kind of cartoonish frenzy. When these lovebirds went at it, they looked like Fred and Wilma Flintstone playing each other's roles. I never bought the argument that *The Jeffersons* was demeaning to blacks or was the most idiotic series in TV history. Every sitcom limits the range of human experience—it's a genre of incidental pleasures—and *The Jeffersons* had one priceless joy: Marla Gibbs. Sanford simply fit into the scheme of the show. She was neither as ambiguous as Esther Rolle *(Good Times)* nor as riotous as LaWanda Page *(Sanford and Son)*. She was a workmanlike Lear Lady.

Jean Stapleton

Jean Stapleton's career would make a good *Twilight Zone*: a respected character actress sells her soul for a classic part that makes her rich and famous only to be seen as that character for the rest of her life. Part of Stapleton's problem in shaking Edith Bunker is that she's never really been able to play a wide variety of roles. Her rattled, loud, working-class women in the stage and screen versions of *Bells Are Ringing* and *Damn Yankees* are not all that different from Edith. Unlike Geraldine Page, who could pass herself off as a rich bitch in her younger days, Stapleton has always been the quintessential prole from a New York borough. Her triumph as Edith is that she

exaggerated all her own mannerisms and made them representative of an entire way of life. When you hear "New York housewife," you think of Edith even before Lucy. Her lovability, undercutting Archie's pomposities with offhand truths, made her a legend. Since *All in the Family* Stapleton has spent all her TV time trying to break Edith's spell, playing everything from Eleanor Roosevelt (hopeless) to Cinderella's fairy godmother (a Southern accent!) to a tap-dancing sleuth (don't ask). Not only did these roles resemble Edith, but they played on our affection for her— they were "nice" characters. Perhaps fed up herself, Stapleton gave a performance in 1985 that may be the richest of her career (and the strangest, too). As the vicious, neurotic matriarch in Showtime's adaptation of Jules Feiffer's *Grown-Ups,* Stapleton incinerated the stereotype of her life. Flailing menacingly and screeching through smirks, she did something trickier than make us forget Edith—she showed us the ugly side of the everpresentable Lear Lady.

Sally Struthers

It's interesting to think what Sally Struthers would be doing today if *All in the Family* hadn't come along. Just before landing the show, she was a regular on *The Smothers Brothers Comedy Hour* and *The Tim Conway Comedy Hour,* as well as Jack Nicholson's pickup in *Five Easy Pieces* and Sam Peckinpah's sexpot in *The Getaway.* Her talents as a variety player and an ironic sidekick never seemed to matter much in Lear's world, which demanded actresses of less variety and far less irony. So Struthers became Gloria—the princess of Queens. The role brought her immortality, but it also brought out the worst in her: a whiny, overbearing sentimentality. The funniest thing about Gloria was that she *looked* like her parents' offspring, combining Archie's piggy-faced pout with

Edith's goofy grins. Struthers also gave Gloria a wonderful get-down silliness, a willingness to go to any length to make a joke work. When she wraps her legs around Rob Reiner's waist, or thrusts her tongue between her lips and goes, "Bthbthbthbthbhthbth!," she's getting at something really nutty. But Struthers believes the Jewish mother in her character. She's a born nurturer with a weight problem. Even after she left *Family,* dumped Reiner, and got her own series *(Gloria),* Struthers still acted like a mother of mercy, playing an aspiring veterinarian. Her TV movies, centering on wife abuse *(Intimate Strangers),* deaf children *(And Your Name Is Jonah),* and MIAs *(My Husband Is Missing),* showcased her grating knack for crying on cue (I'd love to see her and Bonnie Franklin have a weep-off). Lately, she's made tearful TV pitches for starving children and starred in a Broadway revamp of *The Odd Couple.* Boo-hoos and boo-boos: the stuff of the Lear Lady.

TINKER TOOTSIES

Julia Duffy
Veronica Hamel
Valerie Harper
Cloris Leachman
Nancy Marchand

Mary Tyler Moore
Christina Pickles
Suzanne Pleshette
Betty Thomas
Betty White

Grant Tinker not only created a distinctive television universe, he married its premier diva: Mary Tyler Moore. You remember Grant and Mary at the Emmy Awards—he the great stoneface, so chiseled and gray he'd be on Mount Rushmore if only there were room; and she the toothy pixie, all smiles and goodwill. When Grant and Mary eventually divorced, leaving him to run NBC and her to star in *Ordinary People,* it gave the lie to the sophisticated calm of the Tinker Tootsie.

A Tinker Tootsie is a woman of means, brains, and looks. She carries herself with pride, but wonders why her life doesn't offer her more. Usually single, she's TV's first yuppette—she's driven. But she's basically too vulnerable to be classified as a bitch.

Tinker Tootsies belong to an exclusive sorority known as MTM Enterprises. A classy offspring of Grant and Mary's, MTM has produced a tasty variety of award-winning programs, from *The Mary Tyler Moore Show* to *Hill Street Blues*. That MTM is as adept at comedy as drama points up a telling truth about Tinker Tootsies: they're basically dramatic actresses with a redemptive streak of comedic brilliance.

Whether moneyed mavens (Nancy Marchand of *Lou Grant* and Julia Duffy of *Newhart),* uniformed workers (Betty Thomas of *Hill Street* and Christina Pickles of *St. Elsewhere),* urban housewives (Valerie Harper of *Rhoda* and Suzanne Pleshette of *The Bob Newhart Show),* status-seeking shrews (Cloris Leachman and Betty White of *Mary Tyler Moore),* or white-collar professionals (Veronica Hamel of *Hill Street* and Mary herself), a Tinker Tootsie exudes a witty wisdom that transcends the messier aspects of class and culture.

Even the explicitly ethnic Morgenstern family—Harper, mother Nancy Walker, and sister Julie Kavner—is warmly received in the sub-high-couture environment of the Tinker Tootsie: crisply tailored suits with Peter Pan collars, gingerly knit sweaters with geometric designs, soft pastels over vivid hues, cascading manes sprayed firmly into place, and the ever-presentable two-inch pumps. (It seems no accident that Rhoda's job was as a window dresser in a downtown department store.)

This all-accepting quality highlights MTM's predominant feature—ensemble acting. Except possibly for Mary, whose image is enhanced by her production savvy, a Tinker Tootsie is never a star in her own right—she's part of a group. (This is why Leachman and White bombed in their vehicles, *Phyllis* and *The Betty White Show*). Whether toiling in a police precinct, a city hospital, a TV station, a newspaper office, or a Vermont inn, a Tinker Tootsie belongs to a collection of crazies whose follies are connected to the structure of the plot. (Even Mary had the good sense to throw her show to her supporting cast.)

This familial atmosphere allows the Tinker Tootsie to express herself more forcefully. From Walker's yapping yenta to Marchand's iron-willed tycoon, from Pleshette's sharp-tongued helpmate to White's man-hungry homemaker, a Tinker Tootsie seeks power in a man's world. That she continually resorts to wit to get her way is indicative of her precarious position. She's a mass-market heroine and a national treasure: TV's first modern woman.

Julia Duffy

As Stephanie, the spoiled little rich girl on *Newhart*, Julia Duffy can bring tears of joy to your eyes—her timing is sharper than her looks. Tossing her blonde curls and cooing like a baby dove, she rings more changes on a line than any blonde bombshell since Mae West. Like West, Duffy is a physical oddity: her body is part of her comedy. Long-waisted, big-headed, and dangerously tiny, she flounces into scenes with an assurance that's a comment on her character's arrogance. But if West accented syllables to invoke a double entendre, Duffy races through punch lines to make a point about the wealthy, who needn't bother to waste breath on mere language. When, after doing some light cleaning, she's told she looks "mussed,"

Duffy snaps, "Well, that's what happens when you do blue-collar work in silk." Her delivery is breathless, bitter, swift, downplaying the joke to heighten its effect. She's like a Kewpie doll intoxicated by her own cuteness. Her face—sculpted alabaster broken by almond-shaped baby blues and bee-stung lips—is always in repose, except when contorted in a pout. She's matched every step of the way by Peter Scolari's stuck-up yuppie, Michael, whose aspirations seem puny next to his beloved's true worth. Duffy's Stephanie is unique among Tootsies in that she's a gorgeous girl born with money—she's everything Cloris Leachman's Phyllis pretends to be. But like Phyllis, she's a pain in the ass. That she's tolerated at all is a tribute to the Tootsie's ability to transcend self-absorption with personal style. When Duffy brought this style to a tragic-heroic character in the Civil War miniseries, *The Blue and the Gray,* she was faintly ridiculous. She's the kind of woman whose petticoat is never soiled by blood, only because it leaves such a nasty stain.

Veronica Hamel

The only high-couture Tootsie in Tinker's stable, Hamel is a model-turned-actress who can really act. But as Joyce Davenport—Pizza Man's main squeeze on *Hill Street Blues*—she's been robbed of the juiciest material. While the show is sweaty, pretentious, and self-consciously "realistic," Hamel is glacial even in the midst of chaos—she glides through the set like a *Twilight Zone* zombie with a superiority complex. Yes, she plays a respected attorney, a dedicated careerist, a woman of wit and intelligence, but she's not as forceful as the grubbier members of MTM's most celebrated ensemble. Basically, Hamel is a diva in search of a project—she has depths that are unexplored by the male-obsessed sensibilities behind *Hill Street*. In only two TV specials, shot during *Hill Street*

Veronica Hamel in Hill Street Blues

hiatuses, has Hamel been given the chance to strut her stuff. In *Sessions,* a fine TV movie about a Manhattan call girl, Hamel undercuts the pain of her character's double life with an exquisitely wistful irony. And in the remake of *Valley of the Dolls* (even more wretched than the movie), Hamel handles her suicide scene with what can only be described as understated melancholia. This is the key to Hamel's talent: showing us the sadness beneath the cheerful façade of the Tinker Tootsie (Mary Tyler Moore did the same thing in *Ordinary People*). But it's a talent that can be abused easily. In the miniseries *Kane & Abel* Hamel cried on cue while Sam Neill and Peter Strauss went head-to-head. Even in *Hill Street* Hamel is often set against a gray wall, her hair pulled straight back, her eyes full of longing. If she's lost the Emmy five years in a row, it may be because the creators of *Hill Street* simply do not know what to do with that "look."

Valerie Harper

Until recently, Valerie Harper was the saddest casualty of California psychobabble: a gifted comedienne who'd lost her sense of humor. As Rhoda Morgenstern on *The Mary Tyler Moore Show,* and in her own spinoff, *Rhoda,* Harper endeared herself to an ethnically diverse nation by embodying its best traits. Unpretentious, down-to-earth, self-deprecating, Harper proved a social point leavened by wit: it's the sass of the proletariat—not the nuclear family—that's the backbone of America. She won the hearts of women, who identified with her physical insecurity, and seized the affections of men, who responded to her dead-on sarcasm. But after *Rhoda* left the air, Harper zealously set out to separate herself from her character. A fanatical est graduate, she recited pop-therapeutic

(Left to right): *Nancy Walker, Valerie Harper, and Julie Kavner in* Rhoda

buzzwords, robotlike, in interviews. Taking "responsibility" for her own life, Harper slimmed down, dumped her husband of thirteen years, and sought supporting roles in movies. To prepare for her part in *Chapter Two* she worked with physical trainer Tony Cacciotti (who now shares her private life as well as her production company). Her near-anorexic appearance in the film prompted critics to inquire about her health. Gaining a few pounds, Harper continued to polish her image as a concerned actress in high-minded TV movies: *The Shadow Box* (cancer patients), *Fun and Games* (sexual harassment), *The Execution* (Holocaust survivors). But early in 1986, Harper bounced back in *Valerie,* a conspicuously minor sitcom that's also likable and extremely smart. Its appeal rests on Harper's bullheadedness in the face of teenage smugness, embodied by the wonderful young actor Jason Bateman. It seems Harper's pulled off a miracle: she's merged the two Valeries in a way even Rhoda might like.

Cloris Leachman

An actress's actress, Cloris Leachman is an Oscar-winner *(The Last Picture Show),* a cult-movie star *(Kiss Me Deadly),* a *Philco Playhouse* heroine ("Nocturne"), a song-and-dance girl *(Cher),* a Mel Brooks stock player *(Young Frankenstein),* and a Miss America runner-up (1946). It's this dizzying variety that allowed Leachman to bring such detail to her acid portrait of Phyllis Lindstrom on *The Mary Tyler Moore Show* and its spinoff, *Phyllis.* If her own show failed to match the glittering highlights of her appearances with Mary, it's because Leachman's talent is the most concentrated of all Tinker Tootsies: she never forgot an effect she ever achieved. Like the immortal Mildred Natwick, Leachman is best in small doses—her every gesture carries with it the history of the theater. Perhaps Leachman played Phyllis so knowingly

because there's a lot of Phyllis in Leachman. Self-dramatizing, self-centered, and self-consciously colorful, Leachman is continually asserting her dominance over more sensible characters. When Mary complains about the loneliness of her life, Leachman snaps, "You don't know what loneliness is till you get into bed with Lars." When Leachman, freshly widowed, appears at the top of the stairs in a flaming red gown in the first episode of *Phyllis,* a character cracks, "Why do I get the feeling we should be singing 'Hello, Dolly!'?" It's this utter self-possession that makes Leachman such a great Tootsie. She brings dramatic density to punch lines and comic timing to kitchen-sink realism. An incurable ham, she's as indispensable as she is incorrigible.

Nancy Marchand

A Broadway Baby kidnapped by MTM, Nancy Marchand exudes a precise theatricality uncommon among American actresses. Indeed, *Lou Grant* costar Ed Asner says Marchand "puts those English dames to shame." Her imperiousness served her well as Margaret Pynchon, publisher of the *Los Angeles Tribune.* Bitchy, regal, tough-minded, Marchand refused to be one of the boys only because it would be a step down. When Asner lectured Marchand on a point of journalistic integrity, she purred, "You are absolutely right, Mr. Grant. Now get out of here." She wielded power in a man's world, but always retained her catty edge. Based, some say, on the *Washington Post*'s Kay Graham, Marchand's Pynchon is closer in spirit to a godmother of Grant (Tinker, not Lou) and Mary's—she combines their best qualities. Like Grant, she's a tycoon whose severe looks are backed up by clout; like Mary, she's a smartly tailored cookie whose femininity never crumbles. A veteran of the New York stage and the Golden Age of Television (she played opposite Rod Steiger in

Cloris Leachman in Phyllis

Nancy Marchand in Lou Grant

the original "Marty"), Marchand never flinches in the face of complex characters. Her paramount role in Christopher Durang's *Sister Mary Ignatius Explains It All for You* allowed her to flaunt the bitter irony of her own starkly comic presence. A sharp-witted, chain-smoking New Yorker, she commuted to California to appear on *Lou Grant*. She won four Emmys for her trouble, beating out such certified Hollywood personalities as Meredith Baxter Birney and Jessica Walter. She rented herself to MTM, but didn't sell her soul. Her aloofness isn't just a trait of Mrs. Pynchon's—it's a tribute to the coolness of the Tinker Tootsie.

Mary Tyler Moore

The most coolly accomplished comedienne in TV history, Mary Tyler Moore went from a disembodied pair of legs on *Richard Diamond, Private Detective* to an impossibly sexy housewife on *The Dick Van Dyke Show* to a career girl determined to make it after all on *The Mary Tyler Moore Show*. That she made it so big is a testament to the complexity of her own sensibility. With hubby Grant, Mary forged an image that paralleled the

Mary Tyler Moore and Dick Van Dyke in The Dick Van Dyke Show

aspirations of a generation of women. She's a bourgeois lady who wants the good life without being dependent on a man. A semistylish product of Doris Day comedies, *Cosmopolitan* magazine, and Bloomingdale's catalogues, Mary's Mary Richards seeks power from a position of powerlessness. Though an associate producer at a TV station, she performs secretarial duties and can't bring herself to call her boss by his first name. The key to her personality comes when Mr. Grant asks her if she's "been around." Whimpers Mary: "I've been nearby." She's Mrs. Pynchon without maturity, breeding, or a rich, dead husband. But she is, after all, making it on her own. When the real Mary decided to do the same, she left her series, divorced Grant, and became a dramatic actress on TV *(First, You Cry)*, on Broadway *(Whose Life Is It, Anyway?)*, and onscreen *(Ordinary People)*. Stripping away the artifice of her comedic image, Mary showed us the death mask underneath. But she was either a spirited victim of disease or a pitiable sacrifice to family unity. Her performance in *People* was scathingly exact, but it also endorsed the antifeminist bias against her character. Here was a wife and mother who kept a perfect house for twenty years, and all she got in return were two weepy nerds in crewneck sweaters harassing her for not "loving" them (if the movie had had any guts, it would've ended with the father and son trying to figure out how to work the washing machine). Yes, Mary dared to expose a darker side of the Tootsie—the control freak terrified of affection—but she had more independence as Mary Richards, who at least got to keep what she earned (even Laura Petrie got to stay in suburbia with her breast-beating husband and son). In more recent roles, Mary has watched others meet grisly fates: her little daughter in *Six Weeks*, James Garner in *Heartsounds*, Ted Danson in *Just Between Friends*. But she's denying herself the full power of the Tootsie's dramatic flip side—the malicious drive of the prissy wit. In her latest sitcom, *Mary*, she added bitchiness to her old format—Mary "grows up." But the show pretended to a light-spiritedness it didn't really feel. Its mustiness was underscored by *All Is Forgiven*, a sparkling sitcom whose opening credits were more evocative of *MTM* than was all of *Mary*. The show's star, Bess Armstrong, was a delicious update of Mary Richards, partly because she was the appropriate age for a struggling career girl. But America wants Mary to stay its sweetheart forever *(Mary*'s being revamped to meet this demand). While her fans wallow in nostalgia, Mary approaches fifty. But the irony is that Mary's never *been* a sweetheart—like Doris Day, she's an edgy diva. Basically, Mary botched her comeback. She should've taken advantage of the family-sitcom craze by starring as a *People*-type mom who makes life hell for her snotty teenaged kids. It would've merged the Mary we love *(MTM)* and the Mary we respect *(People)* into a Tootsie for tomorrow. But as the Real Mary becomes dwarfed by the Legendary Mary, she may never take the advice of another legendary survivor: Don't Look Back.

Christina Pickles

As Nurse Helen Rosenthal on *St. Elsewhere*, Christina Pickles gives the coolness of the Tinker Tootsie a wry twist: she's warmly ironic. Eyebrows arched in amusement, supremely intelligent, Pickles seems tickled by everything around her. Though far from impervious to the chaos of St. Eligius, she isn't overwhelmed, either—she's a professional. Even when felled by personal tragedy—a mastectomy—Pickles just curls up in her cardigan and gets on with it. In one bright episode Pickles has an affair with a huggable married man. Meeting him at a motel, she reveals her physical condition without a trace of self-pity. This grown-up sensibility makes Pickles the most appealing woman in either of MTM's towering ensemble dramas, *St. Elsewhere* and *Hill Street Blues*. While *Elsewhere* is less offensively brutal than *Hill Street*—it's closer in spirit to *The Mary Tyler Moore Show*—it shares *Hill Street*'s difficulty in creating compelling female characters, who tend to be either

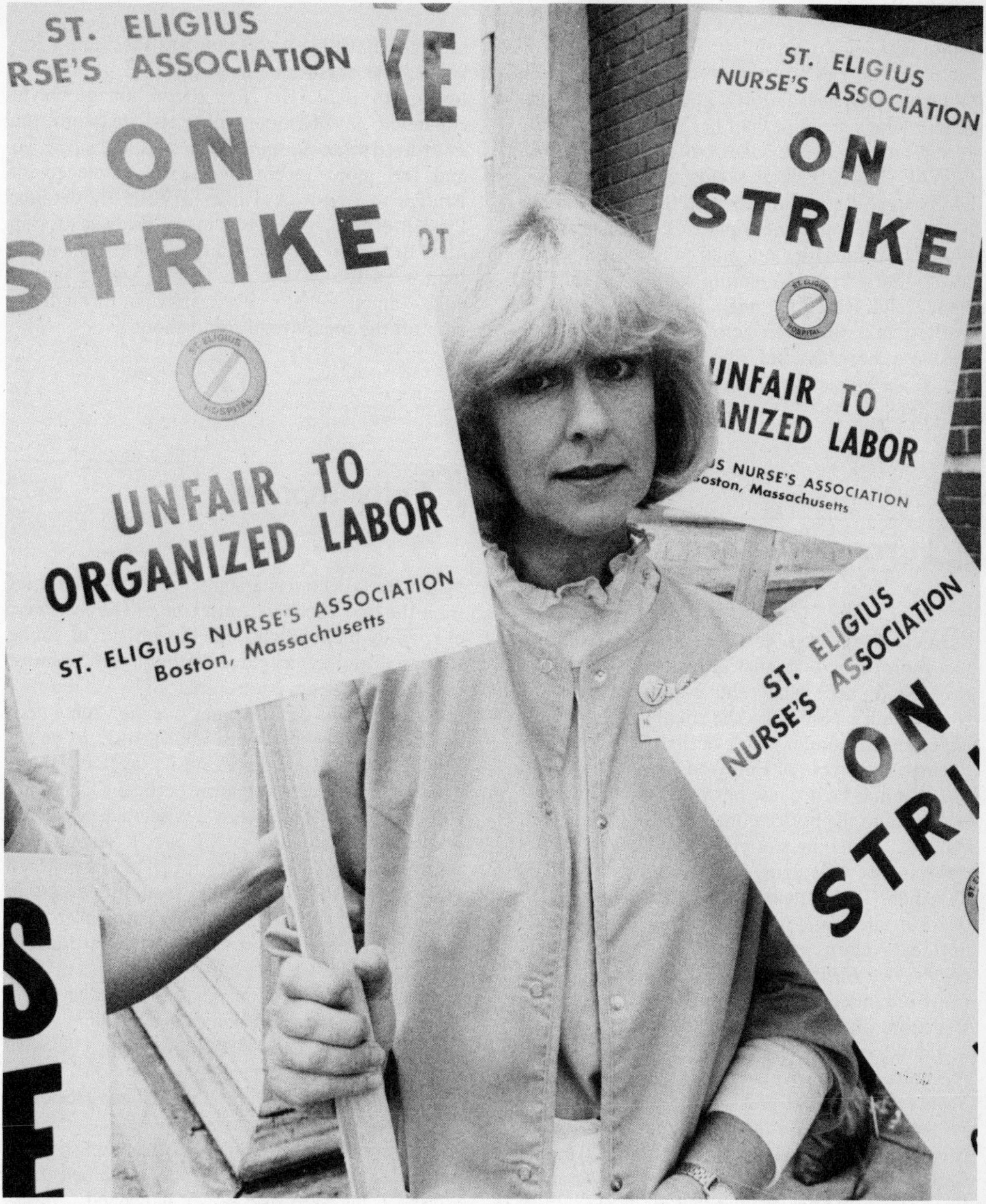

Christina Pickles in St. Elsewhere

polite witnesses to men's problems or just one of the boys. But Pickles is a rarity—a working mother who can assert her identity without losing her femininity (she's smarter than her male colleagues). A veteran of daytime soaps *(Another World, The Guiding Light),* Pickles seems right at home on TV's classiest prime-time serial. She faces trauma head-on. Her directness paid off in an against-type role as the lascivious matron in the miniseries *Space*. Tarted up and leering wildly, she showed what Helen Rosenthal might be with a few bucks in the bank. But even here Pickles brought out the wit of her character. She's a Tootsie with real brains—a woman who sees the comedy in drama.

Suzanne Pleshette

Suzanne Pleshette's voice—a gravelly contralto just short of a growl—has always been older than the rest of her. When she was twenty-five she sounded fifty. Now fifty, she sounds like the most experienced woman who ever lived. If she failed to surpass her role of Emily on *The Bob Newhart Show,* it may be because her voice and body never added up to the bottom-line bozos in Hollywood. Even as a stunning starlet Pleshette was cast as a doormat for male egos, from Jerry Lewis to Troy Donahue. This brutalization sometimes tapped her deepest talents. Her performance, for example, as the lovelorn schoolteacher in Alfred Hitchcock's *The Birds* was steeped in a heavy-lidded irony reminiscent of the young Marlene Dietrich. But more often Pleshette stayed stuck in a series of thankless parts. By the time of *Bob Newhart* Pleshette was a bright, brittle, fearsome-looking beauty with the sharpest tongue this side of Eve Arden's. Allegedly a third-grade teacher, she existed to poke holes in Newhart's inflated hysteria. Married to a psychologist, surrounded by crazies, Pleshette exuded a sane wit that made everything around her look all the more ridiculous. The role

seems to have been conceived as Pleshette's Revenge: she got even for all those years of kow-towing to men. But her sitcom image never expanded in subsequent projects, including the short-lived series *Suzanne Pleshette Is Maggie Briggs* and the more recent mid-season replacement *Bridges to Cross.* A Tinker Tootsie by default, Pleshette has crossed too many bridges to stop now. But she's far more than Maggie Briggs, more than even Emily. She's a Tootsie with a jagged edge—an edge that's never really cut through the crap on the messy road to divahood.

Betty Thomas

When Betty Thomas assumed the roll-call duties from the late Michael Conrad on *Hill Street Blues,* everybody balked: who was this impudent young woman displacing a beloved father figure? Almost immediately Thomas was replaced by yet another crusty old man. But a deeper question remained: what does a Tinker Tootsie have to do to be accepted as one of the guys? Surely, as Lucy Bates, Thomas is the butchest Tootsie of them all: a broad-shouldered six-footer with a wisecrack for every occasion. An alumnus of Chicago's Second City improvisational comedy troupe, Thomas learned early on how to downplay her femininity to attain power. But there's something disconcertingly smirky and false about Thomas—her attitude is skin-deep. She tries so hard to be imposing, she makes her flickering moments of vulnerability look like lapses in concentration. She's a willing victim of MTM's sexual catch-22: a woman must be twice as good as a man to beat him at his own game. The only Tootsie to triumph was Eileen Heckart's Aunt Flo on *The Mary Tyler Moore Show*—a hard-bitten reporter who flaunts her accomplishments before lesser male colleagues. When she beds Lou, a disbelieving Mary asks how it happened. "Well," croons Heckart, "if I was good enough for

Churchill . . ." The problem with Thomas is that she isn't good enough for Churchill. If *Hill Street*'s creators had cared enough to give Lucy Bates a plausible identity, they would have made her a lesbian. Instead, they introduced a lesbian character in 1986 (played by Lindsay Crouse) to team up with Thomas. When Crouse is falsely accused of sexual misconduct, Thomas defends her thusly: "The percentage of lesbian cops is damn low." Thanks, MTM. After six years, Thomas is still the only Tootsie who buries her wit out of fear.

B etty White

Betty White

If Lucille Ball is the Queen of Television, Betty White is its Princess. In the '50s she starred in two sitcoms *(Life With Elizabeth, Date With the Angels),* appeared as a regular on game shows (warming up for *Password),* and won an Emmy as the Most Outstanding Female Personality (Liberace won among men). But as the deliciously malicious Sue Ann Nivens on *The Mary Tyler Moore Show* (two more Emmys), White cashed in on a career of thankless chores. She got the role when MTM producers sent out word for "a Betty White type" until they realized they could get the real thing. A wit, a presence, a pro, Betty White has always been the real thing. When she sashayed onto the set of *MTM,* she brought with her the history of TV. Every leer, every twinkle, every wisecrack was attuned to the dynamics of video. She knew how to fill the box with expressive effect. The shock of Sue Ann was a double-edged gag: White reflected the Happy Homemaker's squeaky-clean image—when she talked dirty, it was as if Marie Osmond were picked up for soliciting. Whether commenting on Mary's chastity, Murray's baldness, or Lou's libido, White bullied her costars by natural right. If her own vehicle, *The Betty White Show,* failed, it's a simple matter of too much of a good thing: White shines brightest among equally luminous stars. After *MTM* left the air, White supported Vicki Lawrence's tour de force on *Mama's Family* and won a fourth Emmy for the lame game show, *Just Men!* Her delightful metamorphosis as a dim-witted Harris Harridan on *The Golden Girls* shows she isn't content to play Sue Ann for the rest of her life. Being a Tootsie is just one step on the road to TV divahood. If she'd married Grant Tinker thirty years ago, she'd be running all three networks.

HENNING HONEYS

Gracie Allen
Bea Benaderet
Ann B. Davis
Rosemary DeCamp
Donna Douglas

Eva Gabor
Nancy Kulp
June Lockhart
Meredith MacRae
Irene Ryan

The shenanigans of Norman Lear and Grant Tinker in the '70s have obscured the antics of the King of '60s Sitcoms: Paul Henning. His brilliant mega-hit *The Beverly Hillbillies* ran for nine years and spawned two spinoffs, *Petticoat Junction* and *Green Acres*. Collectively the three shows racked up a total of twenty-two seasons, made a fortune for CBS, and offered the most perverse collection of divas ever to hit prime time.

If Lear was a social satirist and Tinker a high comedian, Henning was a video vaudevillian—his humor reached back to burlesque. A writer for *The George Burns and Gracie Allen Show* and the force behind *The Bob Cummings Show* in the '50s, Henning resurrected an ancient style of comedy for the Pepsi generation. His view of women was a function of his esthetic: he dramatized the characteristics of gender. If the Lear Lady is red-blooded, and the Tinker Tootsie blue-blooded, the Henning Honey is no-blooded. A theatrical creation, she has greasepaint in her veins.

A Henning Honey is happy to humiliate herself—she'll do anything for a laugh. Living by the motto, "Show business is my life," she never behaves like a normal woman. Just as her male co-stars often appear in drag—Max Baer, Jr., as his cousin Jethrene and Roy Clark as his dipsomaniac mother in *Hillbillies*—a Henning Honey is conspicuously fantastic. Whether dressed as a backwoods bag lady (Irene Ryan in *Hillbillies*) or an East Side matron (Eva Gabor in *Acres*), speaking in non sequiturs (Gracie Allen in *Burns and Allen*) or a Bryn Mawr drawl (Nancy Kulp in *Hillbillies*), a Henning Honey is a disruptive force in her environment.

A Henning Honey is either a barbarian who's basically civilized or a civilized lady who's really a barbarian. This don't-judge-a-book-by-its-cover theme reflects the Honey's showbiz life: she's in a glamorous profession that demands a lot of hard work. It seems no accident that June Lockhart and Meredith MacRae (mid-series replacements on *Junction*) tried to match the reputations of their theatrical parents, that Allen and Ryan (paramount Henning Honeys) were ex-vaudevillians, or that Kulp and Donna Douglas (physical con-

George Burns and Gracie Allen

trasts on *Hillbillies*) all but disappeared from the business.

Even Henning's own daughter Linda appeared in the original cast of *Junction* (and vanished), while Bea Benaderet—Henning's spiritual aunt—went from a continuing part on *Burns and Allen* to frequent guest shots on *Hillbillies* to the starring role on *Junction,* where she died during the run of the series. This generational saga offers famous showbiz names that parallel the familial entanglements of the Clampetts, Bodines, Bradleys, Douglases, and Carsons.

But the Henning Honey refuses to fill a traditional female role. She's neither a passive life-giver nor a civilizing force in her family's life (she's usually crazier than any man in her gunsight). Her independence doesn't spring from wealth or poverty—it comes from the honky-tonk music inside her own head. Like a Broadway gypsy, she may be broke one day and in the chips the next. She may wind up in a Beverly Hills mansion or a rural shack. Either way, she plays for keeps—she's in a business that's trained her to go for broke. Working on the edge of reality, she creates a single, vivid image and then quietly fades away.

G racie Allen

If Gracie Allen had been a painter, she'd have specialized in melting watches. Her breathless monologues—irrational, jumbled, oxymoronic—are riotously surreal, seemingly yanked from the unconscious (she verbalized what Lucy acted out). A product of vaudevillians, Gracie had been on-stage for over a decade when she hooked up with George Burns. For the next twenty-eight years, George and Gracie conquered vaudeville, movies, and radio before landing on television in 1950. Their series, *The George Burns and Gracie Allen Show,* which ran for eight seasons, was the most bizarrely self-reflexive sitcom in TV history—a

deadpan *Twilight Zone* hosted by a stand-up Jean-Luc Godard. As Gracie launched into a convoluted story about the nutty members of her family, George would lean into the camera, explaining it all, or retreat to the den to watch the other characters on his TV set. Gracie's gift was that she never lost the logic of her illogic—she made you think *you* were crazy. Grinning giddily and batting her eyes sweetly, she was a perfect foil for the unflappable George—World War III couldn't throw him. George said recently that Gracie had a helluva time memorizing her voluminous speeches, that he regrets having made her work so hard. Putting an end to the show six years before her death, Gracie had no Emmy to show for her trouble. This is understandable: Gracie was enchanting but not entirely lovable (like Lucy). Gliding on the detached rhythms of her show, she didn't always grab your heart. At the close of each episode there was no comforting "Baby, you're the greatest!"—just "Say good night, Gracie." She was a comic miracle ahead of her time—a Henning Honey with brains.

B ea Benaderet

The housemother of the Henning Honey sorority, Bea Benaderet served eight years on *The George Burns and Gracie Allen Show,* one year on *The Beverly Hillbillies,* and five years on *Petticoat Junction* until her death in 1968. Though her characters changed radically from series to series, her function on each show remained the same: to grapple with impossible divas. Whether dealing with the otherworldly logic of Gracie, the cantankerous sarcasm of Granny, or the spirited antics of Billie Joe, Bobbie Jo, and Betty Jo, Benaderet provided a calm center to centrifugal lunacy. A horse-faced yet handsome wit, Benaderet could play crazy herself—her Pearl Bodine on *Hillbillies* wasn't exactly Margaret Mead—but she was al-

(Left to right): *Bea Benaderet, her girls, and Eva Gabor in* Petticoat Junction

ways confronted by an even more demented personality. Her byplay with Gracie was particularly hilarious and even touching: she understood this woman, though she couldn't explain her. Their misadventures together mystified their husbands. How could two such different women join forces to wreak so much havoc? While the unflappable Burns channeled his confusion into narrated asides, the hysterical husband of Benaderet couldn't hold on to his sanity: four different actors played the role of Harry Morton. On *Hillbillies* Benaderet met her match in Irene Ryan—their bitch fights are a scream. Worse, Benaderet had to endure the ugliest daughter any woman ever had: Max Baer, Jr., in blond curls and pinafore. By the time of *Junction*, Benaderet was coasting. Three fetching daughters were a breeze after Gracie and Granny.

Ann B. Davis

What Charles Nelson Reilly is to men, Ann B. Davis is to women—comically androgynous. As Schultzy, the lovesick secretary on *The Bob Cummings Show*, Davis pursued her boss with a suspicious fervor: why would she want him or he want her? While he slobbered over every gorgeous girl who wandered into his office, she stood behind him, leering. It wasn't at all clear who was after whom. After all, there's a lot of Reilly in Cummings. He's preposterously persnickety, never seems to land a girl, and lives with his older sister. He also hangs out with his cute teenage nephew, who hustles cash from him by commenting on his "sex appeal." Meanwhile Davis is back at the of-

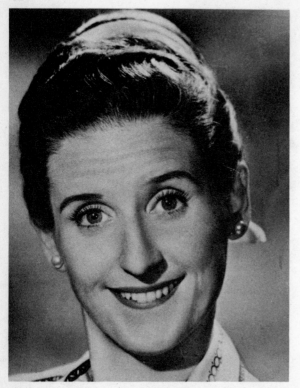

Ann B. Davis in The Bob Cummings Show

Rosemary DeCamp

fice, peeking through a sliding door to Cummings's photographic studio and getting into bitch fights with beautiful babes. When she's called "bitter" by one of these women, Davis barks, "Look, Blondie. Nature gave me everything she gave you— only I didn't ask for seconds!" When Davis asked for seconds in a series, she wound up as the gym teacher—Miss Wilson—on *The John Forsythe Show*. When she asked for thirds, she was put in charge of the brood on *The Brady Bunch*. Though her character, Alice, showed softer sides, Davis made an appearance as Alice's cousin—an Army drill sergeant. Somehow the joke of Davis's image never came across as funnily as it should have (Reilly wasn't a scream in sitcoms, either). Despite her two consecutive Emmys for *Cummings,* Davis didn't bring enough shading to her mugging—she didn't put heartfelt spins on her punch lines, as Nancy Kulp did on *The Beverly Hillbillies*. Professional to a fault, Davis plays better in memory than in reality.

If Rosemary DeCamp doesn't have stigmata on her palms, it's a miracle. As TV's premier doormat, she existed to play stooge to insatiable male egos, first to Jackie Gleason on *The Life of Riley* and then to Bob Cummings on his show. If that weren't humiliation enough, she showed up on *The Beverly Hillbillies* as a historical preservationist, letting Granny and Mrs. Drysdale get all the laughs, and stumped for Borax soap on *Death Valley Days,* watching fellow huckster Ronald Reagan go on to God-knows-what. As Margaret MacDonald on *The Bob Cummings Show,* DeCamp had her liveliest role. A merry widow doting on her nutty teenage son (Dwayne Hickman) and perpetually hysterical brother (Cummings), DeCamp seemed to be the only character whose brains weren't fried. But what she gained in dignity, she lost in laugh lines—she was a tireless straight man. Even when she showed some backbone, insisting on going out with a wolfish pal of her brother's, she still has to say to Cummings, "I was dating while you were still in knickers" (it's more like the other way around). If DeCamp was such a willing patsy, it may have something to do with how she presents herself. There's skittishness, a ladylike self-effacement in her delivery and demeanor—she doesn't want to step on anybody's toes (or lines). Her appearance on *Hillbillies* is particularly sweet—she almost apologizes for being in the frame, and the other actors seem nervous for her. Perhaps understandably, DeCamp's roles as Marlo Thomas's mom on *That Girl* and Shirley Jones's mother on episodes of *The Partridge Family* are all but forgotten. If she's remembered primarily for the campiness of her name, it may be because she was too good for her own good.

Donna Douglas

A video variation on *Li'l Abner*'s Daisy Mae, Donna Douglas was a weirdly erotic presence. Squeezed into button-busting blouses and sprayed-on jeans, she was an innocent in touch with barbarism. Though she had boyfriends (Dash Riprock), she communed with "critters": she talked to them and they seemed to understand. The joke of Elly May was that she didn't know she was a hot number. Her healthy respect of animal lust made her immune to assaults from libidos hooked on *Playboy* centerfolds. A contrast in every way to Nancy Kulp's horny Miss Hathaway, Douglas embodied the civilized virtue of backwoods simplicity. While the cultured Kulp was lasciviously eyeing Jethro, Douglas was sweetly slipping her tongue into a goat's ear. That Kulp looked like a slutty voyeur while Douglas came off like Mother Teresa is a tribute to the goodness of Elly May. This purity was accented by Douglas's willingness to let the other women on *The Beverly Hillbillies* steal the show. As Kulp and Irene Ryan drew the laughs, Douglas smiled benevolently and batted her baby blues. Her diffidence seems to be part of her career: she has virtually no TV credits either before or after *Hillbillies,* except for a reunion special in 1981 and a few guest shots on pre-*Hillbillies* series *(Hennesey, The Adventures of Ozzie and Harriet)*. She became a glittering creation on a single show and then quietly got out of the business.

Eva Gabor

Unlike sister Zsa Zsa, who turned her life into her art, Eva Gabor actually went out and became an actress. Her TV credits include a stint on *Ponds Theater* and a *Masterpiece Playhouse* production of "Uncle Vanya." But it was as Lisa Douglas on *Green Acres* that Gabor gave the performance of her life. She's a Henning Honey at heart. Even in her early movie roles, such as *The Last Time I Saw Paris,* there was a streak of wantonness in Gabor. Her cool was deceptive; here was a woman who'd been around and liked what she saw. On *Acres* she did a parody of the Gabor image—a dizzy dame rolling in dough who isn't as stupid as she seems. You can't help but sympathize with her. Who'd want to trade "a penthouse view" for a Hooterville farm? But when hubby Eddie Albert sang, "You are my wife," and she lamented, "Goodbye, city life!," you realized she was smart enough to give in to her misguided meal ticket. But she exacted her revenge through attitude. Flighty, yakky, unflappably silly, she took years off Albert's life—she seemed to be waiting for the dope to die so she could move back to New York with all his money. Moreover, she adjusted to rural living better than he adjusted to her. While she was skipping through the yard in a silk shift merrily naming all the animals, he was frowning at a broken water pipe with Mr. Haney peering over his shoulder. Her free-spiritedness can flourish anywhere: she can dish the dirt with Park Avenue matrons or high-hat Arnold the pig. Despite her ritzy appearance, she's an indomitable force of Nature.

Nancy Kulp

As Jane Hathaway on *The Beverly Hillbillies,* Nancy Kulp gave homely women hope. She never let her looks stand in the way of what she wanted. What she wanted was about six-feet-four with rippling muscles, supple butt, and curly black hair. Her name was a joke: this Jane couldn't land her Tarzan. Spying, leering, pleading, dressing up in a wild array of exotic outfits, Kulp etched the most hilarious portrait of unrequited love in TV history.

Nancy Kulp in The Beverly Hillbillies

A cross between Ann B. Davis's man-hungry Schultzy and her own Pamela Livingston from *The Bob Cummings Show,* Kulp was an irreproachable Tasteful Lady, except when Jethro was around, and stole every scene she was ever in, except when Granny was around. Using each inch of her scrawny frame to comic effect, Kulp was a physical miracle even when she wasn't given the laugh lines. Often a straight man to Mr. Drysdale, Kulp kept tightening her mouth and clenching her elbows until her scenes were funny. She was nominated only once for the Emmy (a crime) and lost to Frances Bavier's Aunt Bee. But she was an indispensable force behind the success of *Hillbillies.* If Irene Ryan was the soul of the show, Kulp was its brains: her obvious intelligence gave weight to the gags. Though presented as a feminist nightmare, Kulp subverted the stereotype—she made you root for her smarts. After *Hillbillies* left the air, Kulp devoted her smarts to politics, running for Congress in Pennsylvania in 1984. Buddy Ebsen, a right-wing Republican, endorsed her opponent, and she lost in a landslide. But Kulp has the sweetest revenge in reruns: she wipes every man off the screen three times a day. A perfect Henning Honey, she's a lusty spirit inside a civilized body. If she ran for President, I'd vote for her.

June Lockhart

A Mother Figure since the days of Methuselah, June Lockhart is a Henning Honey for her extraordinary showbiz background. Her father, Gene Lockhart, was an early vaudevillian who appeared in over one hundred films. Her mother, Kathleen, was also an actress. She herself was on the stage at eight and made her movie debut (with her parents) in the 1938 version of *A Christmas Carol.* By the time she was thirty-three she was playing the mother on *Lassie* (she replaced Cloris Leachman, who'd replaced Jan Clayton). At forty she originated the role of the mother on *Lost in Space,* and the year that show left the air she joined *Petticoat Junction* when Bea Benaderet died. While Lockhart's image of a pinch-hitting mama is a testament to her professionalism, she never chose to break out of her prescribed role. She's allowed herself to be upstaged by a dog, a robot, and three plunging necklines without ever finding her own key light. Even as a wised-up doctor on *Junction,* she failed to click with TV viewers (the show was canceled the season after her debut). But even in her most innocuous roles, Lockhart projects a toughness that undercuts her image. When, on *Lassie,* she says to Timmy, "I know it's a difficult situation for you, dear," her voice is so laden with irony, you know she'd just as soon see the boy and his dog fall off the nearest cliff. Unlike Vera Miles, who surpassed her early sweet-spirited roles and became a sharp-witted character actress, Lockhart drifted away from the business she'd toiled in for so very long.

Irene Ryan and Donna Douglas in The Beverly Hillbillies

Irene Ryan in The Beverly Hillbillies

Meredith MacRae

Less interesting for her individual performances than for the showbiz references on her spotty résumé, Meredith MacRae disappears for years at a time only to metamorphose into some variation of a Henning Honey. Her earliest TV role, as Tim Considine's love interest on *My Three Sons*, led directly to her replacement of Gunilla Hutton on *Petticoat Junction*, who had already replaced the original Billie Jo, Jeannine Riley. If Riley brought a frank sluttiness to her role, and Hutton was thoroughly forgettable until *Hee Haw*, MacRae exuded a wryness totally at odds with the goings-on in Hooterville. There seems to have been a skeptical grin plastered on MacRae's kisser since birth, perhaps because her parents, Gordon and Sheila, probably conceived her in a trunk. Her knowingness about the industry might have kept her from filling the footprints of mom and dad, who made marks not only in movies, nightclubs, and on Broadway, but matched their daughter's accomplishments in TV: Gordon had his own show in the '50s and Sheila played Alice Kramden in the '60s. MacRae's long marriage to Greg Mullavey, Mary Hartman's husband, adds another kink to her video-drenched history. Her appearances in the '70s as a catty panelist on the game show *Mantrap* and in the '80s as a sneaky reporter on the weepfest *Fantasy* form a curious coda to a greasepaint-soiled career (her fellow reporter on *Fantasy:* Jack Lemmon's son, Chris). MacRae has always been too close to showbiz to be dazzled by its glitz.

Irene Ryan

If *The Beverly Hillbillies* is the most underrated sitcom in TV history (it is! it is!), Irene Ryan is its most undervalued diva. A whirling dervish in bag-lady drag, a malicious bitch in fits of fury, a sneaky drunk in an oversized kitchen, Ryan's Granny is one of the shrewdest, kinkiest, and most beautifully played characters in all of television. There isn't a moment of screen time Ryan doesn't fill: twitches, sneers, grunts, grins, frowns—she seems to have invented mugging. But her hamminess is too wholehearted to be offensive. She just grabs you by the collar and forces you to love her. Her physicality leaps beyond audaciousness. When she tackles Mrs. Drysdale and beats her to a pulp, she doesn't make you feel for the poor woman—she makes you fear for your own life. Her thin, wiry, seemingly fragile frame is a fearsome force when seized by rage: the Chicago Bears couldn't stop her. Her tongue is even more vicious. Infuriated by pretension, skeptical of all human behavior, she hurls barbs sharp enough to make Groucho Marx duck. Her only softness comes when she misinterprets someone's predicament as pitiful—a rich person who looks poor, for instance. Then, "Christian mercy" takes hold: her eyes droop in humility, her lips quiver with grief. She's a riot. Her gender, too, is comically ambiguous. Yes, she's a woman, but there are no visible signs of it. Her body draped in layers of rags, her voice pitched at a perpetual shriek, her gray hair pulled into a tight bun, she could be Norman Bates dressed as his mother. At once a civilized barbarian and a former vaudevillian (she died during the run of Broadway's *Pippin),* Irene Ryan is a transcendent Henning Honey.

HARRIS HARRIDANS & COUNTERCULTURAL CUTIES

Jane Curtin
Cathryn Damon & Katherine Helmond
Estelle Getty & Rue McClanahan
Lee Grant
Goldie Hawn

Ann Jillian
Andrea Martin & Catherine O'Hara
Gilda Radner
Phylicia Rashad & Debbie Allen
Inga Swenson

Harris Harridans and Countercultural Cuties are products of a comic sensibility popular on television only in the past twenty years. Earlier TV comedy tended to be "conservative," drawing on traditional theatrical forms (vaudeville), pretube media (radio), and studio-system hierarchies (Hollywood). Its performers were such veterans of showbiz they'd often starred on Broadway, radio, and the silver screen long before reaching prime time (Jack Benny, Burns and Allen, Lucille Ball). There were rare wild men—Spike Jones, Ernie Kovacs—while at least one wit had prefigured modernism as far back as the '20s (Groucho Marx). But by and large, classic TV comedy depended on decades of tried-and-true conventions. In the '60s structures collapsed, reflecting the social attitudes of the time. *Rowan & Martin's Laugh-In* and *The Monkees* splintered visual forms and injected political satire. In the '70s Norman Lear added something new: instead of presenting professional comedians or semihippie cutups, he hired respected New York actors to play characters whose sociological struggles symbolized conflicts in the culture. In no time at all the Not Ready for Prime Time Players were doing things on television Lenny Bruce would have been sent to jail for. Out of *NBC's Saturday Night Live* and Lear's syndicated smash *Mary Hartman, Mary Hartman* came another mutation: *Soap*. Created and written by Susan Harris, the show was a paean to exaggerated send-up. Soon the comics of the Great White North (*SCTV*) were upstaging *SNL*, while David Letterman was putting heat on Johnny Carson. Today Harris has a Top-10 hit with *The Golden Girls*, while her *Soap* boss, Marcy Carsey, produces *The Cosby Show*. Both shows feature minority characters in conventional situations. Welcome to TV comedy in the '80s.

(Left to right): *Bill Murray, Jane Curtin, Gilda Radner, Garrett Morris, and Laraine Newman in* Saturday Night Live

Jane Curtin

Jane Curtin waited a long time to be anointed Queen of the Countercultural Cuties. For five years on *Saturday Night Live* she supported more male egos than a conference table at the SALT talks. Between John Belushi's belly-busting bellows and Chevy Chase's bone-crunching pratfalls, Curtin seemed static—an ice cube waiting to melt. If her most prized routines involved kooky Coneheads, Dan Aykroyd's put-downs ("Jane, you ignorant slut!"), and a ripped-open blouse ("Try these on for size, Connie Chung!"), it's because they conformed to the style of the show. But Curtin is far from an *Animal House* cutup—her wit is feminine, reserved, sly. Unlike Gilda Radner, who became the diva of *SNL* by joining its rowdy fraternity, Curtin retained a catty detachment (Laraine Newman was more than detached—she was like somebody's girlfriend who'd wandered onto the set). Perhaps sensing her sensibility wouldn't be welcome in movies, Curtin was the only *SNL* alumnus who didn't go Hollywood at the drop of a contract. But as Allie Lowell on *Kate & Allie,* Curtin did something better—she found a voice for her own humor. While her wilder *SNL* cohorts bomb in one kiddie-pic after another, Curtin wins Emmys for the most hilarious portrait of yuppette insecurity in prime time. She's grown up as an actress by taking the counterculture one generation further. Using her exaggerated features as comic crosses to bear, Curtin shows how a smart woman can undermine her own authority. Her self-deprecation is a tribute to her intelligence, and her sarcasm is her only defense. Curtin's timing, faster than a speeding BMW, puts your teeth on edge. She may not be convincing as a loving mother, but she's the sharpest-witted Sitcom Queen since Ann Sothern.

Cathryn Damon & Katherine Helmond

At once half-baked and overripe, the Harris Harridan is a jolt to good taste. She looks like a Dunkin' Donuts waitress, sounds like an agitated donkey, and acts like Yvonne DeCarlo on *The Munsters*. This exaggerated ditziness has become a staple of fictional females, from Swoosie Kurtz in *Fifth of July* to Shirley MacLaine in *Terms of Endearment*. On TV it's those *Soap* sisters, Cathryn Damon and Katherine Helmond. If Damon suggests the emotional instability of the HH, Helmond revels in her comic craziness. Between them, they define Harris's universe: cartoonish, fretful, foolish, witty, garish, melancholic, and sentimental. What Damon and Helmond have in common is a theatrical intensity—they're startlingly vivid presences. While Damon gets laughs through a repressed hysteria, Helmond draws yuks with her blithe silliness. On *Soap* each actress understood her character in an almost kinesthetic way. Damon reached so deeply into Mary Campbell's woes that her own cocker-spaniel eyes drooped in despair. She seems to be a dramatic actress who's often funny because she knows how much grief goes into comedy. Helmond, meanwhile, is strictly joyful. Her Jessica Tate is a cookie with a twinkle, pixilated by life. Helmond has kept this spirit alive as the sex-crazed mama on *Who's the Boss?*, while Damon has been visibly stifled in a subsupporting role on *Webster*. Helmond's challenge will be to show the price one pays for unbridled lasciviousness—her character can't have her beef and eat it, too. But Damon has an entirely different prob-lem—she should go straight to Circle in the Square and take a crack at Eugene O'Neill. Somewhere between Helmond's farce and Damon's tragedy lies the soul of the Harris Harridan.

Estelle Getty & Rue McClanahan

Not so long before *The Golden Girls*, Estelle Getty and Rue McClanahan were Broadway Babies. In *Torch Song Trilogy* Getty stole the show as the Jewish mother of a gay wisecracker (Harvey Fierstein), while in *Sticks and Bones* McClanahan held the fort as the distraught mom of a Vietnam vet (Elizabeth Wilson won a Tony in the role). On *GG* Getty and McClanahan are recalling their stage triumphs: while Getty undercuts an offspring's sarcasm (Bea Arthur even sounds like Fierstein), McClanahan offsets the disadvantaged life experience of a rattled housemate (Betty White). But if Getty is doing a virtual replay of her role in *Torch Song*, McClanahan is reworking the emotional fragility of her character from *Sticks* (she wept at her curtain call). Like Cathryn Damon on *Soap*, McClanahan is a bundle of nerves—her eyes glisten, her mouth tightens, her voice trills up and down. Her volatility is perfect for Blanche, who's really a bit of a fraud. A Southern belle in love with love, Blanche is more come-on than come-across. Unlike Sue Ann Nivens, whom one could imagine bedding down with the Sixth Fleet, Blanche needs romance to cushion the springs. If McClanahan is a better Harris Harridan than a Lear Lady (she supported Arthur on *Maude)*, it's because her feelings can change between commercial breaks. Getty, meanwhile, is the acting equivalent of a tennis machine: feed her one-liners and she'll defeat any seasoned player. Her Sophia doesn't make sense—a glitch in the brain makes her say what's on her mind—but she's not supposed to. She's a monument to sitcom timing. She's also an

Cathryn Damon and Katherine Helmond in Soap

Lee Grant in Fay

example of sitcom expediency—a classic Jewish mother who's passed off as Sicilian. It seems some theatrical traditions still aren't ready for prime time.

Lee Grant

Lear Ladies have Edith Bunker, Desi Dames have Lucy Ricardo, and Tinker Tootsies have Mary Richards. But who's the Queen of Harris Harridans? The golden girls are too recent, the *Benson* babes too passive, and the *Soap* stars too obscure. The real monarch was beheaded in 1976 when *Fay,* a sophisticated sitcom about a freewheeling divorcée, was canceled after only eight episodes. It spawned the production team of Witt/Thomas/

Harris and starred an actress who'd just slept with Warren Beatty in *Shampoo:* Lee Grant. When she went on *The Tonight Show* to rant and rave about *Fay*'s grisly fate, Grant coined the term "Mad Programmer" to describe an NBC executive—she was a Harris Harridan before her time. Blacklisted by McCarthyites, Grant bounced back in the '60s and '70s as a mournful character actress, winning Emmys for *Peyton Place* and *The Neon Ceiling*. But after passing forty, Grant added something new (and hot) to her kitchen-sink collection of Jewish mothers and urban outcasts: a loony eroticism. Half chick and half yenta, she gave Peter Falk a run for his money in the pilot for *Columbo* and won an Oscar for *Shampoo*. If her TV credits don't quite add up to a full-fledged career, it's because Grant never got to fulfill her promise as a Harris Harridan. As Fay, Grant could have pulled together the strands of her career: social persecution (Fay was seen as an oddball for leaving her husband), feminine survival (she insisted on independence), and grown-up sensuality (she had no intention of remaining faithful to her ex). I don't mean to slight Grant's other accomplishments (she's been doing a lot of directing lately) or to suggest that *Fay* was a masterpiece. But the two together might have produced a Queen.

Goldie Hawn

Is Goldie Hawn the captain of her fate or a prisoner of her looks? She once said that an actor can coast for three years on one hit movie, but it's been twice that long since *Private Benjamin,* and she's still coasting. On *Rowan & Martin's Laugh-In* Hawn was a walking time warp—a giggly dumb blonde. But like her spiritual mother, Judy Holliday, Hawn transcended the stereotype: she had a deceptively brainy edge. You couldn't take advantage of her because her guilelessness thwarted deceit. Hawn's Jewishness, like Holliday's, enhanced her appeal. Beneath her Daffy Duck exterior beat the heart of a true-blue yenta (if she'd been white bread, she'd have lacked nourishment). But just as Holliday struggled to find flattering roles after winning her Oscar, so did Hawn—*Cactus Flower* yielded a bushel of thorns. This isn't surprising. After all, which movies could Hawn have starred in? *Klute*? *Chinatown*? *Interiors*? Short of extensive plastic surgery, Goldie will always be Goldie. As producer and star of *Benjamin,* Hawn resurrected her career but created another problem: she became the Sitcom Queen of the Silver Screen. As her comedies decline in quality, the stock of TV sitcoms rises dramatically. In her recent stab at drama *(Swing Shift),* she was upstaged by costar Christine Lahti (Goldie's one "serious" success remains *The Sugarland Express).* Hawn has two choices: she can come back to TV in a sitcom or accept a scene-stealing supporting part in a movie. But she's prideful. She expects top billing, steers clear of TV, and demands complete control. She's like Private Benjamin on her first day of boot camp, inquiring about condos and the color of her uniform. Where's Captain Lewis when we need her?

A nn Jillian

Ann Jillian has gone through too many changes to stop now. She made the transition from child actress (Baby June in the movie *Gypsy)* to leading lady *(Mae West),* from astringent supporting player *(Girls of the White Orchid)* to Sitcom Queen *(Jennifer Slept Here),* from Miniseries Maven *(Ellis Island)* to Harris Harridan *(It's a Living).* But her double mastectomy in 1985 demanded the kind of transitions no one ever anticipates. Luckily Jillian had already proven herself a fine dramatic actress. Her Mae West ranks with Faye Dunaway's Evita Perón and Susan Clark's Babe Didrikson as one of TV's enduring biographical portraits. Stuck with

a soggy script that would have us believe West spent her entire life mooning over some man, Jillian transcended clichés with a performance that went beyond impersonation—she located the point where sarcasm meets sentiment. Her best supporting roles—as the ill-fated whore in *White Orchid* and as the flouncy gold digger in *Ellis Island*—also struck a balance between hard-heartedness and purple passion. In her current transition from victim to heroine, Jillian seems to be separating the nice and nasty sides of her self. In *Killer in the Mirror,* her first starring work since her operation, Jillian plays a good woman besieged by her bad twin. When the latter says to the former, "You got the good genes and I got the evil ones," it's as if Jillian is working through some physiological purge. But if she's going to remain a major actress, Jillian will have to merge all aspects of her personality. She can't go back to being a Harris Harridan and she shouldn't become the Patricia Neal of the '90s. She should use her toughness to tell the truth as a TV diva.

A ndrea Martin & Catherine O'Hara

To say that *SCTV* was a parody of television doesn't quite do justice to its ruthless purity. The idea of lampooning Perry Como or Merv Griffin isn't funny in itself—it's really pretty obvious—but after seeing what *SCTV*'s ensemble did to TV stereotypes, you could never look at the medium in quite the same way again. The strength of the show depended almost entirely on impersonation—not the kind of aping that approximates the look and sound of a performer or program, but exact, full-drag recreations of glitzy celebrities, both real and imagined (the people whom David Letterman calls "showbiz weasels"). You knew *SCTV* was really cooking when you couldn't tell where the show left off and the commercials began—it erased the line between tackiness and taste. Each cast mem-

Ann Jillian in Jennifer Slept Here

ber was superb, especially the two women, Andrea Martin and Catherine O'Hara. While Martin did dead-on impressions of Mother Teresa and Bernadette Peters, O'Hara zeroed in on Brooke Shields and Elizabeth Taylor. The closer their takeoffs were to reality, the funnier they were. O'Hara's skewering of Katharine Hepburn captured all the giddy pomposity and heartbreaking insecurity of one of America's most treasured icons (the *SCTV* cast was all-Canadian, which may account for its chilly love-hate detachment from south-of-the-border pop culture). But the very qualities that made Martin and O'Hara so bracing on *SCTV* are the ones that have limited their careers. They're so adept at impersonation, they've never projected their own personalities. When they screened a satirical home movie about PMS on Letterman's show recently, it was hard to know when to laugh. They'd been looking through other people's eyes for so long, they never developed a point of view.

G ilda Radner

Gilda Radner's lovable imitation of Lucy on *Saturday Night Live*—"Waaaaaaaaaaaa!"—told more about her own screeching vulnerability than her target's. She was the only Not Ready for Prime Time Player whose routines had as much feminine feeling as masculine mauling, which is precisely why she got away with murder—she did things the guys would've been crucified for. Her classic skit as Roseanne Roseannadanna, describing how Gloria Vanderbilt suffered a vaginal itch in her blue jeans and started straddling door knobs and clutching hair brushes, is the kind of humor you wouldn't see outside of a sorority rush party. But unlike Lily Tomlin, who might use such a joke to make a statement about Women, Radner reveled in collegiate comedy to endear herself to fraternities—she'd swallow goldfish to be one of the boys. Her colorful characters had the wit and hi-

larity of Tomlin's, but they minced a fine line between self-expression and self-effacement. Yes, Emily Litella got to rant and rave about "Soviet jewelry," but she eventually had to whimper, "Never mind." True, Ba Ba Wawa delivered pressing reports, but her speech rendered them unintelligible. And sure, Roseanne mouthed off freely, until silenced by an anchorman. Radner even invaded the traditional province of women—romance—and skewered away. When she does a spread-eagled parody (with Steve Martin) of the "Dancing in the Dark" number from *The Band Wagon,* she's surrendering the last vestige of her gender. But Radner relinquishes power in order to be loved. Her recent association with Gene Wilder is sad—she's far too talented to play straight man to a ham-fisted hysteric. She should remember that even Lucy stopped crying, "Riiiiiiicky!"

P hylicia Rashad & Debbie Allen

Phylicia Rashad and Debbie Allen are almost as fearsome as Audrey and Jayne Meadows, but they're nowhere near as funny. Actually, Allen isn't supposed to be funny. Her dance instructor on *Fame* is sexy and "dedicated," but she's a Countercultural Cutie by virtue of her position: Den Mother of Showbiz Brats. I never understood the series or the movie. Its glorification of youthful ambition was always gooey and even a little scary. I felt that if these kids ever made their dreams come true, we might be physically forced to appreciate their talent. Lately Allen has returned to her roots—the Broadway musical—while Rashad has surpassed her sister's more extensive video credits with a single phenomenon: *The Cosby Show.* Her Clair Huxtable is supposed to be a modern black woman—stylish, professional, and takin' no crap from no man. But these qualities may be closer to the Duchess of Windsor than to a married lawyer with five kids in Brooklyn. Rashad has an attitude you couldn't cut with a chainsaw—almost all her laughs come when she's telling off someone. Bobbing her head from side to side and pulling her lips tight over her teeth, Rashad unleashes more righteous anger than Moses. When her daughter complains about wanting a car, Rashad spews, "If you ever take that attitude again, you can take whatever's in that bank account of yours and go discover America." Thanks, Mommie Dearest. When she isn't pissed off, Rashad exists to reflect the fashion sense of her leading man. Rolling around in bed with the luscious Rashad, Bill Cosby seems to be saying, "I have good taste in women, huh?" But his leading lady is no competition to him where it counts: comedy. Rashad is the Annie Hall of the '80s—sporting nifty duds while basking in the light of "genius."

Inga Swenson

Susan Harris's work, like an old Warner Bros. movie, is torn from today's headlines. But unlike Norman Lear, who turned current events into mini-civics lessons, Harris reflects the surface of truth and passes it off for the real thing. There's an air of expediency, superficiality, even exploitation in some of Harris's characterizations. On *Soap* Billy Crystal switched from homosexual to transsexual to heterosexual almost at will. On *The Golden Girls* Estelle Getty blurts whatever's on her mind because she's had a stroke. And on *Benson,* Inga Swenson has to put up with the witless put-downs of Robert Guillaume because she looks and sounds like a Nazi. The show is structured like the 1936 Olympics, with Guillaume as a Jesse Owens–type hero showing up all the Aryan numbskulls. But Guillaume is no Owens. He's a smug, sour, sneering presence—a king-sized Gary Coleman. Keeping one eye on his costars and the other in a mirror, Guillaume gains immediate acceptance into the Bad Actor Hall of Fame, alongside Dick Van Patten and Jack Klugman. His hamminess is all the more distasteful because Swenson is such a fine, smart, and lovely actress. Her brutalization on *Benson* has been going on for so long, even she seems tired of it—when she doesn't have a line, she relaxes out of character and smiles sweetly. Her role as the Yankee matriarch in *North and South* didn't give her anything to do, but she scored a small triumph: she was unrecognizable without the aid of a *TV Guide*. I'd love to see her land a part that would complement her statuesque handsomeness and precise theatricality. If she stays a Harris Harridan, she might wind up a transsexual Nazi war criminal who's saved by Jesus.

9
BROADWAY BABIES & BITCHY BRITS

Jane Alexander
Shirley Booth
Colleen Dewhurst
Julie Harris
Judith Ivey

Glenda Jackson
Angela Lansbury
Geraldine Page
Kim Stanley
Maureen Stapleton

The Broadway Baby and the Bitchy Brit are united by a single passion: the the-uh-tah. Dripping in greasepaint and rhinestones, dropping names and elongated vowels, the BB/BB lives to hear what Anne Baxter in *All About Eve* calls "waves of love coming over the footlights." Unlike the Distinguished Guest & Dramatic Do-Gooder, who selects a project on the basis of its social import, the BB/BB believes in the crispness of her own diction as a justification for civilization. But like the DD/DG, the BB/BB is a revered figure whose appearances on television are viewed as cultural events. Much of this attention is deserved. The theatrical intensity the BB/BB brings to her stage work can be positively explosive when contained by the miniature proscenium in your living room. Some of the greatest performances in television history are not by movie stars slumming for cash, but by theatrical legends transmitting histrionic hysteria through tiny tubes. It's amazing how many BB/BBs have won Tonys and Emmys, but have no Oscars on their makeup tables. The bigger the screen, the greater the problems. First of all, unlike the DD/DG, the BB/BB is never a dish—she is, to be blunt, a bit homely. She's either too big or too small, too butch or too femme, too affected or too plain. She doesn't exude a Hollywood-style glamor or a physical voluptuousness associated with the greatest stars. Her strengths are her voice (rich and varied), diction (clean and clipped), and emotional energy (concentrated and ferocious). She usually lives in or around New York or London, unless "trapped" in an American television series. She's an awful snob, but when given sharp lines to deliver, she can metamorphose from a caterpillar into a butterfly, from a mere BB/BB into a full-blown Grande Dame.

Jane Alexander in Playing for Time

Jane Alexander

As Hedda Hopper in *Malice in Wonderland,* Jane Alexander pulled off a miracle: she gave a joyful performance. After all, this is the woman who committed suicide onstage *(The Great White Hope),* endured social persecution on TV *(A Question of Love),* and suffered radiation poisoning on screen *(Testament).* A borderline Distinguished Guest & Dramatic Do-Gooder, Alexander is a Broadway Baby by virtue of her dramatic fussiness. Every gesture, every inflection, every glance seems rehearsed and re-rehearsed. This thoroughness can be boring or thrilling, depending on the project. If nearly all of Alexander's best work has been on television, it's because the medium offers an arena tiny enough for Alexander's controlled strokes. The delight of her performance in *Malice* didn't come just from her concentrated attention to line readings, but from her unerring eye for ridiculous hats or the way she slapped her silky backside to make a point. It seems no accident that Alexander's finest vehicles—*Malice, Annie Oakley, Blood & Orchids, Eleanor and Franklin* (and its sequel)—are pretty period pieces as well as "serious statements." This is a roundabout way of saying that Alexander isn't half the Plain Jane she seems to think she is—you can see she derives all sorts of guilty pleasure from playing dress-up. Even as she prepares to go to a dinner that results in her death in the wrenching *Playing for Time,* Alexander licks her fingers and wipes the smudges from her ratty dress. Forget raised consciousness. Forget moral purpose. Forget art. Beneath the drab edifice known as Jane Alexander, Actress, is a spirited soul dubbed Diva.

Shirley Booth

Shirley Booth had been bustling down Broadway for twenty-five years when she played Lola De-

Shirley Booth and brood in Hazel

laney, the overbearing wife of a remorseful alcoholic in William Inge's *Come Back, Little Sheba.* Onstage, the role brought her a Tony and a New York Drama Critics Award. Onscreen, it won her an Oscar and a New York Film Critics Award. All over the world, it earned her the reputation as a serious and versatile actress. Well, Booth is nothing less than serious, but she's far from versatile. If she played Lola so convincingly, it's because the part exploited her limited range of expression: sharp whines blunted by pathetic grins, fevered shuffling accompanied by jutting elbows, quivering lower lip hastened by puddling eyes. When Booth schlepped this bag of tricks to TV for the long-running sitcom *Hazel,* she was rewarded with two Emmys. Playing a loudmouthed busybody masquerading as a housemaid, Booth demolished everything within earshot—plots, actors, dialogue, direction, even the sets seemed to quake. Amazingly, nobody noticed that Booth's Hazel looked and acted almost exactly like Booth's

Lola. The only difference was that Hazel guffawed while Lola wept. Even the strain of sentimental smugness that runs through Booth's work like the Orient Express smeared Hazel—this woman was always right. Basically, Booth's horrifying hamminess is the sort that's best left in the theater. It's no accident that Tallulah Bankhead and Gertrude Lawrence bombed onscreen, or that Laurette Taylor and Katharine Cornell shied away from soundstages. Shirley Booth is the only actress in this book who never should have gone Hollywood.

Women's Room and *Silent Victory: The Kitty O'Neil Story* allowed for more wit and variety, but three of her most recent performances—as the stern adoptive mother in *Anne of Green Gables,* the neurotic mother-in-law in *Between Two Women,* and the murderous matriarch in that masterpiece of mixed moods, *Johnny Bull*—may be the finest of her career. In *Women* in particular, Dewhurst stretched her range to the limit. Yes, she showed joy and pain, but she also hit all the points in between. For once she was an Earth Mother with both feet on the ground.

Colleen Dewhurst

Some Broadway Babies are too big for the screen, but Colleen Dewhurst is too big for the *stage*. She was made for town squares, football stadiums, Grand Canyons. Her voice—a raspy, resonant, bellowing growl—is surpassed in dimension only by her head and shoulders, which look like an animated Greek bust. Dewhurst could never play Desdemona—she has the thickest *neck* of any human this side of William "the Refrigerator" Perry. Her size is both a blessing and a curse. She can communicate power and gravity just by showing up, but she's always Colleen Dewhurst, Force of Nature. When in a revival of *Who's Afraid of Virginia Woolf?* she roars, "I am the Earth Mother and you are all flops," she upstages her character. Her range is not as wide as some people think: she's great at droopy-jawed ruefulness and broad-grinned giddiness. But what she does, she does better than anybody—her two classic expressions are replicas of the masks of tragedy and comedy. These flip sides work to Dewhurst's advantage on TV when she recreates Broadway triumphs: her awesome nurturer in *A Moon for the Misbegotten* and her dizzy duchess in *You Can't Take It With You.* But the networks usually cast her as strong-willed mamas, from *The Blue and the Gray* to *Studs Lonigan.* Her more modern roles in *The*

Julie Harris

If Helen Hayes is the First Lady of the American Theater, Julie Harris is its First Daughter. She even reprised Hayes's greatest stage triumph, *Victoria Regina,* for television in 1961 and won an Emmy to match the one she'd already won for "Little Moon of Alban." But if Hayes will retain a regal dignity until the last footlight dims, Harris has always been the unruly heir exiled to a boarding school. After all, her earliest stage and film triumph embraced a rural neurotic (Frankie in *The Member of the Wedding),* while her most popular theatrical success in later life focused on an intense recluse (Emily Dickinson in *The Belle of Amherst).* In between, Harris wavered between tried-and-true vehicles *(Anastasia)* and skid-row shockers *(How Awful About Allan).* Only John Huston's movie *Reflections in a Golden Eye* gave Harris the chance to weld the wild-eyed and regressive sides of her personality—Frankie Goes to Amherst. By the late '70s Harris let her backwoods side win out, starring as a Ma Walton clone in the short-lived series *The Family Holvak.* But in 1981 she accepted a role that many thought a comedown, but has come to define Harris better than any character ever has: Lilimae Clements on *Knots Landing.* At first, Lilimae was a corn-pone

Colleen Dewhurst in A Moon for the Misbegotten

Julie Harris in Anastasia

hearts of mush, Ivey dawdles over her lines with an ironic intonation that falls somewhere between a sarcastic singsong and a Texas twang. When in the TV version of *The Long Hot Summer* she addresses Don Johnson (Ben Quick) as "Meeestahhh Queeeyuuuck," Ivey expresses her character's contempt for animal lust as well as her attraction to it. Cast against type as a cultured spinster, Ivey delicately shifts between shoot-from-the-hip toughness and gun-shy vulnerability. Her scenes with Johnson—subtle, electric, erotic—are the only times this miniseries transcends its clichés. If NBC really wants to capitalize on Johnson's megastardom, it should cast him and Ivey in a new series called *Mississippi Vice*. The big treat is that Ivey makes the most of her leading-lady role, outshining a pair of certified goddesses. Cybill Shepherd, so dazzling in *Moonlighting,* is stuck with a thin, one-note part, while the great Ava Gardner, so glorious in *Knots Landing,* is squeezed into a drab cameo. But it's a tribute to Ivey's ironclad technique that she can suggest levels of eroticism beneath her overwhelmingly dowdy appearance. Her coup is enhanced because television telescopes every physical imperfection. Onstage Ivey can play Shepherd-like roles, but on TV she's forced to tackle characters closer to herself. She's a Broadway Baby with a very bright future as a TV diva.

mama—a camp. She then entered a period of quiet solicitude—the Julie Harris bit. But last season all hell broke loose: Lilimae yelled at her crackpot-evangelist son with such primal fury, he toppled off a roof and went squish. No longer a wallflower, Harris is just beginning to blossom into a TV diva.

J udith Ivey

In the second act of David Rabe's *Hurlyburly,* a preposterously overrated travesty of human experience passing for a Broadway play, Judith Ivey marches onstage and takes over. Striking but not pretty, zaftig but not fat, Ivey projects herself almost entirely through her dazzlingly deadpan delivery. Often playing sharp-tongued bimbos with

G lenda Jackson

Glenda Jackson has pulled off what no other actress of the English theater ever has—not Margaret Leighton before her, Kate Nelligan after her, Rosemary Harris during her, or Judith Anderson before them all. For more than fifteen years Jackson has scored multimedia, leading-role, trans-Atlantic triumphs, winning Oscars (two!), Emmys (two more), and just about everything else. Yes, there's Deborah Kerr, but she became a movie

Glenda Jackson in The Patricia Neal Story

star. Yes, there's Jessica Tandy, but she became an American actress. Yes, there's Maggie Smith, but she became a supporting player. Only Glenda— the Good Witch of the West End—transcended her homeliness and became a showbiz phenomenon. What's amazing is that Jackson turned her back on superstardom and insisted on remaining an Actress. Her two great TV roles, as the embattled empress in the *Masterpiece Theatre* miniseries "Elizabeth R" and as another embattled empress in *The Patricia Neal Story,* spanned the years when Jackson was the toast of Tinseltown (the early '70s) and persona non grata in the Land of Streep (ten years later). But the ever-exciting aspect of Jackson, apart from her uncompromisingly unstarry attitude, is the ferocious cattiness of her performances. A big fan of Bette Davis (as Davis is a big fan of hers), Jackson makes diva power palatable to the PBS crowd. Let's not forget that Davis herself played Elizabeth the Queen, but Jackson played the part with a theatrical precision that made Bette seem lowbrow. My only gripe with Jackson is her recent selection of projects. Why impersonate Patricia Neal or Yelena Bonner (in HBO's *Sakharov*)? She should star in the vehicle she was born for: *Bitch Goddess: The Bette Davis Story.*

Angela Lansbury

It's one of the ironies of modern media that more people see Angela Lansbury in a single episode of the tediously conventional smash *Murder, She Wrote* than in all her other works combined. Her career is as delectable and wide-ranging as any Broadway Baby: a string of sizzling supporting roles in classic movies (*Gaslight, The Manchurian Candidate*) segueing into a series of legendary musicals (*Mame, Sweeney Todd*). In many of these roles Lansbury played women far older than herself. Her seeming worldliness allowed her to etch

portraits of villainy unmatched by any actress of her generation. She made conventional morality seem sinful. When she goes nose-to-nose with a revoltingly virtuous Spencer Tracy in *State of the Union,* you yearn to see evil win. But long after her movie roles dried up, even after her Broadway projects grew scarce, Lansbury continued playing older characters—but with a change. Instead of tackling icy matrons, Lansbury became Margaret Rutherford, playing cutesy, crotchety sleuths in *The Lady Vanishes* and *The Mirror Crack'd*. Taking this act to TV, Lansbury bridged the age gap, but remained a banal presence. Her Jessica Fletcher is a paragon of pure thoughts and good intentions—a neutered know-it-all. There's nothing technically wrong with Lansbury's performance— it's just a waste of her talents. At the same time Lansbury has done some of the best work of her career in scintillating parts on TV specials: as the murderous Mrs. Lovett in Stephen Sondheim's *Sweeney Todd* and as the conniving aunt in *Little Gloria . . . Happy at Last*. These shows might not bring the mass-cult attention of *Murder, She Wrote,* but they gloriously recall the lascivious Lansbury of yesteryear.

Geraldine Page

If Geraldine Page had retired twenty years ago, she'd still be a legend today. Her back-to-back movie roles as the sweet-souled Alma in *Summer and Smoke* and the rapacious Alexandra Del Lago in *Sweet Bird of Youth* set the tone for the rest of her career and made histrionic history. Here was an actress who could play meek-ugly (Alma) and bold-gorgeous (Alexandra) through the sheer force of her full-throttled mannerisms. When Tennessee Williams in his *Playboy* interview said that of all his characters he most identified not with Blanche and Stanley, but with Alma and Alexandra, he was paying an indirect compliment to one of the

Angela Lansbury in Murder, She Wrote

seminal actresses of our time. It was fashionable back in the '60s to pooh-pooh Page's visible technique, her anti-"cinematic" style. But Page has proven the Chinese proverb that if you sit by the river long enough all your enemies will float by. Her major TV performances in *A Christmas Memory* and *The Thanksgiving Visitor,* which followed her early movie triumphs, fused Alma and Alexandra—a good woman inside a harridan's body. This bracing combo has influenced almost every role Page has played ever since. But as inspiring as her television work has been, it's not as cutting

as her supporting work in offbeat movies. Yes, her dim-witted, kind-hearted cousin in *Christmas Memory* is touching and memorable, but her furious cancer patient in *I'm Dancing as Fast as I Can* burns a hole in your forehead (her overrated work in *The Trip to Bountiful* was a big-screen replay of her TV roles). Even when Page was cast in a disease-of-the-week TV movie *(Something for Joey),* she played the long-suffering mother of a leukemia victim. If she'd played the lead, they'd have had to put warning labels on TV sets: APPROACH WITH CAUTION.

Geraldine Page in The Thanksgiving Visitor

Kim Stanley

Mention Kim Stanley's name in theatrical circles and you'll incite a riot: "She's the best!" "She's the worst!" "Have you *seen* what she *looks* like?" Part of this dialectical delirium is due to Stanley's peekaboo career: four or five movies, a few TV guest shots, and several plays long ago—the skimpiest résumé of any theatrical legend. Stanley's disappearances from the limelight for years at a time, accompanied by dramatic weight gains, are all part of her myth. A frighteningly chunky, square-jawed blonde, Stanley is the closest thing to a female Brando. She makes Anne Bancroft look like a wimp. Her training in The Method cements her style—she has more mannerisms than Tallulah. But when Stanley is hot (like her spiritual sister, Geraldine Page), nobody can touch her. Her greatest recorded performance can't be found in her big-screen stabs at stardom—*The Goddess, Seance on a Wet Afternoon*—but in a two-part episode of *Ben Casey,* "A Cardinal Act of Mercy," directed by a twenty-nine-year-old Sydney Pollack. As Faith Parsons, a morphine-addicted attorney, Stanley crystallized an entire school of acting. Dragging herself across the floor in a sweat-drenched nightgown, spewing unspeakably caustic barbs, Stanley exposed the demon inside her wheedling, little girl's voice and the frightened soul inside her imposing, big mama's body. When she finally played Big Mama in a disastrous version of *Cat on a Hot Tin Roof* on Showtime in 1985, winning a second Emmy, Stanley was too big, physically and emotionally, for her role. She seemed ready to tackle Medea, or maybe Martha Mitchell.

Maureen Stapleton

Maybe because she's blowsy and used to be black-haired, maybe because she's as skilled at comedy as at drama, maybe because she scored an early success in *The Rose Tattoo,* Maureen Stapleton has been called the American Anna Magnani. But if Magnani achieved her greatest effects through shrewd overplaying, Stapleton has been at her best with an economy of expression. Her highly touted roles as Amanda Wingfield on Broadway *(The Glass Menagerie)* and Big Mama on television *(Cat on a Hot Tin Roof)* showed that Stapleton has little poetry in her soul—when she gets "passionate" she looks rattled and sweaty. What she's great at is mining the wit of her consistently colorful characters. Her supporting performances in the movies *Reds* and *Interiors* reveal a remarkable ability to bring out the comedy in the drama and vice versa (like Magnani, she's a riotous farceur). But the source of laughter is often linked with tears, and in prime time Stapleton has become a purveyor of weepies, much in the same way that Magnani became a heroine of Italian Neorealism. Her celebrated work in *Tell Me Where It Hurts* (a drab drama about a blue-collar housewife who "finds" herself) and *Queen of the Stardust Ballroom* (a brilliantly inspired romance despite its gratuitously downbeat ending) is affecting, but perhaps a bit too easy. Her best TV performance is as the sensible matriarch whose estranged husband is mysteriously dying in *The Gathering*. In a project that cries out for scenery chewing, Stapleton keeps pulling back to the point where everybody around her looks foolishly sentimental. That's Stapleton's secret: she looks Italian but thinks Equity Showcase.

10

SERIES SIRENS

Barbara Bain
Barbara Eden
Anne Francis
Sharon Gless & Tyne Daly
Peggy Lipton

Tina Louise
Stefanie Powers
Diana Rigg
Susan Saint James
Lindsay Wagner

The Series Siren is adored for her sexy image in a single program: she's a one-show woman. Unlike the Soap Star, whose big emotional scenes make viewers forget her measurements for five seconds, or the Reformed Bimbo, whose off-screen time is devoted to becoming an extremely serious actress, the SS is a thing of beauty forever. The key word here is "thing" because an SS never quite transcends her appearance. If she tries to look "realistic"—i.e., ugly—she seems something more than a siren, but something less than an actress. The only way an SS can retain her power is to stay glamorous, and to comment on that glamor as she grows older. Instead of playing frumpy victims of wife abuse, an SS should remain lethal—she ain't a femme fatale for nothin'. She isn't necessarily a B-girl, but her drop-dead looks put everybody on edge. When Norman Lear wanted to spice up *All in the Family* he had the glorious Janis Paige lure Archie away from Edith. When Grant Tinker needed to heat up *Hill Street Blues*, he let a panting Barbara Babcock seduce Sergeant Esterhaus. And when Captain Kirk took off for the stratosphere, he made sure Nichelle Nichols was wearing a microskirt. Even the runners-up in this category are rapturous: Julie Newmar (*Batman*), Dorothy Provine (*The Roaring Twenties*), Connie Stevens (*Hawaiian Eye*), Abby Dalton (*Hennesey*), Julie London (*Emergency!*), Lynda Day George (*Mission: Impossible*), Linda Cristal (*The High Chaparral*), Amanda Blake (*Gunsmoke*), Barbara Anderson (*Ironside*), Gail Fisher (*Mannix*), Lee Meriwether (*Barnaby Jones*), Phyllis Davis (*Vegas*), and maybe even Barbara Hale

(Perry Mason). I'd go so far as to include Joan Blondell in *Here Come the Brides,* though I'd stop short of Elena Verdugo in *Marcus Welby, M.D.*

barbara Bain

The fictional names of Series Sirens are a tasty smorgasbord: Honey West, Ginger Grant, Emma Peel. But the most luscious of all is Cinnamon Carter—a drag queen's alias if I ever heard one. The actress who played C.C. isn't a transvestite, but she's the next best thing: Barbara Bain. If her name on *Mission: Impossible* evokes an exotic pastry in a display window—spicy, rich, cold to the touch—that's exactly how Bain was showcased on the show. Decked out in a dizzying variety of *Vogue* ensembles and Weimar Republic garter belts, Bain made the world safe for democracy through the sheer electricity of lace on nylon. Her makeup, applied to alter her age by decades depending on the mission, reflected the show's artificiality and infatuation with surfaces— Bain was to '60s TV what Marlene Dietrich was to '30s movies. But while Dietrich was mistaken as a talentless zombie by Oscar voters, Bain won three Emmys in a row: her changes of clothes and hair styles were appreciated as feats of acting. After she and husband Martin Landau left *Mission* in a contract dispute, they went to England to star in a dismal futuristic soap, *Space: 1999.* As Dr. Helena Russell, Bain was expected to register normal human emotion: fear, concern, pride. These tedious feelings are best left to Meryl Streep. Bain has spent more than twenty-five years constructing a mask she should never let slip (she began in TV as Richard Diamond's paramour). So it came as one of the sparkling delights of last season to see Bain in a brilliant episode of *Moonlighting* as a painted matron wearing ten tons of face powder and plotting the death of her weaselly son. Once again Bain was a monument to sensuousness, doing justice to the name Cinnamon.

Barbara Bain in Mission: Impossible

barbara Eden

When I was a kid my absolute favorite show wasn't *Howdy Doody, Romper Room,* or *Captain Kangaroo*—it was *How to Marry a Millionaire,* a syndicated sitcom based on the hit movie (which I also loved). If the movie was gingerly divided among its three stars—Lauren Bacall, Betty Grable, and Marilyn Monroe—the series belonged to a single bombshell: Barbara Eden. Playing Loco, the part made famous by Monroe, Eden upstaged her co-stars (Merry Anders, Lori Nelson) and brought a down-to-earth craziness to her flighty character. By the time of *I Dream of Jeannie,* she was a processed pro in a schematic sitcom—a block of Velveeta with a navel. Actually her navel couldn't be shown, which is the most interesting thing about this inexplicably popular show. The usual charges

Fannie Flagg (left) *and Barbara Eden in* I Dream of Jeannie—15 Years Later

of "sexism"—Jeannie is a "slave" to her "master"—are pretty lame. Eden is too savvy an actress to be anybody's slave. The problem with *Jeannie* was a thin concept overlaid with frantic overplaying. While Larry Hagman saved face by racing through his routines, Eden lost dignity by savoring every shtick (Hagman didn't turn into Velveeta until *Dallas*). When she materialized recently in a TV movie updating Jeannie's life, Eden didn't comment on the grotesquerie of her char-

acter. Instead she became a subfeminist yenta, yapping about being an independent woman to her exhausted husband. The irony was that Eden, at fifty-one, finally got to show her navel. In between *Jeannie* escapades, Eden followed in the footsteps of yet another Jeannie (C. Riley) in a movie and series based on Riley's smash single, *Harper Valley P.T.A.* Again Eden conformed to the mustiness of the material. You'd never guess she began her career positively Loco.

A nne Francis

If I owned a network, I'd give Anne Francis a series tomorrow. No flash in the pan, this Anne, she was a perky pitchwoman for floor covering at the dawn of television *(Versatile Varieties)*, a semi-regular character on three hit series *(My Three Sons, Dallas, Riptide)*, a dependable guest star on countless shows (name one, she's been on it), and a pungent presence in dozens of TV movies (vive *Mongo's Back in Town*!). Best of all, she starred in *Honey West,* an all-but-forgotten series about a slinky sleuth who made Napoleon Solo look like Mr. Peepers. The show, which lasted a single season, was the only American series that rivaled *The Avengers* in erotic perversity. Just as Diana Rigg's leather jumpsuits and karate kicks enlivened the latter, Francis's peccadillos made *Honey* hot: a spread-eagled judo jump, a lipstick cum radio transmitter, a pet ocelot named Bruce. Francis was born for the role, because she'd been re-hearsing for it all her life (amazingly, she was thirty-five when she played it). A child star in radio—she was dubbed "The Little Queen of Soap Opera"—Francis landed roles that demanded increasing viciousness as she got older. Deep-voiced and acid-tongued, she seemed to turn off mainstream audiences. But her ironic, hard-edged portrayals have made her one of TV's enduring cult divas. More recently, her work has been laced with humor—she seems to be lampooning her own tough-gal image. In a *Murder, She Wrote* she played a federal food inspector appalled by the homespun morsels in Cabot's Cove. When questioned by Jessica Fletcher, she barks, "My job is bad food—not murder." Francis's gift is that she always gives stale shows a taste of Honey.

S haron Gless & Tyne Daly

Cagney & Lacey has a production history more fascinating than the show itself. It's based on a 1981 TV movie starring Loretta Swit and Tyne Daly, but Swit bowed out when it went to series because she was already a regular on *M*A*S*H.* So Meg Foster played opposite Daly in the spring 1982 episodes. When the show was renewed for the fall, Foster was fired and replaced by Sharon Gless. A CBS executive was quoted describing the characters as "dykes." Canceled in 1983, the show was brought back by popular demand. Basically it's a distaff *Kojak* with a dash of feminism. Gloria Steinem has praised it for showing "two women working together," but the real political battles have been fought behind the scenes. The show itself exists as a study in acting styles: Swit's sweaty earnestness, Foster's translucent glare, and Gless's studied swagger. The glue that's held it all together from the beginning is Daly. The extraordinary alertness and concentration of this kitchen-sink diva make even the most mundane scenes seem compelling. Daughter of James Daly *(Medical Center)* and sister of Timothy Daly (the movie *Diner*), Tyne may have ham juice in her veins. She's mannered as all get-out—sorta like Ratso Rizzo in *Midnight Cowboy*—but she's so utterly *there*, even in reaction shots: her eyes flicker and dart like a frightened doe's. Her path to Mary Beth Lacey was littered with a string of do-gooding TV movies. Daly thrives on Truth: the uglier her environment, the purer her purpose. Her looks reflect her esthetic. Was it only 1976 when she played Dirty Harry's cute rookie in *The Enforcer*? Now she looks like Maureen Stapleton's sister (and acts like her, too). Daly isn't a true Series Siren because she's never been beautiful enough to carry a show. But she's talented enough to overcome her appearance. Gless's struggles are entirely different. She used to be prime time's premier pinch hitter, following Lynn Redgrave on *House Calls,* Foster in *C & L,* and even herself in the sequel to *All My Darling Daughters*. She also played sexy helpmates to leading men in three series, including *Marcus Welby, M.D.*, and appeared as pretty young things in male-dominated miniseries, including *The Last Convertible*. This image of availability and sensuality must have rankled Gless: she isn't the sort of Siren to enjoy such a role. So she went out and won a role for which she was thoroughly unsuited—Chris Cagney. As the hot-tempered Irish cop with a rocky love life, Gless is about as convincing as Claudette Colbert would have been in *The Grapes of Wrath*. Her ladylike attempts at being tough—fierce frowns, pursed lips, fiery glares—are too forced to be convincing. Gless's true claim to Sirenhood is romantic comedy. She shined in the classic TV movie, *Hardhat and Legs,* an updated Tracy-Hepburnesque vehicle by Ruth Gordon and Garson Kanin, and saved face in the short-lived series, *Turnabout,* in which she inhabited her husband's body and vice versa. *C & L*'s creators, whose idea of feminism is curling up in goose down and talking about relationships, don't understand the delicacies of erotic intrigue. Rather, they fashion scripts for actresses who live and breathe Social Realism, such as Daly, who's beaten Gless for the Emmy three years in a row. When Gless did star recently in a romantic comedy with John Ritter, she lost her lightness of spirit. Having tried so hard for so long to be a "serious" actress, she forgot how to capitalize on her looks without selling out.

P eggy Lipton

Leave it to Aaron Spelling to trivialize the counterculture even before it got under way. *The Mod Squad*, a conspicuously contrived melodrama masquerading as a social statement, was to the late '60s what later Spelling cop shows—*T.J. Hooker, MacGruder & Loud*—were to the early '80s: pseudo–character studies setting up slam-bang action. The show's most attractive character, Julie Barnes, was played by Peggy Lipton with a sour-faced petulance often mistaken for political concern. But she was a dish, too. Men put up with her to find out if she was a natural blonde (she wasn't a whore's daughter for nothing). Lipton is fascinating not only because she's TV's first hippie diva, but because she's a Charlie's Angel (another Spelling creation) filtered through '60s icons—a psychedelic siren. I don't think it's an accident Lipton is a ringer for the young Michelle Phillips or that the series debuted during the glory days of Grace Slick and Janis Joplin. The men on the show, Michael Cole and Clarence Williams III, resembled Bob Dylan and Jimi Hendrix, respectively. This overwhelmingly rock-and-roll imagery makes Lipton a precursor to MTV divas—she's something less than a Video Vixen because she doesn't sing, but something more than a VJ because she can act (well, sulk). That she eventually married Quincy Jones and all but vanished from the business, except for a reunion special in 1979, adds to her allure as a pop princess. As skimpy as it is, her career parallels the course of youth culture from post-Camelot (a high school student on *The John Forsythe Show*) to hippie *(Mod Squad)* to yuppie—via Quincy ("We Are the World"). Even Spelling, with all his commercial savvy, couldn't have anticipated that.

T ina Louise

As movie star Ginger Grant on *Gilligan's Island,* Tina Louise did a delicious parody of every Hollywood sexpot you ever loved (especially Marilyn Monroe). Dizzy, breathless, impossibly beautiful, Louise wallowed in self-absorption even as she exuded compassion for homelier beings. She wasn't deep—a broken heel was more upsetting than a shipwreck—but she was justified in her vanity. Surrounded by the most repulsive collection of

(Left to right): *Clarence Williams III, Michael Cole, Peggy Lipton, and Tige Andrews in* The Mod Squad

men ever assembled for a sitcom, Louise had grounds for suicide. If she wasn't being hassled by the beer-bellied captain (Alan Hale, Jr.) or the loudmouthed millionaire (Jim Backus), she was being bored by the hysterical Gilligan (Bob Denver) or the plodding professor (Russell Johnson). Worse, Louise was the only character who wasn't paired with somebody else: there was Backus and his wife (Natalie Schafer), Johnson and his groupie (Dawn Wells), and Hale and Denver (don't ask).

All Louise had were her clothes, which were deservedly limitless. After *Gilligan* Louise appeared in a series of TV shockers *(Death Scream, Look What's Happened to Rosemary's Baby)*, a nifty movie thriller *(The Stepford Wives)*, and a prime-time soap *(Dallas)*, though she didn't star in a sequel to *Gilligan* because she reportedly asked for too much money (impossible!). There's always been a sad quality to Louise—let's call it the Abused Goddess Syndrome. It's been part of every

(Left to right): *Alan Hale, Jr., Tina Louise, Bob Denver in* Gilligan's Island

bombshell from Hayworth to Monroe, from Mansfield to Carol Wayne. But in an episode of *Blacke's Magic* Louise played a movie star fed up with T & A roles—she still believes in glamor but yearns to grow up. Similarly, Louise can't play Ginger anymore, but she's smart enough to comment on her. She ought to have her own series: *Ginger's Roots.*

Stefanie Powers

Everything about Stefanie Powers screams artifice: her hair, clothes, acting style, even her name (b. Stephania Federkiewicz). She's thoroughly self-created in the way that Hedy Lamarr was, or Lana Turner, or Joan Crawford—a shimmering siren. But the miracle of Powers is that she isn't cold. People genuinely like her. In the First Annual Nettie Awards in 1985, in which I asked readers of *The Village Voice* to pick their TV favorites in twenty categories, Powers handily won as Best Actress in a Miniseries against a field of heavy competition: Angie Dickinson, Faye Dunaway, Ava Gardner, and Lesley Ann Warren. Her margin of victory had to do with a remarkable coup, starring in hit miniseries on all three networks in a single season *(Mistral's Daughter, Deceptions,* and *Hollywood Wives).* This sensory overload is part of Powers's appeal: she never starves your eyes. Like Lola Falana at Caesar's Palace, Powers knows the power of quick-change artistry. Her radiant narcissism couldn't redeem *The Girl From U.N.C.L.E.,* but it fueled her smash series *Hart to Hart.* Created by Sidney *(I Dream of Jeannie)* Sheldon and produced by Aaron *(Dynasty)* Spelling, *Hart* gave Powers the chance to work the two sides of her image—the shapely innocent (Jeannie) and the heavily made-up diva (Alexis). *Deceptions* was even more telling. Powers played twin sisters—one a beleaguered housewife, the other a jet-set glamor queen—who exchange identities.

Stefanie Powers in The Girl From U.N.C.L.E.

Powers's own identity can be confusing, especially to Powers. She began in the business as Taffy Paul and last year tried to sing and dance on the Tony Awards. But if she's a major figure in diva cults, it's because she recognizes the importance of hair spray in keeping a career firmly in place.

D iana Rigg

Diana Rigg was to *The Avengers* what Joan Collins is to *Dynasty,* Cybill Shepherd is to *Moonlighting,* and Natasha is to *Rocky and His Friends*. Her rapturously witty portrayal of Emma Peel, Series Siren extraordinaire, provided the kink that gave *The Avengers* its kick. Yes, the show had delicious setups, demented villains, and dazzling credits, but without Rigg it would have been a TV tortilla: cold, flat, and foreign. Even so, Rigg wasn't the show's first female lead; Honor Blackman originally played opposite Patrick Macnee's John Steed. But by the time the series hit the States, Rigg had stepped in, and Americans never saw anything like her. Zipped into leather jumpsuits, flinging her auburn locks over her lipsticked puss, kicking her karate-crazed jackboots at the camera, Rigg was a paragon of perversity: Diana Dominatrix. Her opponents—a comical collection of zombies, psychos, sickos, drooling despots, and mechanical monsters—completed a circle of sadomasochism: Emma's chains on twisted brains. Rigg's appeal as an actress is rare. She brings a sexy grandeur to her glamorous roles, but can dress down for classy parts without seeming pretentious. As the well-to-do-widow-turned-novice-nun in *In This House of Brede,* and as Mrs. Dedlock in "Bleak House," Rigg balanced the two sides of her talent with a teasing delicacy. She even starred in a sitcom *(Diana),* a form for which she's too large, physically and emotionally. But short of a juicy character part in her old age (Dame Diana?), Rigg will always be remembered for *The Avengers*. After

Diana Rigg in The Avengers

she left the show, all the Linda Thorsons in the world couldn't put it back together again. Evil men needed to be punished by a woman who packed pleasure in every painful punch.

Susan Saint James

Susan Saint James's résumé is enough to make an actress drool. She's the only Siren to score spectacular successes in three separate series. Her transformation from a kooky secretary (The Name of the Game) to a dizzy housewife (McMillan and Wife) to a divorced mother (Kate & Allie) parallels her progression from a supporting player to a leading lady to a top-billed star. But her advancement has always been impeded somehow. On Name she had to play second fiddle to three operatic hams: Gene Barry, Robert Stack, and Anthony Franciosa. On McMillan she had a nice rapport with Rock Hudson, but after leaving the series in a contract dispute she didn't land another for seven years. And on K & A she's consistently upstaged by the more gifted comedienne, Jane Curtin. Through it all Saint James's ace in the hole has been a throaty sensuality reminiscent of Jean Arthur's. Even as a pudgy-faced half hippie in Name, she was more of a siren than the conventionally glamorous Jill St. John, who appeared with her in the series pilot. You identified with her fumbling insecurities and scatterbrained schemes. She was a working-class cutie holding onto her dignity, though not necessarily her virginity. Saint James's recent metamorphosis as a full-fledged yuppie goddess on K & A is pleasant enough, but also a bit of a comedown. Not only does Curtin get the laughs, she gets the audience's sympathy the same way Saint James did on Name and McMillan. While Saint James's Kate attracts her ex-husband, breaks off affairs with studs, and attends her high school reunion to rekindle an old flame, Curtin's Allie repulses her ex, scares off men, and goes to her reunion to hide in the bathroom. Saint James's only comfort is that Curtin will never be mistaken for a Series Siren.

Lindsay Wagner

In an episode of The Bionic Woman Lindsay Wagner plays a scene with John Houseman. He's in profile on the left of the screen, she's in full face on the right. As he delivers a little speech, the emphasis is on her. So on the word "optimistic" (always a loaded term), Houseman folds his arms, rocks forward, cocks his chin away from Wagner, and all but peers into the camera. Not to be outdone, Wagner smiles, looks away, runs her fingers through her hair, shakes her head, puts her hands on her hips, and smiles again. All this takes about ten seconds, but it's very telling: don't mess with Lindsay Wagner. She's a marvelous actress, but she seldom accepts the roles that might reveal her personality. Even as a long-haired Siren in Bionic— for which she won an Emmy over Angie Dickinson, Kate Jackson, Michael Learned, and Sada Thompson—Wagner seemed to be slumming: there's an imperious air about her. When she tried for big-screen superstardom (Two People), she stubbed her toe—she wasn't built for cloying romance. With her high forehead, prominent cheekbones, Greek-goddess nose, and fierce, baloney-slice lips, Wagner should be playing anything but conventional heroines. Two of her most recent TV roles, as a distraught adoptive mother (This Child Is Mine) and a compassionate social worker (Child's Cry), don't jibe with the impression she leaves: hoarse, tense, and angry (Lynda Carter she ain't). When she tongue-lashes a wife beater in Child's Cry, you want to see her do it again. If she had done Bionic not as a distaff version of Lee Majors's Six Million Dollar Man, but as a variation of Arnold Schwarzenegger's The Terminator, she might be doing more interesting work today.

SOAP STARS

11

Diahann Carroll
Linda Evans
Linda Gray
Michele Lee
Dorothy Malone

Pamela Sue Martin
Donna Mills
Victoria Principal
Susan Sullivan
Joan Van Ark

A Soap Star is a Series Siren filtered through a Daytime Diva. Daytime surely has its stars, but the prime-time princess has a patina of glamor that sets her apart from her workaday sisters. She's a link in a chain of ambition: Daytime Divas (Susan Lucci, Genie Francis) want to be Soap Stars, Soap Stars (Pamela Sue Martin, Barbara Parkins) want to be Movie Goddesses, and Movie Goddesses (Jane Wyman, Dorothy Malone) wind up as Soap Stars. The irony is that the best movie actress in ten years—Kathleen Turner—jumped from daytime *(The Doctors)* to goddess *(Body Heat)* in a single bound. After a certain point, it's all luck, and part of that luck is landing in the right vehicle. The list of failed nighttime soaps is longer than J.R.'s life line: *Paper Dolls, Glitter, Berrenger's, Bracken's World, Bare Essence, Flamingo Road, The Yellow Rose, Emerald Point, N.A.S., Secrets of Midland Heights, Beacon Hill,* and *Our Family Honor*, which tarnished the reputations of such exciting actresses as Stella Stevens, Anita Morris, Susan Anspach, Jennifer Warren, and Sheree J. Wilson. Soaps produced as in-house artworks, such as *Masterpiece Theatre*'s "Upstairs Downstairs" and MTM's *Hill Street Blues,* fare much better, though their divas (Jean Marsh, Barbara Bosson) leave much to be desired. When we talk prime-time soaps, we're talking about only five shows: *Dallas, Dynasty, Knots Landing, Falcon Crest,* and *Peyton Place* (the jury's still out on *The Colbys*). What's remarkable is not the quantity of soaps, but how each soap's quality is determined by its divas: the fainthearted fillies of *Dallas,* the costumed cats of *Dynasty,* the leering ladies of *Falcon,* the soulful sirens of *Knots,* and the heavy-lidded honeys of *Peyton.* Tune in to see what happens next.

Diahann Carroll, Irene Cara, and Rosalind Cash in Sister, Sister

Diahann Carroll

Diahann Carroll always seems to be fuming. Her singing, punctuated by fierce jabs and truculent head twists, is the last word in chilly stylization: she makes Lena Horne look like Bessie Smith. Much of Carroll's haughty dignity (like Horne's) is understandable. For more than twenty-five years she struck blows for integration onstage *(No Strings)*, onscreen *(Paris Blues)*, and on TV *(Julia)*. By the time Whoopi Goldberg charmed Broadway, Eddie Murphy conquered Hollywood, and Bill Cosby owned NBC, Carroll seemed unemployable—a glitzy chanteuse. So she begged to be prime time's first "black bitch" (her words). As Dominique Deveraux on *Dynasty*, Carroll is less pioneer than superfluity. Initially an Alexis-style schemer, she was repeatedly outwitted by Joan Collins. She then became a Krystle-like sufferer, complete with a disease and a more relaxed hairdo. Now she's back to glaring again. But if Collins's fury is lyrical, and Linda Evans's is functional, Carroll's is sociological—she's one of the few glamor queens who should strip off the makeup to make a point. Her Oscar-nominated role in *Claudine* as a hardworking mother of six tapped levels of warmth and regret in her own personality. But it was her electric performance in *Sister, Sister,* a biting TV movie by Maya Angelou, that revealed the real Carroll. As the resentful, straitlaced sister of an easygoing urbanite (Rosalind Cash) and a well-meaning teen (Irene Cara), Carroll was a black bitch all right, but her anger had a context. Folding her arms firmly and raising her chin for combat, Carroll told the truth about a woman who kept the home fires burning only to be singed by the flames. If Carroll has wound up on *Dynasty,* it's because she's been burned too often waiting for her career to catch fire.

Linda Evans

Linda Evans has come full circle without moving an inch. In the '60s she played a girlfriend of John Forsythe's niece in an episode of *Bachelor Father* and starred as Barbara Stanwyck's daughter on *The Big Valley.* Twenty years later she married Forsythe on *Dynasty* and supported Stanwyck on *The Colbys.* Even her private life seemed repetitious. When she left John Derek, he went out and married a young Evans look-alike (Bo). This remarkable consistency has been the hallmark of Evans's career; she seldom has a hair out of place. Her Krystle Carrington is a paragon of fidelity—an earnest Earth Mother. Much has been made of how Evans looks great at forty-plus, but I think Lee Remick looks better at fifty-plus, Cyd Char-

isse at sixty-plus, and Claudette Colbert at eighty-plus. Part of the problem is that Evans always acts older than her characters. Her Audra on *Big Valley* was supposed to be a feisty colt, but she seemed sedate next to her mother. While Stanwyck roped steers and foiled bank robbers, Evans leaned against a pillar and looked unspoiled. Krystle is an update of Audra, though she's still the slowest draw in the West—a thickheaded goody-goody. If audiences respond so enthusiastically to Krystle's cat fights with Alexis, it's because they want to see Evans with her hair messed up. It came as no surprise last season, when *Dynasty*'s creators needed to boost the show's sagging ratings, that Evans had a knock-down-drag-out fight with her evil twin—two Krystles for the price of one. Still, it's a tribute to Evans that she's triumphed in two epochs without losing her likability. Even at her stickiest she's never contemptible. Twenty years from now, she'll probably star as Stanwyck's daughter in a new sitcom: *Bachelor Mother.*

Linda Gray

Adultery, divorce, drunk tanks, sanitariums, vehicular manslaughter, Christopher Atkins—you name it, Sue Ellen's been through it. But her rocky road seems built on contrivance. I always feel Sue Ellen suffers not because J.R.'s a meanie, but because Linda Gray wants an Emmy. Her wild-eyed leaps into Sarah Bernhardt country—hair-pulling, screeching, conspicuous perspiration—are never quite convincing and sometimes hilarious. One knee-slapping shot from last season showed J.R. and Cliff Barnes arguing when—bam!—Gray pops up between them and screams, "Aaaaaaaaaaaaaaaaaa!" (she looked like Liza Minnelli hitting the last note of "New York, New York"). Why is Gray so wacky? First, she tries too hard—she's so eager to impress, she's over the top before she knows it. Second, she doesn't

Christopher Atkins and Linda Gray in Dallas

seem to take any pleasure from her self-destructive impulses—she's a doe-eyed victim of insidious forces. And third, she can't overcome *Dallas*'s voyeuristic treatment of women. You're not expected to identify with Sue Ellen's pain—you're invited to lick your lips over Gray's humiliation. Just before *Dallas* Gray's forte was sophisticated light comedy. She played a transsexual model in Norman Lear's satire *All That Glitters* and supported Carol Burnett in the TV adaptation of Erma Bombeck's *The Grass Is Always Greener Over the Septic Tank*. Gray's exaggerated features were made for farce. Whether she can recapture her lightness of spirit after *Dallas* is anybody's guess. But at least she'll be free of silly Sue Ellen.

M ichele Lee

Michele Lee is the heart of prime-time's greatest soap. As Karen Fairgate MacKenzie on *Knots Landing*, Lee provides a common ground for earthy goings-on. She's a buffer, the only thing between good and evil. She's had problems herself in the years since the series began, but she's gotten out into the world and become a stabilizing force in other people's lives. The sensitivity of Lee's portrayal is easy to underestimate—the only time she was up for an Emmy was when Karen battled drug addiction. But Lee is on to something more subtle: she's the Myrna Loy of television—the Perfect Wife, the understated sexpot. If Loy's joyously sane contribution to American movies for more than half a century failed not only to garner her an Oscar, but even a single nomination, Lee's work on *Knots* will look better in retrospect. Her relationship with Kevin Dobson is rivaled in warmth and wit only by *St. Elsewhere*'s Bonnie Bartlett and William Daniels, married in real life. When Lee and Dobson turn down the covers of their bed without missing a beat in their conversation, you know they're wed for keeps. Maybe Lee's

training in musical comedy—she got her break as the ingenue in *How to Succeed in Business Without Really Trying*—helped her to develop the lyrical tempo she has on *Knots*. And maybe her long marriage to James Farentino, which ended in divorce, gave her the rhythmic rapport she has with Dobson. But whatever her influences, Lee has located the point where timing meets feeling. Her performance as the wifely writer in the TV remake of *A Letter to Three Wives* struck the perfect balance between commitment and self-affirmation. She's a Star who puts the hope in Soap.

D orothy Malone

The Academy of Motion Picture Arts and Sciences has made lots of mistakes, but its existence is justified by a single selection: Dorothy Malone as Best Supporting Actress for *Written on the Wind*. As Marylee Hadley, the hot-pants heiress of a Texas oil dynasty, Malone gave one of those rare performances that gets you high. I don't think any actress has ever used her eyes as lyrically as Malone. When she glared, she made a normal-sized screen look like Cinerama. Her breath control was amazing—she seemed to exhale completely before delivering a line so that each zinger rang with a deep, bitter tone. Her Marylee was a demented diva with a streak of decency, a character Malone perfected during her Hollywood career. But when she accepted the role of Constance MacKenzie on *Peyton Place*, the character Lana Turner put a hammerlock on in the movies, Malone emphasized the decent at the expense of the demented. Even Lola Albright, who filled in for an ailing Malone for a season, couldn't make the circumstances of Mia Farrow's birth seem seamy. Constance is a bore, a vacuous bombshell who suffers too heartily. If Turner won her only Oscar nomination as Constance, it's because she herself is a vacuous bombshell who suffers too heartily. But

Dorothy Malone and Tim O'Connor in Peyton Place

Malone has a dreamy delirium. When she swallows a vial of acid in *Man of a Thousand Faces*, she does it with a glee alien to Turner. She was used on *Peyton* as a den mother for more alluring sirens, especially Barbara Parkins—a raven-haired Malone look-alike. Malone's juiciest TV turn was as Van Johnson's alcoholic wife in *Rich Man, Poor Man*. It was a brief role, but it showed that Marylee Hadley still breathed inside the soul of Dorothy Malone.

stepped out of *Dynasty* to pursue other interests, including a feature film about cocaine abuse that sank so fast even Nancy Drew couldn't find it. Martin's brazen attitude served her well as Fallon Carrington Colby, the most outrageous spoiled brat since Chatsworth Osborne, Jr. With her ripe, downcast lips, giant baby blues, and perpetually upturned nose, Martin made petulance palpable: she looked like Daisy Duck with PMS. In early episodes Fallon was Denver's premier B-girl, sleeping with a tasty assortment of creamy studs. But after Alexis showed up, Fallon's nymphomania seemed tame. So Fallon became softer, even sympathetic. As the showdown between Alexis and Krystle crystallized, Fallon occupied a middle ground: a rebellious girl with a troubled soul. Martin made you understand why Jeff Colby (John James) was so crazy about her—she provoked craziness in everybody. By the time she drove off a cliff, Martin was an integral part of the show, more alluring than Pamela Bellwood (who isn't?) and more likable than Heather Locklear (ditto). Her replacement, Emma Samms, is woefully miscast—a cool, sweet zombie who mirrors the conventional acting style of leading man James (even Universal had the sense to cast edgy divas opposite Rock Hudson). Only Catherine Oxenburg, as Alexis's wayward daughter, rivaled Martin in the Junior Bitch Sweepstakes. Still, there's been a hole in *Dynasty* ever since Martin left, just as there's a gap in *The Colbys* with Samms at the center. I wouldn't go so far as to say that Martin's a first-class actress, but her uppity personality fit Fallon like a mink-lined glove.

P amela Sue Martin

Pamela Sue Martin has walked out on more shows than Jack Paar. She left *The Nancy Drew Mysteries* after its merger with *The Hardy Boys* and

D onna Mills

Donna Mills is a monument to mousse and makeup. Her hair, which has no apparent source and no definable end (except split ones), is symbolic of her character, Abby Cunningham Ewing, on *Knots*

Landing: determinedly appalling. Still, her hair is relatively serene next to her eyes—enormous pools of Easter-egg blue surrounded by immaculate white circles. These circles are highlighted by wiry black lashes, which are further encircled by matching blue shadow. When Abby walks into a room, she looks like a raccoon at the Academy Awards. Mills's character—a scheming rich bitch à la Alexis and Angela—wasn't on the first season of *Knots Landing,* which began in 1979 as a middle-class spinoff of *Dallas* but slid continuously upscale. At its best the show evokes a '50s concern with the tortured personal relationships of bourgeois life, centering on adultery, missing children, and wayward parents. At its worst it gets bogged down in the same corporate power struggles as the fuddy-duddy Ewings or the high-flying Carringtons. Though Mills is tied to the worst of *Knots,* she brings a needed element to the show: sleaze. Her early scenes with Ted Shackelford, whom she lured away from Joan Van Ark, are some of the steamiest ever to hit prime time. But as the years slip by, Mills has become as weird as she is evil—she's freaked by the idea of anybody finding out what a rotten human being she is. Her casting as Abby is a double-edged joke: she began as a fresh-faced virginal type in movies *(The Incident)* and played Larry Hagman's wife in a pre-*Dallas* sitcom *(The Good Life),* all about a middle-class couple who take jobs as a cook and butler on a millionaire's estate. In that show, all Mills did with the mousse was serve it.

Victoria Principal

Victoria Principal brings out the beast in me. Every time I see her I want to slap her around. She's the yin to Chuck Norris's yang: revoltingly feminine. It's funny how Norris and Schwarzenegger and Eastwood are attacked for being too macho, while Principal is adored as an ideal of female beauty. I think it's because women like Principal are eroticized as objects of desire, while men like Norris are distanced as forces of aggression. Principal is a walking *Playboy* centerfold—passive, willing, airbrushed. When she talks, I expect her to say her favorite singer is Billy Joel and her biggest turnoffs are loud music and rude people. That she's a dead ringer for Priscilla Presley seems to be some sort of joke: these girls have staples in their navels. Whether Principal can act remains to be seen, as she spends most of her time away from *Dallas* doing commercials for Jhirmack shampoo. But whatever she does, she'll have a hard time overcoming her image as Pamela Barnes Ewing. She began on the show as a willful Juliet, marrying Bobby against the wishes of the warring Barnes and Ewing families, and has become an iron-willed businesswoman. Her attempts at playing a tough-minded tycoon going nose-to-nose with J.R. consist of pursing her lips and stomping her foot. Part of Principal's problem is her inability to overcome *Dallas*'s dialectic: men are men, women are women, and men are more interesting. The show's obsession with corporate deeds over emotional needs makes it an anti–soap opera. It may be the only classically styled soap with a violent male lead. The young women of *Dallas* are decorative and tangential; they should all be doing shampoo commercials.

Susan Sullivan

Susan Sullivan seems the least likely of nurturers. Her lips are too thin, her voice too sharp, her eyes too cool. But that's exactly what she's become—a sensible mama. Her portrait of a compassionate doctor in *Having Babies II* and *Having Babies III* led directly to her own series, *Julie Farr, M.D.,* which instantly disappeared. Sullivan's strengths as an actress—straightforward intelligence, common sense, a certain malicious wit—are always at

Victoria Principal and Larry Hagman in Dallas

Joan Van Ark (left) *and Michele Lee in* Knots Landing

odds with her weaknesses—lack of warmth and erotic appeal. But the image of Sullivan as life giver persists. She plays Maggie Gioberti, preeminent wife and mother of *Falcon Crest*. Miscast, Sullivan is thwarted at every turn. Her relationship with Robert Foxworth is meant to be warm and wise, like Michele Lee's with Kevin Dobson on *Knots Landing*, but she's oddly detached and he's about as responsive as a drunken sailor. They're both upstaged by the soap world's best supporting couple—William R. Moses, a wonderfully naturalistic actor, and Ana-Alicia, a sharply intense femme fatale. And then there's The Truth about *Falcon*: it's Jane Wyman's show. So where does this leave Sullivan? Locked in the wine cellar without a corkscrew. Her most convincing moments come when she loses patience with Wyman—she enjoys zinging the old crow. Indeed, Sullivan's best performances have been sadistic guest shots as the doctor who rejects a lovesick Bernie Kopell on *The Love Boat* ("You'll get over it") and as the theatrical manager who maneuvers Jeff Conaway onto her casting couch in *Taxi*. Maternal? Yeah, like Joan Crawford.

J oan Van Ark

If Michele Lee is the heart of *Knots Landing*, Joan Van Ark is its soul. A thin, tremulous blonde with the most pouty lower lip since Jackie Cooper's in *The Champ*, Van Ark follows in a long line of virtuous victims from Janet Gaynor's put-upon hausfrau in the silent classic *Sunrise* to Olivia De Havilland's sacrificial mama in *To Each His Own* to Nastassja Kinski's lovelorn lass in Roman Polanski's *Tess*. It's an almost extinct type of heroine, but Van Ark plays it better than anybody has in years. Quivering with vulnerability, Van Ark's Valene is a three-hankie diva. Look at her the wrong way and she cries. The entire show is wired to her emotions—when Valene suffers, everybody short-circuits. Only the disappearance of Val's babies could precipitate suicide, insanity, amnesia, marital discord, generational conflict, financial ruin, and the discovery of dirty deeds (it was a wonderful season). Van Ark knows she's the centerpiece of a classic series; she carries herself with the pride of a melancholy monarch. Her scenes with Julie Harris, who plays her mother, are little masterpieces of pristine poses—the Princess of the Prime-Time Soap meets the Princess of the American Theater. Sometimes Van Ark's studied delicacy can be a pain. But just when you get tired of her shtick, she freaks out—screaming at her wacko brother (beautifully played by Alec Baldwin) or pounding on the front door of the couple who adopted her kidnapped twins: "I want my babies! *Give me my babies!*" Van Ark is essential to the greatness of *Knots Landing* because her spirit complements the earthiness of Michele Lee and pierces the wickedness of Donna Mills. If Lee is human and Mills demonic, Van Ark is angelic—a wispy wimp on the brink of transcendence.

MOTHER FIGURES
(and Their Darling Daughters)

Frances Bavier
Barbara Billingsley
Beulah Bondi &
Spring Byington
Florence Henderson
Shirley Jones

Michael Learned
Harriet Nelson
Donna Reed
Sada Thompson
Jane Wyatt

The world of the Mother Figure and her Darling Daughter is one of memory and loss, repression and release, submission and ambition. Frozen into images of goodness and purity, the MF/DD either breaks out or breaks down, subverting expectations or conforming to them. Her difficulty in deciding which way to go isn't just the risk of losing work, but the psychic price she's already paid during a particularly vulnerable period in her life. If the DD endures the embarrassment of growing up in public, the MF experiences the awkwardness of growing old in public. While the DD frets about the future, the MF meditates on the past. Somewhere in the present, each reflects the other—two sweet females wondering how to sell their images in an ever-changing marketplace. Some DDs pose for *Playboy* to flaunt their adulthood (Judy Norton-Taylor of *The Waltons*), while others become larger versions of their younger selves (Elinor

Donahue of *Father Knows Best*). Almost all MFs seem frozen in place, whether Broadway Babies (Sada Thompson, Barbara Bel Geddes) or Hollywood pros (Jane Wyatt, Harriet Nelson). That most DDs grow up to be mothers themselves while most MFs become divorcées or widows may be the weirdest irony of all. But there are always dramatic stories of transcendence among MF/DDs. Elizabeth Taylor, the reigning DD of postwar Hollywood, grew up to be a certified Grande Dame after forty years of heaven and hell. Her heir, Natalie Wood, struggled all her glorious youth to be a serious actress, only to give her best "straight" performance as the alcoholic wife and mother in the TV movie *The Cracker Factory*. And then there's Annette Funicello in a 1986 episode of *Growing Pains* doing a devastating parody of a Moral Majority mama. Only a Disney DD posing as a grisly MF could wreak such joyful havoc.

Mother & Daughter Quiz

Match the TV mother's first name in column A to her daughter's in column B and then select the appropriate last name in column C (proper names only—no nicknames). Finally, name all actresses and their respective shows.

A	B	C
1. Carol	a. Letitia	A. Anderson
2. Donna	b. Kathy	B. Williams
3. Olivia	c. Lucy	C. Brady
4. Lily	d. Marcia	D. Miller
5. Joan	e. Mary	E. Lawrence
6. Margaret	f. Elizabeth	F. Stone
7. Kate	g. Nancy	G. Ruskin
8. Valene	h. Ruth	H. Walton
9. Shirley	i. Debra	I. Bradford
10. Kathy	j. Linda	J. Ewing

Frances Bavier in The Andy Griffith Show

ANSWERS: 1-d-C, Florence Henderson & Maureen McCormick, *The Brady Bunch*; 2-e-F, Donna Reed & Shelley Fabares, *The Donna Reed Show*; 3-f-H, Michael Learned & Kami Cotler, *The Waltons*; 4-h-G, Spring Byington & Frances Rafferty, *December Bride*; 5-g-I, Diana Hyland & Dianne Kay, *Eight Is Enough*; 6-b-A, Jane Wyatt & Lauren Chapin, *Father Knows Best*; 7-a-E, Sada Thompson & Kristy McNichol, *Family*; 8-c-J, Joan Van Ark & Charlene Tilton, *Dallas*; 9-i-B, Shirley Jones & Rosanna Arquette, *Shirley*; 10-j-B, Marjorie Lord & Angela Cartwright, *The Danny Thomas Show*.

Frances Bavier

Aunt Bee is not a well woman. More than addled or frazzled, she's one step from the Mayberry loony bin. In one episode of *The Andy Griffith Show* Aunt Bee invests four hundred dollars in a Chinese restaurant, but when counting the receipts at night's end, she's slipped a fortune cookie warning she'll lose a lot of money. Taking it as gospel, she suffers a near-collapse, cowering in the kitchen like Agnes Moorehead in *The Twilight Zone*. Her behavior is accepted as normal—if she suddenly announced she was Marie Antoinette, her family would chip in for a powdered wig. Along with the town's predominantly crazy citizens—a hysterical deputy sheriff, a brain-damaged gas-station attendant, a spastic-psychotic barber—Aunt Bee makes one wonder if a chemical spill didn't contaminate the town's drinking water. Unlike *The Beverly Hillbillies,* which presented its characters as robust vaudevillians, *The Andy Griffith Show* paraded comical "little people" who triumphed over nervousness. Frances Bavier played Aunt Bee with enormous concentration. She plugged right into this plump woman's fears and hostilities. When she lies about having a date so as not to tag along with Andy and his girlfriend, you feel like cradling her until the shrink arrives. But Andy, who's incapable of treating a fellow human being as an equal, insists on coddling his aunt as a dear, sweet soul. No wonder he's a widower who resists marriage—he has Aunt Bee to condescend to (Barney Fife undercuts Andy's smugness with his sublime silliness). Bavier's best scenes are with Ron Howard, who doesn't know how to act superior to anybody. When Aunt Bee smiles at Opie, she seems free—her eyes aren't clouded, and she isn't intimidated. She's face-to-face with another motherless imp.

Barbara Billingsley and the Cleaver clan in Leave It to Beaver

B arbara Billingsley

Whenever I watch *Leave It to Beaver*, a justly celebrated sitcom classic, I have a persistent fantasy: after Ward and "the boys" leave the house, I slip into the Cleaver kitchen and spend the day with Barbara Billingsley. The coolest and sharpest of all Mother Figures, Billingsley is what Mary Tyler Moore would have become if she'd been born twenty years earlier. June's perennial pearls and pumps, worn amid even the most daunting crises, are symbols of feminine survival in an oppressively masculine environment. Almost all of Billingsley's touches in the show have been over-

looked by the *Animal House*/David Letterman school of slobby collegiates that's adopted The Beav as its prime-time mascot. In one subversive episode Billingsley lounges on a divan in a Doris Day frock reading an oversized magazine called *Style*—a dead ringer for Andy Warhol's *Interview*. The supercute but eternally dumb Tony Dow lumbers into the room, startled to find his "mom" immersed in something so ritzy. Defensively, Billingsley launches into a rapturous rap about visiting New York as a young woman, attending the opera, and wearing beautiful clothes. When Dow, more perplexed than ever, expresses disbelief, Billingsley spins around and snaps, "I wasn't *born* a mother, Wally!" The ferocity of her delivery shows how much June gave up to become the warden to Ward and the boys. Billingsley, too, gave up the hope of a movie career to become a Sitcom Queen (remember her as Lana Turner's costume designer in *The Bad and the Beautiful*?). Lately, she's turned up in *Airplane!* as a jive-talking baritone and in a series of *Beaver* sequels. But I'd love to see Billingsley fulfill June's Broadway dreams—as Elaine Stritch's sister in a new musical: *The Ladies Who Lunch.*

B eulah Bondi & Spring Byington

The 1938 Oscar race for Best Supporting Actress was a battle of the Mother Figures: Bainter, Bondi, Burke, and Byington. That's Fay, Beulah, Billie, and Spring, respectively. The fifth contestant, Miliza Korjus, never made a movie before or after the one she was nominated for *(The Great Waltz),* leaving the field clear for nurturers of Bette Davis (Bainter in *Jezebel*), Jimmy Stewart (Bondi in *Of Human Hearts*), Constance Bennett (Burke in *Merrily We Live*), and Jean Arthur (Byington in *You Can't Take It With You*). Burke and Byington are lighthearted, Bainter and Bondi deep-spirited, but all four are sublime. Only two—Byington and Bondi—made the transition to television. In doing so they became the premier Mother Figures of our time, making final comments on their images in a medium that will mean more to the next century than to the current one. If Bondi seizes the heart, Byington tickles the funny bone. In *December Bride* she sparkled as Lily Ruskin, a captivating mother-in-law whose irrepressible wit makes everybody think she's still marriageable (take that, Golden Girls). She also popped up on *Make Room for Daddy* as an escaped nursing home patient who believes she's Alice in Wonderland (Danny Thomas and Jean Hagen throw a tea party for her). And very late in her life she bustled in as Larry Hagman's mom on *I Dream of Jeannie,* dropping catty remarks about Barbara Eden's

Spring Byington

housekeeping. Complementing this giddy imagery is Bondi's wrenching work as the fierce matriarch who comes home to die in an episode of *The Waltons*. At eighty-five Bondi seized the strands of her extraordinary career by falling to the ground to grasp the last gasp of life. She won an Emmy for her performance and accepted it in person. Oh, yes: Bainter won the Oscar in '38.

F lorence Henderson

On *The Tonight Show* in 1985 Florence Henderson took center stage in a tight, sequined gown, brought down the house with a hot, sultry song, and then sat down with Joan Rivers to tell all about her new life: divorcing her longtime husband and dating for the first time in decades. Grilled on the grisly details, Henderson handled herself well, fielding Rivers's questions with a merry, albeit forced, maliciousness. But then, almost as a non sequitur, Henderson blurted that she'd had a hysterectomy. A hush swept the audience and even Rivers was thrown. What Henderson tried to do was find out whether America would accept a life-long Mother Figure as a tart-tongued, swinging single. Well, why not? Jessica Fletcher and the Golden Girls aren't exactly yesterday's mashed potatoes. But Henderson's charm is that she doesn't push—she's pleasantly nonchalant. It's hard to think of another actress who could bound into a bevy of Bradys and burble, "Hi, kids, would you like to watch some TV with me?" without coming across as a horse's ass. Seldom has a Mother Figure been given so little to work with, but Henderson was never contemptible on *The Brady Bunch*—she got the job done. A veteran Variety Player (*The Jack Paar Show, Oldsmobile Music Theatre*), Henderson always seemed like an American Julie Andrews (she even did *The Sound of Music* onstage). But just as Andrews reversed her image in the movie *S.O.B.*, Henderson is taking her first faltering steps on the road to a New Attitude. All she needs is a cable sitcom based on *S.O.B.: Screw Off, Brady!*

Shirley Jones

The irony of Shirley Jones's career used to be that she went from playing a virginal ingenue in *Oklahoma!* to laying a tainted hero in *Elmer Gantry*. "Give that girl an Oscar!" audiences cried, and the Academy did just that. But no sooner was her name inscribed on the trophy than Jones was off being Smilin' Shirley again, merrily supporting male egos in *The Music Man* and *The Courtship of Eddie's Father*. Even when she landed her own series,

Shirley Jones in The Partridge Family

The Partridge Family and *Shirley*, she played single mothers in charge of all-American broods. In *Partridge*, she looked and acted more like an elder sibling than an abandoned mama. Starring opposite her own stepson, David Cassidy, Jones waited for her reaction shots to express motherly concern. But the deeper irony of Jones's image is that she's always been closer to *Elmer Gantry*'s B-girl than *Oklahoma!*'s A-material. There's a malicious glint in Jones's eye that has less to do with Rodgers and Hammerstein than Bonnie and Clyde. Her best performance, as Lloyd Bridges' clear-eyed mistress in the movie *The Happy Ending,* reunited her with *Gantry* collaborators Richard Brooks and Jean Simmons, married at the time in real life. Jones's own marriages to Jack Cassidy and Marty Ingels suggest all sorts of unexplored regions in her sensibility. She's dealt with marital tension in a number of TV movies, especially as the wayward wife in *Silent Night, Lonely Night* (also opposite Bridges in the same year as *Happy Ending*), but Jones insists on accenting the fresh-faced side of her personality at the expense of the dirty-minded. It's hard to guess whether Jones feels trapped by her image or she just enjoys playing innocuous characters. Maybe she and Bridges can team up for a revival of *Who's Afraid of Virginia Woolf?*

M ichael Learned

Once described as "a mothering bucket of slop" by a distinguished movie critic who dumps on television every chance she gets, Olivia Walton is an original Mother Figure. Before *The Waltons* TV moms maintained an upper-middle-class lifestyle without working up a sweat. In their postwar paradise everybody liked Ike. But *The Waltons* embraced extremes, romanticizing a Depression-era dream of family unity but recognizing a recession-era reality of blue-collar blues. It may be the only smash series that was at once reactionary and progressive (if John Ford had gone into television, he'd have been right at home on Walton's Mountain). Michael Learned made a perfect Olivia because she reflected the split in the show—a dressed-down character actress playing an idealized Fordian heroine. After all, Maureen O'Hara starred in *Spencer's Mountain,* a backwoods weeper based on the novel by *Waltons* creator Earl Hamner, while Patricia Neal headlined *The Homecoming,* a TV movie written by Hamner that became the pilot for *The Waltons*. If O'Hara was a tremulous Leading Lady and Neal a stone-faced Grande Dame, Learned was a Quixotic Queen—she brought a sullen tenseness to Walton's Mountain. Her Olivia was really rather a bitch—intolerant, inflexible, aggressively pious (Ellen Corby was even worse). I don't think the part was written that way, but that's how Learned played it. Lately, she's had trouble shaking Olivia in *Nurse* (a series) and *Widow* (a TV movie), both contemporary pieces. In 1986's *A Deadly Business* she submitted to a degradation worse than unemployment: she threw

Michael Learned in The Waltons

herself at Alan Arkin. The irony is that Olivia seems to be getting even with Learned for portraying her as something other than a mothering bucket of slop.

H arriet Nelson

If the auteur theory applied to television, *The Adventures of Ozzie and Harriet* would be the *Citizen Kane* of sitcoms. Every frame of every episode for fourteen years was wholly expressive of its

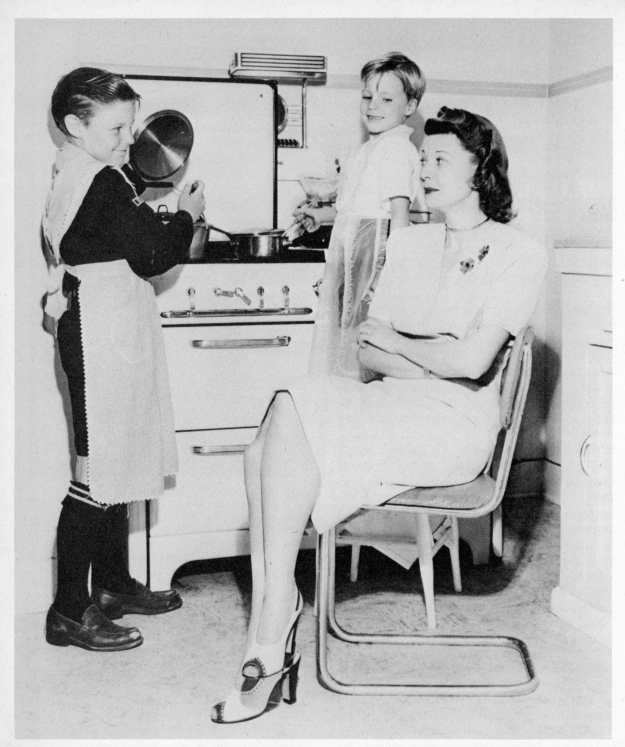

(Left to right): *David, Ricky, and Harriet Nelson*

creator, Ozzie Nelson, who produced, directed, headlined, and cowrote (with his brother!) the entire series. Ozzie even cast his wife as his wife, his sons as his sons, his daughters-in-law as his daughters-in-law, and probably his sweater as his sweater. The show was filled with startlingly personal touches: Ozzie addressing the camera, Harriet watching Ricky sing on TV, an incongruent jazz riff over the closing credits. If this art-reflecting-life imagery gave *Ozzie and Harriet* an esthetic purity, the life-reflecting-art reality behind the show has given it an elegiac quality in retrospect. It's hard watching the reruns today without focusing on Harriet, the most steadfast of all Mother Figures, who survived her husband and now her younger son, a boy so heartbreakingly beautiful

and lyrically savvy he anticipated rock video by two decades. Harriet's role on the show reflected her real-life one: to support the men in her life. She never hogged a scene or lingered over a line. She gave until it hurt. Yes, she embodied the ethos of the '50s housewife, all cheery and efficient, but she wasn't a cloying presence—there was an air of detachment in the way she treated her family, just like a real mother. Overall, the show was too tame for my taste—I always yearned for Sue Ann Nivens to sashay onto the set and run her fingers through Ricky's hair. But Ozzie and Harriet's integrity and commitment can't be brushed aside. They held a mirror to the American family without making us feel arrogant about our triumphs or devastated by our tragedies.

Donna Reed and family in The Donna Reed Show

Donna Reed

Donna Reed's life ended on a particularly sad note. Dumped from *Dallas* just before her death, she sued the producers, seeming like an embittered and desolated TV diva. Public sympathy was with her (deservedly), but one cruel fact remained: the role of Miss Ellie belongs to Barbara Bel Geddes. A respected and pampered Broadway Baby, Bel Geddes strikes the perfect balance between patrician snootiness and tough-minded naturalism. She *looks* like a queen of the Old-New South—you could drive a tractor through the creases in her face. But Reed played the part like a PTA chairwoman from Orange County. Her unctuous dignity embalmed her later work, such as *The Best Place to Be*—a mere TV movie *and* "A Ross Hunter Production"—which made Lana Turner's bourgeois idealism in *Imitation of Life* seem subversive. But Reed's two great movie roles—as Jimmy Stewart's wife in *It's a Wonderful Life* and as Montgomery Clift's lover in *From Here to Eternity*—glorified the two sides of her image: the girl-next-door and the hussy-down-the-block. She was never, in her prime, the lady-on-the-hill. But with *The Donna Reed Show* Reed began her rise to respectability and her decline as an actress. The show, which was surprisingly mild, erased the dramatic tension from Reed's handsome brow. As her face grew calmer, her hair became wilder. Throughout the series, Reed sported a heavily sprayed, layered bouffant. She retained this style to the bitter end, perhaps thinking it fitting for a Hollywood matron. But the Reed who saved Stewart's soul in *Life* and turned tricks in *Eternity* shouldn't have been stuck with such hair.

Sada Thompson

Produced by Mike Nichols, *Family* began as a trenchant study of power relationships and ended as a smug endorsement of conventional behavior. One early episode, directed by Mark Rydell, is positively surgical in its dissection of upper-middle-class despair: Sada Thompson, quivering with rage, tells her plodding husband she sought an abortion when pregnant with their youngest child (Kristy McNichol). "Why can't men understand that women sometimes just want *out*?" she howls. Thompson's delivery is extraordinary—she doesn't yell the line at top speed, but spews each syllable, spitting out the last word with a subhuman sound that's half hissing and half squealing. Such moments grew rarer as the sanctity of the Lawrence clan was contrasted with the soullessness of the outside world. By the third season Thompson and her brood were besieged by a legion of antifamily fiends—drug dealers, child molesters, ex-convicts, slinky dames, and unkempt neighbors (one shining exception: an episode with Blair Brown as a persecuted lesbian schoolteacher). Thompson conformed to the mustiness of the proceedings with a look that can only be described as shell-shocked, drifting through the Lawrence manse like an opening-night understudy in a Tennessee Williams one-acter. Her cameos in the miniseries *Marco Polo* and *Princess Daisy* confirmed this image, though she was marvelous in 1986 in PBS's *Painting Churches*. A former Broadway Baby (she won a Tony for *Twigs*), Thompson needs meaty material to sink her teeth into. Her electric rapport with McNichol is as touching as it is telling—both are powerhouse actresses who've been unable to channel their anxieties into worthy roles. At the very least Thompson's Kate was the only Mother Figure who could read Virginia Woolf and still have time to take out the garbage.

Sada Thompson and her Family

Jane Wyatt

To win her three consecutive Emmys for *Father Knows Best* Jane Wyatt beat out Gracie Allen, Eve Arden, Ann Sothern, Loretta Young, Jan Clayton, Ida Lupino (twice), Donna Reed (ditto), and Spring Byington (ditto again). Moreover, she won in three different categories: Best Continuing Performance by an Actress in a Leading Role in a Dramatic or Comedy Series, Best Actress in a Leading Role (Continuing Character) in a Comedy Series, and Outstanding Performance by an Actress in a Series (Lead or Support). This combination of impressive victory and fuzzy imagery probably has less to do with Emmy's renowned schiziness than with Wyatt's own ambiguity. Her

Lauren Chapin, Robert Young, Elinor Donahue, Jane Wyatt, and Billy Gray in Father Knows Best

Margaret Anderson is at once unbelievable (i.e., perfect) and instantly immediate (i.e., human). She's the most determinedly unflappable Mother Figure in all of television—brisk, cheerful, capable, thorough—but she also comes across as a real woman. I'm convinced that Wyatt pulls this off through a quirk of nature: she has a fixed facial expression that can only be described as "twinkly." She seems to be laughing at the world, albeit sympathetically. Her eyes sparkle, her mouth crinkles, her dimples dance—she's tickled. She's as much defined by her looks as Goldie Hawn or Anna Magnani—a born bourgeois mama. After *Father* Wyatt seemed to play everybody's mother short of Abraham Lincoln's: Susan Clark's in *Amelia Earhart*, Blythe Danner's in *A Love Affair: The Eleanor and Lou Gehrig Story,* and Mr. Spock's in *Star Trek*. But as Sissy Spacek's distraught mother in *Katherine,* a heartbreaking TV movie about a well-bred girl who joins the Weather underground, Wyatt let her façade crack. She still looked twinkly, but her tears were well-earned. She enhanced her humanity by being less than perfect.

UNDERRATED ODDITIES

Bonnie Bedelia
Meredith Baxter Birney
Joanna Cassidy
Susan Clark
Mariette Hartley

Kay Lenz
Linda Purl
Lynn Redgrave
Jessica Walter
Stephanie Zimbalist

An Underrated Oddity is odd because she seldom gets the parts she deserves. In a profession with too few roles and too many divas, the UO keeps a stiff upper lip while lesser actresses land on the cover of *People*. A tireless team player, she never makes the jump to big-screen superstardom and usually steers clear of Broadway—she's a California girl. She seems to stay on television forever, though her roles grow scarcer and less important as the years slip by. Often scoring a major success early in her career, she doesn't capitalize on the impact, whether through bad luck, bad timing, bad manners, or simply impossible choices women are sometimes forced to make. Part of the problem is her looks. Neither a glamor puss nor a sourpuss, she doesn't always get to play the leading lady or the juiciest character part. If she's past forty she's automatically considered past her prime. Her handsomeness is too frank and her eroticism

too subtle. If she isn't defeated by inferior material or distracted by her personal life, the UO can be the best actress around—she learns resourcefulness the hard way. Her defeats can strengthen her resolve and sharpen her talents. Vera Miles, the den mother of all UOs, began to be a great actress when pregnancy forced her to surrender the lead in Alfred Hitchcock's *Vertigo* to the sublime Kim Novak. Since then she's singlehandedly saved scores of TV movies and series episodes through her acrid portraits of complex women. Her generation of TV actresses—Jeanette Nolan, Dina Merrill, Shirley Knight, Sheree North, Hope Lange, Janet Leigh, Nina Foch, Diane Baker, Beverly Garland, Lois Nettleton, Barbara Rush, Bethel Leslie, and so many others—set the stage for the current cast of UOs. In many ways, the Underrated Oddity is the noblest TV diva.

Bonnie Bedelia

An ingenue with an edge, Bonnie Bedelia got better with age. Her early roles as Michael Parks's companion in the TV movie *Then Came Bronson* and Bruce Dern's pregnant bride in the feature film *They Shoot Horses, Don't They?* showed her ability to be sexy and pathetic at the same time. You didn't know whether to hold her or just put her out of her misery. Her tremulousness and desperation were always a little scary—there was danger in her eroticism. As the years went by, Bedelia seemed stuck. Everybody knew she could play sweet and helpless, but nobody sensed the sharpness behind the eyes. She was even cast in the doomed series, *The New Land,* based on the film about nineteenth-century Swedish immigrants. That's how producers saw Bedelia: an American Liv Ullmann, all earthy and teary-eyed. But director Jonathan Kaplan saw something else, and gave Bedelia the lead in *Heart Like a Wheel,* a nifty B-movie about drag racer Shirley Muldowney. In one of the great film performances of recent years, Bedelia unleashed a lifetime of caustic wit. You could still see the shapely girl inside the tough woman, but you also saw the eagerness of an actress who just couldn't wait to show off. Still, the roles to match Bedelia's maturity haven't come along. Her best work since *Heart* was in *The Lady From Yesterday,* a memorable TV movie about a married man (Wayne Rogers) whose lover from the Vietnam war (Tina Chen) shows up to say she has a son by Rogers *and* she's dying. As Rogers's wife, Bedelia gave a keenly ambiguous performance, showing the intolerance of a woman babied since birth by her fat-cat father (Pat Hingle). This is, of course, Bedelia's own problem: she's been babied too long. It's time she started playing with the grown-ups.

Meredith Baxter Birney

Meredith Baxter Birney shows what happens when an Underrated Oddity sells out. As Nancy Lawrence Maitland, the eldest sibling on *Family,* Birney was a tart presence. Spoiled, pretty, and pissed, she made the rest of the family look like sweet-potato pies. I invariably sided with her against what Bette Davis in *All About Eve* calls "unyielding good taste." Whenever her noble mother or cutesy sister would criticize her selfishness, I felt like screaming, "Give the girl a break! She's too beautiful to be normal!" Her life, of course, was a mess: an estranged husband, broken love affairs, flimsy friendships. On top of it all, she was a lawyer *and* a mother (quelle yuppette!). But Birney didn't get credit for her hard-edged portrayal. Unlike her cuddly costars, Gary Frank and Kristy McNichol, she never won an Emmy. So it came as no surprise that when Birney landed on another close-knit series, *Family Ties,* she played the sympathetic mother of a raging spoiled brat. But the brat, played by Michael J. Fox, has become such a sensation that scripts are tailored for him, pushing Birney off center stage. Meanwhile she's having (more) babies with husband David Birney (twins!). Suddenly she seems content to let Fox do the heavy work on the set. After all, she remembers the pressures of a sitcom, when she and David starred in *Bridget Loves Bernie,* taken off the air after religious groups protested its plot of a rich Catholic girl marrying a poor Jewish boy. But with *Family Ties* Meredith Baxter Birney finally has a hit, even though it isn't *her* hit. That's the catch-22 of the Underrated Oddity: she can become a household name, but only if she mellows herself out to the point where her name is no longer special.

Dabney Coleman and Joanna Cassidy in Buffalo Bill

Joanna Cassidy

Buffalo Bill was one of those shows America just hated. Like *He & She,* which enjoyed the cushy time slot right after *The Beverly Hillbillies* and *Green Acres* but was still canceled after a single season, *Bill* was plopped between *Cheers* and *Hill Street Blues* and still couldn't squeeze out a rating. I loved the show, but I understood the hostility. In a genre that depends on familial coziness *(Lucy/ Mary/Cosby), Bill* offered a thoroughly contemptible protagonist (Dabney Coleman) in a position of authority (talk-show host). This kinkiness was compounded by a central mystery: why would Joanna Cassidy allow herself to be Coleman's lover? A stunning, full-figured redhead with sharp, pale eyes, Cassidy played the intelligent and competent director of Coleman's tacky show. In one episode she confessed that she stayed with Coleman because he was predictable—she knew he'd always be a bastard. But Cassidy is too alluring and provocative a presence to be a victim of such simple masochism. *Bill,* as savvy a project as it was, exploited only one side of Cassidy—the noble sexpot. The movie *Under Fire,* released during the run of *Bill,* showed a denim-clad variation of the same image. *Code Name: Foxfire,* a tawdry, primetime vehicle for Cassidy, accented the sexpot and played down the noble. And *Pleasures,* a supersensual TV movie from 1986, tried to make nobility sexy by flaunting a disheveled Cassidy (she's never looked so crummy on screen). But somewhere between the wants of the body and the demands of the marketplace lies the talent of Joanna Cassidy. I hope she finds that place before producers forget how much she has to offer a medium in desperate need of brainy beauty.

Susan Clark

As Babe Didrikson Zaharias in the TV movie *Babe,* Susan Clark gave the kind of immaculate performance that movie actresses copy without giving credit. It seems to have influenced everybody from Sissy Spacek *(Coal Miner's Daughter)* to Jessica Lange *(Sweet Dreams).* Bringing a modern rhythm to the backstage bio without losing control of her material, Clark embodied a spirit instead of doing a drag routine—her speech and body movements were related to her clothes and hair styles. Let's face it: Susan Hayward was a ball in *I'll Cry Tomorrow,* but her histrionics had about as much to do with Lillian Roth as Little Orphan Annie. In *Babe* Clark used impersonation as the first step in revelation; her mannerisms were so concentrated, they became inseparable from her emotions. Even her death scene, which cried out for throat-clutching, was played in a kind of ghastly hush. Her performance may lack the ferocity of Faye Dunaway's in *Evita Perón,* but its exactitude is more than impressive—it's thrilling. Yet despite beating Jane Alexander, Colleen Dewhurst, and Sada Thompson for the Emmy, Clark didn't go far after *Babe.* Her *Amelia Earhart* was affecting but didn't show us anything new. Since 1983 she's supported Emmanuel Lewis in the lame sitcom *Webster,* as has her husband and *Babe* costar, Alex Karras. Decked out in a crisp array of pseudochic outfits and sporting a David Bowie haircut circa 1975, Clark delivers her lines with a distressingly dispassionate professionalism. She isn't bad, but she isn't challenged, either. It's like watching Babe Didrikson play miniature golf.

Mariette Hartley

There's nothing wrong with Mariette Hartley that a little common sense won't cure. Her transition from Hollywood ingenue (*Ride the High Country*) to TV diva (continuous employment) hinged on a series of spots for Polaroid opposite James Garner. Her easygoing sarcasm was so convincing, everybody thought the two were married in real life. Parlaying this image into pivotal roles on series episodes, Hartley was up for an Emmy for *The Rockford Files,* won the award as Bill Bixby's bride on *The Incredible Hulk,* and landed her own sitcom, *Goodnight, Beantown,* also opposite Bixby. If Garner and Bixby were such enchanting leading men for Hartley, it's because they have a warmly paternal appeal—they're daddies you can go to bed with. Maybe Hartley's feeling for her own father, who committed suicide while she was still a young woman, contributed to the wit and passion she brought to these early TV triumphs (even in *Country,* she was protected by Joel McCrea and Randolph Scott). But as she matured as an actress, Hartley squeezed the humor out of her performances and replaced it with a crusading weepiness. Her grandstanding roles in *M.A.D.D.. Mothers Against Drunk Drivers* (the mother of a drunk-driving victim) and *Silence of the Heart* (the mother of a teen suicide) accented a Puritan force at the expense of a wry eroticism. Even when she tackled an explicitly sexual role in *My Two Loves* as a widow who has affairs with her husband's best friend and her female employer, Hartley was such a bedraggled wreck you couldn't figure out why either lover was interested in her. But Hartley, who's enormously witty about her own marriage to a Frenchman, is suppressing the best in herself. Nobody wants to see the Jean Arthur of TV turn into another Loretta Young.

Nolte's widow in *Rich Man, Poor Man,* won an Emmy for a daytime special *(Heart in Hiding),* and was once married to David Cassidy. Lenz's bio is littered with pretty men, captivating directors, and offbeat projects that never caught on with what Garbo in *Ninotchka* calls "the messes." This is particularly ironic, since Lenz has always been an exemplary proletarian heroine. Her work with B-movie wunderkind Jonathan Kaplan on the TV movie *The Hustler of Muscle Beach* (opposite Richard Hatch) and the feature film *White Line Fever* (with Jan-Michael Vincent) gave her the chance to do what she does best—express feminine frustration with masculine megalomania. While her blue-collar lovers get sucked into power games, Lenz gets at something more complex: how a woman can still respect a man who's being brutalized by the System. Her fidelity enhanced *Escape,* in which she sprung Timothy Bottoms from a Mexican prison, and *Journey From Darkness,* in which she put a blind Marc Singer through medical school. There's an extraordinary mixture of spiritual resignation (Sylvia Sidney) and social anger (Ida Lupino) in Lenz's work. *Here's* the actress who should have played Karen Silkwood. Instead, Lenz has become a tireless TV diva. Her biggest recent success was as Rod Stewart's obscure object of desire in the rock video "Infatuation." Tarted up and strutting like a teen, Lenz seems to have found a bit of immortality in the '80s. But in my heart, she'll always be the heavy-lidded soulmate eulogizing Nolte in *Rich Man, Poor Man:* "It doesn't even out. It never has, and it never will."

Kay Lenz

Kay Lenz ties with Linda Purl as the most underrated oddity of her generation. A sharp-featured brunette with huge, liquid eyes, Lenz played Nick

Linda Purl

The world of the Underrated Oddity is an incestuous one. Linda Purl's best performance was as the mentally retarded girl who fights for the right to marry her equally impaired boyfriend, Shaun

Lynn Redgrave

Cassidy, in *Like Normal People.* Shaun's half-brother, David Cassidy, was once married to Kay Lenz, a certified UO whose acting style is strikingly similar to Purl's. Shaun's costar on *The Hardy Boys,* Parker Stevenson, is married to Kirstie Alley, a scintillating UO who salvaged the second half of *North and South.* Purl herself is divorced from Desi Arnaz, Jr., while David's sister on *The Partridge Family,* Susan Dey, is a classic UO who bears a remarkable resemblance to Lenz. And one of Purl's costars in *Little Ladies of the Night,* all about teenage prostitution, was Kathleen Quinlan, a great UO who reprised the *Ladies* theme in 1985 in *Children of the Night* opposite a budding UO, Lar Park Lincoln. So what does all this have to do with the price of greasepaint? Simple. UOs form a close-knit repertory not unlike off-Broadway actors. But while New York thespians walk off with Oscars, UOs are taken for granted as "Hollywood actors." How many culture vultures know that Purl can be heartrending *(Normal People),* hard-edged *(Little Ladies),* or sly (as the teenage Alice Roosevelt in *Eleanor and Franklin*)? How many pop cultists recall that she was a fresh-faced ingenue who won Richie's heart in *Happy Days* and then showed up seven years later as a sharp-eyed divorcée to wow Fonzie? And how many Nielsen families remember that she excelled as the blind slave girl in *The Last Days of Pompeii,* the mad rape victim in the opening episode of *Alfred Hitchcock Presents,* and the besieged mother-to-be in *Black Market Baby?* That Purl carries off these myriad roles with her own peculiar mix of doe-eyed delicacy and twinkling wit is a tribute to the resourcefulness of the Underrated Oddity.

Lynn Redgrave

Long after becoming one of the world's finest actresses, Lynn Redgrave is still remembered for two things: *Georgy Girl* and her sister. Maybe that's why she moved to Hollywood years ago for the seemingly sole purpose of being a TV diva. She didn't want to be typecast as a youngish Margaret Rutherford—pert, plump, and poignant—and she didn't want to be paired with her sister as an artsy, European radical. But her plan backfired: she never made the minions forget *Georgy* or the critics forget Vanessa. If anything, she was branded a crass capitalist while her sibling was hailed as an uncompromising genius. But Lynn is every bit as great as Vanessa, though in projects far less tony. If Vanessa's supreme strength is a kind of otherworldly looniness, Lynn's ace in the hole is a unbridled braininess—a witty passion. When she verbally tangles with a romantic rival in 1986's *My Two Loves,* she brings just enough precision to her speech to let you know how much she's hurting. Redgrave is one of the few actresses to give first-rate performances in a TV movie *(The Seduction of Miss Leona),* a miniseries *(Centennial),* and a comedy series *(House Calls).* It was, of course, the contract dispute in 1981 between Redgrave and her *House Calls* producers that resulted in her departure from the show. Her career has never quite recovered. She's done another sitcom *(Teachers Only),* a Broadway play *(Aren't We All?),* and a series of spots for Weight Watchers. But one misses the wrenching Redgrave of *Leona* shamelessly begging her married lover to stay with her and knowing all the while that intelligent women should never subject themselves to such humiliation. In an odd way, Lynn lives what Vanessa dreams.

Jessica Walter

Jessica Walter's career has been cluttered with too many other women. In her movie debut, *The Group,* she shared screen time with Candice Bergen, Joan Hackett, Joanna Pettet, Shirley Knight, and Kathleen Widdoes. In *All That Glitters,* a typ-

Jessica Walter in Trapper John, M.D.

Stephanie Zimbalist in Remington Steele

ically Learian series in which men and women switched societal roles, she costarred with Lois Nettleton, Barbara Baxley, Anita Gillette, and Linda Gray. And on *Trapper John, M.D.*, as Pernell Roberts's ex-wife, she joined TV's sturdiest collection of regular, semiregular, and guest-starring gals: Janis Paige, Pat Carroll, Elaine Stritch, Mary McCarty, Barbara Barrie, Lorna Luft, Madge Sinclair, Celeste Holm, Marcia Rodd, and Patti

Davis. But when given center stage, Walter can be astounding. As the sexually obsessed mad slasher in Clint Eastwood's *Play Misty for Me,* she did the scariest, funniest, and most brilliant variation on Norman Bates since Marion Crane was hoisted out of the swamp. And when she landed her own series, *Amy Prentiss,* she won an Emmy, though the show failed to attract an audience. There's something too threatening about Walter for mass-cult taste (can you imagine Tony Perkins as the father on *Family Ties?*). After all, her *Bare Essence* barely lasted ten weeks. But it would be a crime to relegate Walter to rattled divorcées *(Trapper)*, crisp professionals *(Amy)*, and soapy bitches *(Bare)*. She's simply not like other women, and she's too devastating for most men. When a murderous Lothario in the TV movie *Secrets of Three Hungry Wives* calls Walter "coldly exciting," we know just what he means. She should really have her own series: *Lady Macbeth in the Twilight Zone.* It might not beat *The Cosby Show,* but it would take TV divahood into another dimension.

S tephanie Zimbalist

I can never remember what Stephanie Zimbalist looks like. I think of her character, Laura Holt, on *Remington Steele.* I concentrate on her costar, Pierce Brosnan. I flash on her father, Efrem. No luck. Her features always dissolve into an auburn blur. Then I saw a TV movie in 1985 that made everything (except Zimbalist) clear. *Love on the Run,* a disgracefully underrated melodrama about a lonely lawyer who helps her convict-lover escape, showed Zimbalist for what she is: an actress. She's not an actress who has the physical presence and comic savvy to carry off *Remington*'s repartee (like Cybill Shepherd on *Moonlighting*), but she's one who can change shape and color at the beat of a heart. In *Love* she must alter her appearance and attitude from an uptight girl to a giddy lover to a paranoid prey to a grown-up woman who understands that every pleasure has its price. Her transitions aren't just convincing, they're moving, frightening, and sexy, sometimes all at once (her eyes kept shifting between blank and cloudy). Zimbalist's pre-*Steele* characters ranged from nice girls (*Elvis and the Beauty Queen,* opposite Don Johnson's appropriately grotesque Presley) to crazed cuties *(The Babysitter)*. *Love* brought the two sides together. Moonlighting as a Tinker Tootsie (*Steele*'s an MTM production), Zimbalist is a bit like Mary Tyler Moore's kid sister. But she seems far more comfortable with dramatic flourishes than comedic setups. Her role in the TV version of *A Letter to Three Wives* didn't give her much to do, laugh-wise or cry-wise. After it was over I couldn't remember what she looked like. But this amorphous quality will be Zimbalist's trump card so long as she keeps playing with an emotionally full deck.

14

MINISERIES MAVENS

Brooke Adams   Lesley-Anne Down
Jane Badler   Lee Remick
Susan Blakely   Jane Seymour
Blair Brown   Rachel Ward
Olivia Cole   Lesley Ann Warren

In *North and South,* a compulsively enjoyable travesty of history, Terri Garber plays Ashton, an unscrupulous Southern belle Vivien Leigh would be afraid to tangle with. Flouncing into scenes in a flurry of petticoats and pushed-up bazooms, Garber holds center court, commanding her co-stars by the sheer audacity of her viciousness. A cartoon femme fatale, Garber collects brass buttons from West Point cadets she's seduced, but on her wedding night to a rising politician she feigns innocence. "I had no idea it would be so discomfortin'," she coos.

Garber is a classic Miniseries Maven—an exaggeration of her gender and an emblem of her genre. If she seems a compendium of emotional extremes, so is the miniseries. But the scathing reviews *North and South* received show that a lot of people have lost sight of what the genre—and its Mavens—should be.

In 1974 the miniseries meant only one thing: extended pilots for cop shows. The Emmy nominees as Best Limited Series for the 1973–74 season were *Columbo, McCloud,* and *The Blue Knight.*

But two years later a sprawling epic forever changed the face of a fledgling form.

Rich Man, Poor Man is *The Birth of a Nation* of the miniseries—a wrenching social history of white America as seen through an embattled family. At once a revolutionary assault and a reactionary weepie, *RM,PM* debuted at a time when the best American cinema had become a solipsistic playground for astringent auteurs. It did what no movie, except for *The Godfather,* had done since the collapse of the studio system—told an immense story that was physically majestic and emotionally overwhelming.

This, more than anything, is what the miniseries needs: shmaltz. A miniseries is not a treatise, a polemic, a strategem, or a history lesson. It's a symphony of shared feeling composed on human faces. Like the prewar movies it emulates, the miniseries recalls Norma Desmond's nostalgic lament: "We had faces!" Also like these movies, it's a star system run by producers. Writers and directors are positively obscure next to the glittering array of gods and goddesses enacting the lives of mere mortals. And like TV itself, the miniseries is all foreground. It may be set in distant climes and romantic epochs—in ancient Japan or the Australian outback—but the miniseries tells the same tragic-heroic story of defeat and triumph, despair and hope, death and transfiguration.

The miniseries is a majority genre—it works within the ruling culture. If *Roots* and *Holocaust* are less than great, it's because they spend too much time pleading the cases of minority characters. A miniseries doesn't cry over spilled milk—it milks the cow, sells the product at a hefty profit, and then cries that money can't buy you love. It's classically tragic in that it charts the fall of powerful people crippled by pride.

The masterpieces of the genre—*RM,PM, The Thorn Birds, Celebrity,* and possibly *Captains and the Kings*—center on characters who win an earthly paradise only to lose their souls. Like the greatest American movie, *The Magnificent Ambersons,* these dramas show us the folly of our dreams. They are less repositories of collective guilt than reflections of our ambivalence about success. If *Death of a Salesman* had been a miniseries, Willy Loman would have died an adulterous CEO of a multinational, leaving a boozy wife and two sons dabbling in sodomy and cocaine.

A good miniseries should make you cry at least twice, once in the middle and once at the end. This is why *Space* was such a dud. It took thirteen hours of aeronautical nattering to elicit one solid boo-hoo (Beau Bridges' death scene). The only way around this sentimental imperative is to create pathological characters whose social predicaments are so horrifying that you're too spellbound to cry, as in *Inside the Third Reich* and *Evita Perón. Sybil* and *V,* which turned victims of pathological monsters into heroic freedom fighters, had the best of both worlds: they made you cry *and* scared the hell out of you.

Grotesquerie notwithstanding, the heart of a miniseries is the strength of its heart. *Evergreen,* for all its faults, was the best network epic of its year because it knew how to keep you clutching the Kleenex. Yes, you'd hardly know its characters were Jewish, despite accents as thick as a corned-beef sandwich; but the sight of an intran-

sigent patriarch driving his virtuous offspring into early graves carried tsouris to the max. In a great miniseries sociopolitical themes are always buried in the texture of the character's relationships, not pumped up in order to give human feeling the dignity of "larger themes."

Compare the climactic deathbed scenes in *RM,PM,* and PBS's exceptionally handsome *Brideshead Revisited.* In *Brideshead* Laurence Olivier's death exists for the sole purpose of showing us that Diana Quick can't marry Jeremy Irons because Irons doesn't believe in God. But in *RM,PM,* the redeemed poor brother (Nick Nolte) dies so the corrupt rich brother (Peter Strauss) can come to terms with himself and go on. "Go get 'em, Rudy—the bad guys," Nolte gasps, and his brother weeps, "I don't know who they are anymore—I think I'm one of them." The religion-obsessed *Brideshead* ends in denial, but the secular *RM,PM* is suffused with affirmation.

In its own brazen way a great miniseries manages to side with the angels. More often than not it treats organized religions as either a life-denying delusion *(Thorn Birds)* or a bourgeois plot to thwart sensual pleasure *(RM,PM).* The characters may be put through hell, but they arrive at a purgatory of sorts—and their lives, like the length of the miniseries itself, should seem to go on forever.

This is why most good miniseries are concerned with the tangled and tortured relationships of families—the generational saga. *Shogun, Marco Polo, Christopher Columbus*—all intelligent productions—relied too heavily on historicity and not enough on histrionics. The unrelenting tension in a miniseries, amidst all the warring nations, should be: "Who's sleeping with whom?" This is how families—and the melodrama—survive.

But the image of the family should never reflect Norman Rockwell's. Babies must be made, yes, but the characters who make them must be sleazy along the way. In the first episode of *The Thorn Birds*—perhaps the finest three hours of miniseries TV—a septuagenarian matron (Barbara Stanwyck) lusts after a Catholic priest (Richard Chamberlain) who pants for a little girl who's stuck on her teenage brother who hungers for his mother (Jean Simmons) who's in love with her husband (Richard Kiley) who's devoted to Simmons, but who also wants Stanwyck's money, as does Chamberlain. This is the stuff of miniseries art: civilization born of lust and greed.

Dealing with flesh-and-blood characters, a true miniseries is never afraid to go for the jugular—it's unabashedly vulgar. The distancing devices in *Brideshead*—ominous voice-overs, stately long shots, unspoken feelings—are lethal to the genre. Emotions must be acted out and played in close-up. The most electrifying moment in *A.D.*, with its endless bull sessions on the fate of the world, is when Ava Gardner glares at son Nero and purrs, "You're a *loathsome* little boy, *aren't* you?"

A miniseries dishes dirt and reads beads—it tells the truth about its characters. It's richly textured, not necessarily in furnishings, but in feeling. When Angie Dickinson discovers the identity of her long-lost son in *Hollywood Wives,* the scene creaks with the hoariest conventions of dime novels. But when Chamberlain plays a similar scene in *Thorn Birds,* there's a resonance that shakes your picture tube out of its box. In *Wives* the truth of Dickinson's life is a lie: parents who abandon their children produce psycho killers. But in *Thorn Birds* the lie of Chamberlain's life is the truth: parents who deny their humanity lose their children.

An outsized soap opera, the miniseries allows the TV diva to express herself on the grandest possible scale. It seems no accident that some of greatest miniseries performances are by Grande Dames—Dunaway, Gardner, Simmons, McGuire, Dickinson—or the Prima Donna herself, Stanwyck. A Miniseries Maven, more than any TV diva, has the best shot at Grande Damehood. If she's sinful enough to achieve immortality, her genre made her do it.

Brooke Adams

Lace began with the immortal question, "Which one of you bitches is my mother?" *Lace II* posed the implicit question, "Which one of you bastards is my father?" *Lace III,* if they're ever crazy enough to make it, would probably ask the eternal question, "Isn't it lucky we have only two parents?" The importance of Brooke Adams, who starred in both *Lace* sagas, is that she's so theatrically intense, she turns trash into triumph. A darling of artsy auteurs in the late '70s—Terrence Malick *(Days of Heaven)* and Philip Kaufman *(Invasion of the Body Snatchers)*—Adams turned to television in the '80s when her star failed to take off at the box office. What she brought to miniseries glitz was a kitchen-sink realism: a New York actress slumming for cash. As Pagan (love that name!) in *Lace* and *Lace II,* she showed passion and pain beneath tons of powder and gloss—she was never afraid to let her mascara run. This is no mean feat, considering the ice-cold conventions borrowed from Shirley Conran's original smash novel. In the Conran Chronicles, rape, kidnapping, and blackmail are all forgiven in the name of unrequited love and female solidarity. Conran deliberately diminishes every "masculine" concern while exalting every "feminine" feeling. As one woman in *Lace II* muses, "When Judy returned from Vietnam, she was awfully upset—not only from the death and carnage, but because she met Nick there." This distaff dialectic is driven home by *Lace II*'s predominant motif: pastel pink. There's more pink in this miniseries than in Jayne Mansfield's bedroom. Fur coats, terry-cloth robes, tennis shoes, magazine logos, babushkas, lipstick, silk scarves, wool hats, earmuffs, leather purses, blouses, jeans, T-shirts. The stars, too, are uniformly fuchsia: Phoebe Cates, who gave carrot-sucking lessons in the movie *Fast Times at Ridgemont High,* and Arielle Dombasle, who stretched bikinis to eye-popping lengths in Eric Rohmer's *Pauline at the Beach.* But it's Adams, full of fire and stinging sarcasm, who makes you believe in *Lace*'s magnificent obsession with feminine truth and beauty.

Jane Badler in V

Jane Badler

An intergalactic Alexis Carrington, Jane Badler starred in the most brazenly witty miniseries in the history of television, *V,* and its equally dazzling sequel, *V: The Final Battle.* What the *V* saga showed was that a miniseries needn't be based on historical characters or a hit novel to attract otherworldly ratings. It can be an antifascist thriller-comedy serving as a parable for our times. As Diana, the brilliantly wicked alien with a taste for live rodents, Badler lampooned both her beauty and her youth—she was comically efficient. A riotous combo of a *Batman* villain, a mysterious stranger, and an avenging *Playboy* centerfold, Badler reveled in her evil—she enjoyed torturing lower beings. The frequent target of her sadistic lust was delectable Marc Singer, whose chiseled

torso was so placidly perfect you'd swear there was a lizard underneath. Imprisoning her half-naked prey in humiliating conditions, Badler leered with pleasure. She made you think Myra Breckinridge had moved to another galaxy and come back to earth for total domination. The strength of Badler's performance was that she never lost control of her loony character; she didn't wait for her close-ups to play Diana to the hilt. But her image was so strong, she may never transcend it. When she turned up as Perry King's girlfriend on an episode of *Riptide* last season, she was attractive and intelligent, but far from sublime. Similarly, when *V* was made into a weekly series, the power of Badler's portrayal was dissipated. How many times could she lift a live hamster to her lips and devour it whole? It was the miniseries, with its peaks of concentrated lyricism, that allowed Badler to create one of the most sheerly enjoyable Shady Ladies in the TV universe.

Susan Blakely

As Julie Prescott Jordache in *Rich Man, Poor Man,* Susan Blakely gave the kind of performance that a young actress spends the rest of her career trying to top. An ex-model who'd wanted to be a movie actress, Blakely had a lot to prove when she agreed to play Julie—that she wasn't just another pretty face and that she wasn't just a "TV actress." Watching her in *RM,PM,* you weren't aware of either: Blakely *was* Julie. Playing a composite of three different characters from the Irwin Shaw novel, Blakely changed from a small-town ingenue to a cockeyed career girl to an embittered symbol of what is known in *Who's Afraid of Virginia Woolf?* as dashed hopes and good intentions. The miracle of Blakely's performance was that her transitions carried distinct sets of characteristics, deepening as they went along. Vocal inflections dropped, reactions slowed, features tightened. As

Julie got older, Blakely went deader behind the eyes. By the end she was a wreck of a drunk, smashing up things around her without remembering the damage. Her slide precipitated the tragic climax, where the redeemed poor brother dies so the corrupt rich one can come to terms with himself and go on. Married to the corrupt brother, Julie must go on, too, but to what? The mournful ending, with Julie and hubby holding hands on a death ship, doesn't promise anything. Like Julie, Blakely had to go on after *RM,PM* but never fulfilled the promise of her one, great role. Her interpretation of Frances Farmer *(Will There Really Be a Morning?)* was upstaged by Jessica Lange's movie version; her role in the TV movie *International Airport* was drab and puny; and her recent stint on *Hotel* was hackneyed even by Aaron Spelling's standards. C'mon, even Julie had a brighter future.

Blair Brown

Brimming with intelligence, sanity, and goodwill, Blair Brown may be too tasteful for the messy passion of the miniseries. Her lovely lass in *Captains and the Kings* was upstaged by the fiery histrionics of Patty Duke, who got the leading man, Richard Jordan, though Brown got Jordan in real life. She landed the female lead in *Space,* playing a professional woman par excellence, but seemed pallid next to Harry Hamlin's hairy chest and Barbara Sukowa's Wagnerian hysterics (at least she held her own with the easygoing James Garner). Her most vivid performance, as Jackie Kennedy in *Kennedy,* did justice to her braininess: her set-apart eyes and broad smile filled the screen with mythic splendor. These projects are nothing less than respectable—*Captains* is a rousing and grave adventure, *Space* an honorable failure, and *Kennedy* an underrated ode. But maybe Brown can use a little more juice on her miniseries menu.

Her best movie role, as the never-say-die wife of William Hurt in Ken Russell's smashing *Altered States,* gave her the chance to get mean and mean it. Yes, she played a Noble Hausfrau, a subcategory of the Intelligent Ingenue, but her final grapple with her deluded husband, kneeling naked in her psychedelic hallway and howling from a pit of primal fury, expressed a force she's been reticent to show on television. Maybe instead of doing "The Skin of Our Teeth" on *American Playhouse* (a mistake she made with several other distinguished actors), Brown can bring a little more Russell-mania to her miniseries work. She's one of the few actresses with the smarts to take the mushiness out of the Maven.

Olivia Cole

The most telling fault of *The Color Purple* was Steven Spielberg's casting of the women's roles: a stand-up comic (Whoopi Goldberg), a morning talk-show host (Oprah Winfrey), and an actress obscure even by cult standards (Margaret Avery). He didn't want actors who could use dialogue and movement to clarify his jittery style and jumbled narrative. He wanted re-actors—human puppets who could beam or weep while Quincy Jones's ego swelled on the soundtrack. *Purple* should return as a *Roots*-style sequel with a TV diva cast: Pam Grier as Shug, Theresa Merritt as Sofia, and, as Celie, Olivia Cole. A calm-faced wit with cool, wry eyes, Cole won an Emmy (as Mathilda) for *Roots,* and was nominated for *Backstairs at the White House* but lost to Bette Davis. Cole is too subtle an actress to score obvious points—she waits for her audience to come to her. When, as the doomed maid in *North and South,* Cole witnesses social horrors, she neither pities herself nor gives comfort to the enemy. Her predicament in *N and S* is strikingly similar to Celie's—dealing with institutional racism and patriarchal oppression. But

Lesley-Anne Down, Linda Purl, and Olivia Hussey in The Last Days of Pompeii

Cole doesn't emote in close-up to show us how much her character is suffering or to impress us with how well she's "acting." She keeps pulling back, giving ironic perspective to persecution and drawing us in with her wide-open stare. Her understatement has graced failed sitcoms—*Szysznyk, Report to Murphy*—as well as respectable projects. Like her characters, Olivia Cole is neither a snob nor a sellout.

L esley-Anne Down

Lesley-Anne Down puts masochistic madness in the Miniseries Maven. Her performance as the put-upon belle in *North and South* was suffused with such eloquent suffering, it made slavery look like a Sunday in the country. A mere sexy tart in movies *(The Great Train Robbery)*, Down came to television with a backlog of unexpressed anguish. In the superb TV movie *Arch of Triumph* she pulled off an amazing feat: she played the irony of despair. Her limpid, sliced-almond eyes on the verge of flooding, she'd lean against a railing, let a shock of frizzy hair fall against her face, and sigh heavily. She made you cry before you knew you were moved. Her performance, which subtly achieved everything Faye Dunaway tried to do in *Eyes of Laura Mars*, changed the spirit and direction of her career. She was transformed in the role the way Dunaway was by *Mommie Dearest* (though nobody seemed to notice). Bringing some of this dreamy languor to her role in *North and South*, Down was often subverted by the material. The delicacy of her masochism brutalized, she came off looking like a doormat; the depth of her pain made larger-than-life, she seemed like a cartoon. She can't beg for mercy because her wounds are too raw. She was left gazing at Patrick Swayze, who (unfortunately for her) was giving the performance of his life. Basically, Down isn't an ideal Miniseries Maven because she's too

refined for the form—only her features fit the oversized passion of the genre. She's a potentially great actress without a trace of vulgarity: she looks like a slut, but she's really a saint. If Diane Keaton doesn't beat her to it, she'll make a terrific Mary Tyrone. In the interim, she'll have a hell of a time finding roles to match her very special talents.

L ee Remick

In PBS's *Jennie: Lady Randolph Churchill*, Lee Remick etched a sharp portrait of a complex woman: a semipagan amid pseudosophisticates. Remick herself is a hot-blooded American who made her movie debut as a horny drum majorette in Elia Kazan's *A Face in the Crowd* but who's spent a lot of time in England polishing her image as a civilized lady. More than any TV diva, Remick is a case of fire under ice—she encases her passion in blocks of reserve. Though sexy in *Ike*, sleazy in *Wheels*, and hysterical in *Haywire*, Remick always seems to be waiting for more divine inspiration. If she's most fondly remembered for her wrenching work in *Days of Wine and Roses*, it may be because she was still young enough to not care how she looked when she got down. But last season's fascistic TV movie *Toughlove* brought out the worst in her: the puritanical American *and* the pretentious Englishwoman. Basically, Remick is too much in control of being out of control— she just can't wipe the smarts off her face (she's so beautiful, you almost don't want her to). A ravenous culture vulture, Remick is infatuated with genius, having acted with Orson Welles and interpreted Henry James. Her recent association with Stephen Sondheim in the *Follies* revival let her play both sides of her character to fascinating effect. As Phyllis, the ex-showgirl turned embittered matron, Remick dons a slinky, red-sequined gown and sings about the two women inside her: "Lucy is juicy/But terribly drab/Jessie is dressy/But cold as a slab/Lucy wants to be dressy/Jessie wants to be juicy/Lucy wants to be Jessie/And Jessie Lucy." If Remick ever reconciles the Lucy and Jessie parts of her personality, she'll be a Maven of phenomenal force.

J ane Seymour

Jane Seymour is Lesley-Anne Down without a soul—a glacier goddess. Her starring roles in *East of Eden, The Sun Also Rises,* and *Crossings* gave her the chance to do what she does best: dress beautifully and slice up men with her tongue. That she does it with such panache is less a tribute to her polished technique than her perfect teeth. Her pearly whites are dazzling enough to make oysters clam up in shame. Often cast against equally gorgeous and shallow leading men (Bruce Boxleitner, Hart Bochner, Christopher Reeve), Seymour seems to be gazing at her own reflection—Ms. Pretty meets Mr. Pretty. It's not that Seymour has been kept from breaking through the gloss of her image— she just doesn't seem very interested in doing it. Like the young Joan Collins, she's infatuated with surfaces, with the effect of her "style." When, in her Max Factor commercial, she delivers the simple line, "I say it never went out," she hits every T so hard, she seems to be spitting at the camera. If she mistakes this deliberate artifice for emotion, she's not entirely to blame. The miniseries encourages narcissistic glitz. But great Mavens, like the greatest miniseries, strip away the artifice to show the feeling underneath. While Seymour is sharpening her letter-perfect barbs, her homelier costars are stealing scenes. When, in *Sun,* Seymour verbally rips apart the vicious count (Leonard Nimoy), you don't concentrate on her beautiful face—you wait for Nimoy's chilling reaction shots (he upstages Seymour the same way Zeljko Ivanek wipes Hart Bochner off the screen). This is a fact Seymour might keep in mind. She's too vain to let any mere mortal steal the spotlight.

Lee Remick in The Letter

Jane Seymour in The Sun Also Rises

Rachel Ward with Richard Chamberlain in The Thorn Birds

Rachel Ward

In *The Thorn Birds,* Rachel Ward was a lamb among wolves. While Barbara Stanwyck, Richard Chamberlain, Jean Simmons, Richard Kiley, Christopher Plummer, and the ever-versatile Mare Winningham were dining on the scenery, Ward could barely manage a nibble at the tablecloth— she never sank her teeth into the role meaty enough to feed a thousand hungry starlets. Her performance is one of the most disconcerting in mini-series history. Not only was her delivery uneven from line to line, it varied *within* lines. She'd either start off poorly and end well or start off well and end poorly. Sometimes she'd even start and finish all right only to stumble in the middle. If her role were less important, one could dismiss her as an English Ali McGraw doing a guest shot on an

Australian *Dynasty*. But Ward had to hold her own (for seven hours!) with Mr. Technique himself, Richard Chamberlain (poor Dick: he must have wanted to strangle this girl). A great, broad-backed beauty, Ward makes physical sense as Meggie, Temptress of the Outback—she *looks* like a woman a priest would go to hell for. Her easiness-on-the-eyes, which has landed her starring roles in major movies, puts her a cut above such consistently bad actresses as Karen Allen, Margot Kidder, Talia Shire, Carrie Fisher, Nancy Allen, Linda Blair, Tatum O'Neal, and Kate Burton. But the irony is that Ward got to play the female lead in the otherwise most perfectly cast miniseries in TV history. Maybe her marriage to *Thorn Birds* costar Bryan Brown (a fine actor) will present a new choice: she can either learn from him or go live with the kangaroos.

Lesley Ann Warren

If Richard Chamberlain is the King of the Miniseries, Lesley Ann Warren is its Queen. Though she played second fiddle to Angie Dickinson in *Pearl,* she gave full-scale performances in two very different and underrated epics: *Harold Robbins'*

79 Park Avenue and *Evergreen.* The common denominator to these sagas—one about a high-class call girl, the other about a Jewish-American matriarch—was an unbridled emotionalism. Scenes were played at high pitch and Warren soared in every one of them (though sometimes she crashed). The pleasure of Warren is that she doesn't know how to hold back—she goes for broke on every line. Her Yiddish accent in *Evergreen* is as silly as it is affecting, while her slutty sarcasm in *79 Park Avenue* is as campy as it is pointed. In between these roles Warren did a brilliant variation on the dumb blonde in Blake Edwards's *Victor/Victoria.* Lately she's become a cult-movie diva in Alan Rudolph's low-budget wonders, *Choose Me* and *Songwriter.* This is pretty heady stuff for a girl who began her TV career as Cinderella and just a few years ago was known as the wife of Jon Peters after he got his fingers stuck in Barbra Streisand's hair. But Warren remains a marvelous Maven because there's a disreputable quality about her. She lost her Oscar for *Victor* and has never even been nominated for an Emmy. Her triumphs in Rudolph's films were unheralded by an industry ignorant of any production that costs less than $12 million. Her talent is too raw and vivid to be fully appreciated in the Age of Streep. As she grows older, her feelings become richer, her looks wilder, her tastes more eccentric. She may be the only ingenue from the '60s who'll be able to play character parts till she's ninety.

SITCOM PRINCESSES

Loni Anderson
Jackee Harry
Marilu Henner
Polly Holliday
Marion Lorne
Rose. Marie

Audrey Meadows &
Jayne Meadows Allen
Alice Pearce
Rhea Perlman
Loretta Swit

A Sitcom Princess exists to serve her king or queen. Often a scene-stealer, she's seldom a show in herself. At the same time, she's an exaggerated presence—she stands out in her environment. Her function is to offset the conventionality of the leading players. If a sitcom star is a figure of identification, the Sitcom Princess is a source of pleasure. She brings the stars down to earth with an outsider's logic. She's on the fringe as a supporting player, a contrasting personality, and a woman (the Sitcom Prince is often the best pal of his king or queen). Her personal life is almost never drawn in detail, unless she's part of a family unit. Usually defined by what she does for a living, the SP is a professional, both as a character and as an actress. The list of jobs among SPs reads like the want ads: receptionist, waitress, barmaid, taxi driver, Army major, comedy writer, witch, and housewife. Some shows are multileveled divafests, such as *The Many Loves of Dobie Gillis,* which highlights the roles of a moneyed matron (Doris Packer), a grocery clerk/mom (Florida Friebus), a studious student (Sheila James), and a classroom B-girl (Tuesday Weld). Other shows produced as in-house artworks, such as *The Mary Tyler Moore Show* or *The Beverly Hillbillies,* are also top-heavy with a ravishing assortment of Princesses. But generally the SP is a freelancer—she's at the mercy of powers who may not recognize her greatest strengths. Her biggest problem is having enough opportunities for self-expression without upsetting the symmetry of the sitcom. After all, she's not very effective on her own. Remember: Mary Tyler Moore was considered a Leading Lady as far back as *The Dick Van Dyke Show.* An SP is a Lady, too, but she's a Lady-in-Waiting until a throne is abdicated.

Loni Anderson

You can see Loni Anderson thinking a mile away. Her eyes are fixed, her jaw is set, and her head goes "click-click-click." Her utter self-possession was the joke behind her bombshell looks in *WKRP in Cincinnati*. As Jennifer Marlowe, receptionist supreme, Anderson showed that somebody who looks like a dumb blonde needn't be one. Smarter than her boss, sharper than her colleagues, successful in deflecting the advances of office creeps, Anderson was a monument to impregnability and self-respect. But her coup inspired so much high-minded praise that Anderson is in danger of becoming the coldest fish this side of Orca the Killer Whale. Her casting in the TV movie about Jayne Mansfield seemed perfect—one bright beauty portraying another—but Anderson was so intent on showing how smart Mansfield was, she forgot to revel in the giddy vulgarity that made Mansfield a star. A Tinker Tootsie deep down (*WKRP* was an MTM show), Anderson doesn't seem to take pleasure in her own sex appeal. As she grows older, she looks harder and more severe. Her hair has become so brittle it looks as if it could be used to insulate an attic. Her recent work in the witless remake of *A Letter to Three Wives* was typically ill-conceived. Tackling the role immortalized by Linda Darnell, Anderson changed one of the great lines in Hollywood history—"What I got don't need beads"—to "What I got doesn't need beads." Whether she altered the line herself is irrelevant because she played the part less like a tough dame than a Rhodes scholar. Anderson should either reverse her image or just face facts: she didn't get where she is by cramming for a Ph.D.

Jackee Harry

Sashaying her too-wide hips and slipping her tongue between her teeth, Jackee Harry is a sitcom mar-vel. Her sassy temptress Sandra on *227* has shades of Sue Ann Nivens, Florence the maid, and *Newhart*'s Stephanie, but she's also a composite of other showbiz personalities: Mae West, Bette Midler, Betty Boop, Little Richard, Pearl Bailey, R. Crumb's cartoon characters, and any number of female impressionists from Charles Pierce to *La Cage aux Folles*'s Zaza. The more I watch Harry, the more people I see. Harry herself says she based Sandra on an aunt, a schoolgirl chum, and an actress she worked with on *Another World*. But who knows where these influences got *their* influences? The strength of Harry's portrayal is that she's absorbed the lyrical mannerisms of generations of minority comics. Everything she does on *227* is funny because every expression, every inflection, every exaggerated gesture evokes a dozen unexpected associations. Even the way she pronounces Marla Gibbs's name on the show—"Mayyyyyuuuuurrrrreeeee!"—makes you laugh before you know you're amused. Harry knows the impact she's having: she's made no bones about wanting her own series. But I can't imagine an entire show built around Sandra—it would be like making a meal of cotton candy. Harry's great struggle will be to bring shadings to Sandra without losing her seductiveness. She has to keep mincing a fine line between frivolity and reality. The only thing worse than a slick Sandra would be a "serious" Sandra. The world already has Nell Carter and Oprah Winfrey.

Marilu Henner

What was Marilu Henner doing on *Taxi?* She wasn't dressed beautifully enough to be decorative and wasn't defined clearly enough to be interesting. We all knew Tony Danza played a boxer, Jeff Conaway an actor, Andy Kaufman a foreigner, and Christopher Lloyd a weirdo. But what was Elaine Nardo? Answer: an aspiring art dealer (score

Polly Holliday and Linda Lavin in Alice

50 points if you got that one right). The problem with Elaine was that *Taxi*'s creators didn't know how to draw on Henner's image, as they did with Danza (a real-life boxer), Conaway (a Broadway gypsy), Kaufman (an otherworldly comic), and Lloyd (an off-the-wall character actor). But what *is* Henner's image? Her best role, as Richard Gere's girlfriend in the movie *Bloodbrothers*, showcased her strengths: an unpretentious sexuality, a streetwise directness, and a self-deprecating humor. When she sits up in bed and tells Gere that her reputation as the "town pump" doesn't bother her because she enjoys sex, she's encapsulating her likability. Also in Henner is an ease with pretty hunks: onscreen with Gere and Burt Reynolds *(The Man Who Loved Women)*, onstage with Conaway and John Travolta *(Grease)*, and on *Taxi* with a pre-*Magnum* Tom Selleck (Elaine resists his charms). But her part in 1986 in Showtime's *Grown-Ups*, as the uneducated wife of an "intellectual" New York writer (Charles Grodin) unnecessarily abused her. Grodin's whiny, embittered

character seemed wholly unworthy of Henner's body (not to mention her soul). Basically, Henner is much too much one of the boys to be believable as one wimp's victim. If she was invisible on *Taxi,* it's because she was never made special enough as a girl.

P olly Holliday

When the news broke that Polly Holliday had coached Dustin Hoffman on his creation of Dorothy Michaels for *Tootsie,* nobody thought to mention Flo. But if you look at *Tootsie* and *Alice,* you'll see how much Hoffman owes Holliday. First, Dorothy's hair is strikingly like Flo's—a tightly teased clump of unruly waves. Their mouths are their most active features, breaking into toothy grins that crinkle into crow's feet. Both favor exaggeratedly feminine outfits—silk scarves, ruffled collars, almost audible girdles. And each is an indomitable force of Nature, disrupting her environment and exercising power over men ("Kiss my grits!"). While there are differences between Dorothy and Flo, the characterizational detail of each is a tribute to a certain kind of theatrical acting. If Holliday is less known as a New York actress than a Sitcom Princess, it's because Flo's image has become part of our collective memory. Like her *Alice* costar, Linda Lavin, who was once an enormously respected stage actress, Holliday applied a lifetime of greasepaint to a long-running character. But while Lavin keeps stripping off the makeup to be a serious thespian, Holliday has been smart enough to play footsie with the specter of Flo. Her own spinoff, *Flo,* trod old territory, but in replacing Eileen Brennan on *Private Benjamin,* she was on to something new. Appearing in only one episode before the series was canceled, Holliday didn't imitate herself, Brennan, or Hoffman—she was a military Tootsie with the heart of a hash-slinging temptress. Her recent stint on

Marion Lorne in Bewitched

The Golden Girls as Rose's blind sister showed a more serious side. Though shrewdly underplaying, Holliday wasn't entirely effective—she was still funny-looking. Please, Polly: send in the clowns.

M arion Lorne

Marion Lorne gave new meaning to the word "ditz". She made Aunt Bee look like June Cleaver. Mumbling, giggly, self-interrupting, Lorne seemed lost on another plane of thought. Her almost otherworldly confusion made her a perfect Aunt Clara, the addle-brained witch with failing powers on *Bewitched.* She'd developed the character through years of scene-stealing, from *Mr. Peepers* to *The Garry Moore Show.* Her competition in the Senior Ditz Sweepstakes included ZaSu Pitts, Gale Storm's dizzy sidekick on *Oh! Susanna,* and Elsa Lanchester, John Forsythe's foil on *The John Forsythe Show* and Juliet Mills's aunt on *Nanny and the Professor.* But while Pitts and Lanchester scored great dramatic triumphs in films and evolved into Sitcom Princesses, Lorne added elements of pathos to her purely comedic image. On *Bewitched* Lorne became the only Sitcom Princess who might be called Chaplinesque. Aunt Clara's incompetence wasn't just a source of comedy, it was a sign of senility. Dismissed by mortals as a blithering old bag, scorned by peers as a dangerous embarrassment, Clara highlighted the plight of old people in two different worlds. Her sole defender was Samantha, who treated her aunt with a mixture of tenderness and firmness a mother might reserve for a handicapped child (she felt closer to Clara than she ever did to Darrin). Lorne's supreme achievement was that she never let the tears drown the laughs. Beneath all her quivering smiles was a ruthless sense of timing. Her best gags came between punch lines. She'd cut herself off in mid-sentence, gurgle some indecipherable syllables, and then bob her head like a newborn babe. Utterly bewitched, she left everybody bothered and bewildered.

R ose Marie

John Byner once joked that when the Greeks built the first stage, Rose Marie held a hammer. A child star in vaudeville and a veteran of virtually everything, Marie felt right at home on *The Dick Van Dyke Show,* the most showbiz-drenched sitcom of its day. Between its creator (Carl Reiner) and its star, the show embraced every tradition from the Golden Age of Television *(Your Show of Shows)* to Broadway musicals *(Bye, Bye Birdie).* It also prefigured the sitcoms of artist-as-protagonist *(My*

World and Welcome to It), dashing husband-and-wife *(He & She),* and TV-as-backdrop *(The Mary Tyler Moore Show). DVD*'s sophistication gave Rose Marie the chance to play something other than the secretary-sidekick of the leading lady—her role for Elaine Stritch in *My Sister Eileen* (pre-*DVD*) and Doris Day in *The Doris Day Show* (post-*DVD*). As comedy writer Sally Rogers, Marie held her own as the professional associate of the leading man. Gruff-voiced, man-hungry, rough-faced, and very blonde, Sally was a living-and-breathing homage to Selma Diamond (whom Reiner had known from the old days). Marie never looked more comfortable than she did on *DVD*—she got to be one of the guys, but she got to be vulnerable, too. Her likability always depended on our spotting the little trouper inside the tough-talking dame. When she joked about wanting a man, she wasn't saying, "I'm horny," she was saying, "Take care of me." On a recent episode of *Remington Steele,* a series rife with showbiz references, Marie played a beloved TV star who disappears for decades. When she's rediscovered, she redeems her past. It wasn't exactly *The Rose Marie Story,* but it put a sharply dramatic twist on a lifetime of comedic mugging.

A udrey Meadows & Jayne Meadows Allen

If you could harness the fierceness of the Meadows sisters, you could do away with nuclear power. Jayne's Big Freakout Scene in the film noir curio *Lady in the Lake* was one of the highpoints of high '40s histrionics, while Audrey's tongue-lashing duets with Jackie Gleason on *The Honeymooners* set a standard for marital discord in prime time. If Jayne began as a Hollywood harridan and wound up an outrageously funny TV presence, Audrey scored her greatest success as a Sitcom Princess and never surpassed herself. Her immortality as Alice Kramden has less to do with her cultish show or her

Jackie Gleason, Art Carney and Audrey Meadows in The Honeymooners

Jayne Meadows Allen in Meeting of Minds

leading man than her own dogged concentration. Because Gleason hated rehearsal and often resorted to hammy overstatement on camera, Audrey was forced to pounce on every one of her cues as if it were the last meal on Earth. Her speed, her electricity—her real brilliance, I think—came from her instinct to pull her weight in a sitcom top-heavy with locker-room grubbiness and vaudevillian mugging. At the same time she needed to suggest levels of bitterness over Alice's childlessness. That she expressed her character's personality without seeming monstrous is the truest testament to her professionalism. Jayne, meanwhile, is a Sitcom Princess by virtue of *Meeting of Minds*, an unintentionally hilarious series in which ham-fisted actors posing as historical figures sit around and shoot the breeze (it's the ultimate creation of hubby Steve Allen). There's something mind-bogglingly silly about Jayne done up as Cleopatra chatting up Teddy Roosevelt. But cos-

metic excess has always been the source of Jayne's humor. Her riotous turn last year as a Mary Kay-ish tycoon on *Murder, She Wrote* showed that Meadows Madness will live as long as there's TV.

A lice Pearce

I laugh just thinking about Alice Pearce. Her face, which has more elasticity than a steel-belted radial, is never in repose. Her upper lip curls into her nostrils, her nose twitches from side to side, her eyes bug out and crawl back into their sockets. Her voice, which could drown out a police siren, starts in an upper register denying normal pitch

Alice Pearce in The Frank Sinatra Show

was drunk with confusion. By the time she played Gladys, Pearce was considered past her prime. Fifteen years earlier, she'd starred as Frank Sinatra's blind date in the movie *On the Town* and had her own musical variety series. But the *Bewitched* producers, whose eye for comedic divas was sharper than a broken broomstick, knew what Pearce could do. Appearing on the show for only two seasons, Pearce died of cancer just weeks before winning an Emmy. Not a rerun goes by that I don't miss her.

R hea Perlman

Only in the '80s could Rhea Perlman be considered a scream. Her Carla Tortelli on *Cheers* is supposed to be refreshingly lippy, but she strikes me as the most obnoxious Sitcom Princess ever to wear a crown. Loudmouthed, uneducated, proudly pigheaded, she's symbolic of a modern Comedy of Cruelty, combining the dim-witted smears of Eddie Murphy, the misogynist wisecracks of Joan Rivers, and the bully-boy barbs of David Letterman. Carla's personality is traceable to *Taxi,* in which Perlman guest-starred as the good-hearted girlfriend to Louie DiPalma, the loathsome dispatcher played by Perlman's real-life husband, Danny DeVito. When some of *Taxi*'s talents put together *Cheers,* they apparently had Perlman do a female impersonation of her husband's alter ego. But while Louie was universally despised, Carla is generally well-liked. And unlike Ted Baxter, who endured humiliations because of his stupidities, Carla is prized for her honesty. But when she endlessly needles Diane about staying in a mental hospital, it just isn't funny. Basically, Carla exists to poke holes in Diane's pretension—if a man treated Diane the way Carla does, he'd be seen as a brute. But isn't this a bit of a cheat? After all, nothing else about Carla makes sense. She's considered a good waitress but insults all

and ends in a screech denying human pleasure. Her body, a spindly collection of birdlike appendages, can do anything. Her legs buckle and bow into a near-perfect circle, her arms go limp and twist at the elbows, her hips sway to and fro. As Gladys Kravitz, Samantha's nosy neighbor on *Bewitched,* Pearce pulled together a lifetime of physical shtick for one of the most purely lyrical comic creations in TV history. Climbing over hedges, peering into windows, stumbling over lawn tools, Pearce was every goofy busybody you ever wished would go away. She was funny, not only because she got her comeuppance, but because she was *right:* Samantha *was* a witch (though nobody would believe her). The capper to every joke was when weary Mr. Kravitz (George Tobias) dragged his babbling wife home. The look of disorientation on Pearce's face went beyond puzzlement—she

Rhea Perlman in Cheers

her customers. She's strict with her children but can't keep a husband. She's seen as a sage but never reads a book. She's loved by all but is thoroughly unforgiving. Perlman's problem as an actress is that she doesn't undercut Carla's hypocrisies—she plays every scene with a self-congratulatory loudness. She should realize that if she doesn't read Carla's beads, nobody else will dare to.

Loretta Swit

Somebody, someday, may make a marvelous *M*A*S*H*. The movie, by Robert Altman, had a heady, voluptuous style but also expressed the most gleeful sexism this side of Eddie Murphy. The TV series, which ran for eleven years, began as an antidote to Altman and ended as a paean to Alan Alda's namby-pamby liberalism. The pivotal character in both versions was Hot Lips Houlihan, a serious-minded major surrounded by minor men. If Sally Kellerman was the ideal Altmanian heroine in her acquiescence to male camaraderie, Loretta Swit was the perfect Aldavian feminist in her straining for self-affirmation. But while Kellerman seemed too easy, Swit made one queasy. Less hot-lipped than big-lipped, Swit seemed incapable of communicating erotic tension in a show that insisted on high-minded moralizing. At first Swit was a hard-nosed harridan, plotting deceits and thwarting goodwill. But then we learned that she yearned to be loved—invited to parties, let in on secrets, that sort of thing. Gradually the battleground of the Korean War, which was really a metaphor for Vietnam, became a therapy group for Hollywood actors. Egos collided but sins were forgiven because we all belong to the Family of Man. Alda, not content with mere acting, wrote and directed episodes, and was rewarded with Emmys. During it all, Swit worked up a sweat—the more she asserted her identity, the more her eyes flooded. Her comedic ace-in-the-hole—a high-pitched, hysterical howl—began to be used as much for sorrow as for happiness. She was finally defeated by the role in the way Sally Struthers was by *All in the Family*. Her more recent work has demanded only two emotions: self-righteous rage and beatific joy. She started as Hot Lips and is finishing as Wet Eyes.

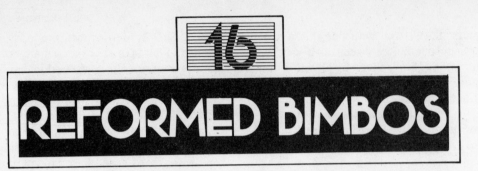

16
REFORMED BIMBOS

Cher
Morgan Fairchild
Farrah Fawcett
Sally Field
Kate Jackson

Cheryl Ladd
Jennifer O'Neill
Cybill Shepherd
Suzanne Somers
Tuesday Weld

David Letterman has beautiful women on his show for the seemingly sole purpose of humiliating them. He ridiculed Nastassja Kinski's hairdo to the point where she all but refused to speak, needled Raquel Welch about a provocative pose in her exercise book, grilled Mariel Hemingway on her motives for appearing, and tried to show up Bo Derek, who isn't half the airhead Letterman is. At the same time, mousy yuppettes from Teri Garr to Mary Beth Hurt are treated with respect, while almost any appearance by a male jock, from Wayne Gretzky on down, is viewed as second only to the Second Coming (Letterman was so smitten with George Brett, he crossed his legs at the knee). This locker-room hierarchy—(a) Best Buddy, (b) Gal Friday, (c) Town Pump—has created what I call the Sluts & Ditz Syndrome. It happens when a female sex symbol develops a pathetic self-hatred because homely women envy her beauty and childish men feel threatened by her sexuality (the women want to hold on to their men and the men want to hold on to their fantasies). At first an object of desire, the sexpot evolves into an object of derision relegated to that most despised stratum of Hollywood icon: the Bimbo. Driven by dreams of redemption, the Bimbo strives to be accepted as a "serious" actress. Betting all on a single career move, she becomes a Reformed Bimbo—the chanciest of all divas. She either makes the grade or dons a bigger dunce cap. She may cram for years to win a gold star (Tuesday Weld), transfer to tougher schools (Farrah Fawcett), or score a 100 her first time out (Cher). Most, however, stay in kindergarten forever. The irony is that RBs aren't markedly better or worse than most other types of actresses—they just have longer to wait for power-brokering bozos to put away their centerfolds and pay attention.

her

On a *Good Morning, America* a couple of years ago, Cher appeared with Meryl Streep to publicize *Silkwood.* The subtext to Cher's conversation was: "I'm so thrilled to be sitting here with Meryl Streep." The subtext to Streep's stint was: "I have Oscars at home, but why be a bitch about it?" Overcome with joy, Cher blurted that she had two best friends in the whole wide world, Josie Schmo from Kokomo (or somebody) and "Meryl." Asked how many best friends *she* had, Streep replied, "I have . . ." (dramatic pause, radiant smile) ". . . *six* best friends!" I fell off the couch in laughter. It was the perfect punch line to a classic joke—the Bimbo seeking Reformation at the feet of a cultural guru. I doubt neither Cher's closeness to Streep nor her recently expressed dramatic talent, but I do wish she'd inject some other earlier TV lightness into her current movie epics. On *The Sonny and Cher Show* and in her own variety series (*Cher*) and TV specials, Cher exhibited a wicked flair for comedic excesses in general and parody in particular. She held her own with Carol Burnett and, more remarkably, matched Bette Midler. There's a likably game quality to Cher, a willingness to try anything. Her comical collection of TV-skit characters, like Burnett's and Midler's, were grotesque and funny at the same time; her screechy-voiced vulgarian on *S and C* prefigured Andrea Martin's leopard-skinned crone on *SCTV* by a decade. I remember a number she did on *The Tonight Show,* borrowed from her Vegas stage act, where she slides through a gigantic high heel singing a slinky tune while chorus boys dance around the toe. This surrealistic quality has always been present in Cher's clothes and hairdos, but it's depressingly absent from a dingy dirge like *Silkwood. Mask* combined the best and worst of Cher: the ironic diva and the weepy thespian. Her Big Crying Scene at the kitchen table isn't the most difficult feat of acting, but her languid moments as a drugged-out shrew are extremely dicey to do without losing the audience's sympathy (she pulled it off, but lost out in the Oscar nominations, which are awarded to actresses who play "nice" characters). Cher's best performance remains her first bid for dramatic respectability, *Come Back to the Five and Dime, Jimmy Dean, Jimmy Dean,* directed onstage and onscreen by Robert Altman. A few months after the movie opened, I spotted Altman at a party and went over to introduce myself. While we were talking, Raquel Welch sidled up and told Altman how much she loved *Popeye.* Altman did not return the compliment. Then Jules Feiffer, who'd written the script for *Popeye,* wandered into our merry group. Welch expressed interest in *his* work, and he, too, kept the niceties to himself. For the next fifteen minutes, Welch burbled desperately, while Altman and Feiffer reversed her words in such a way that she sounded like a complete idiot (they laughed in her face). Finally, she said, "I can't seem to say anything right," at which point I headed to the bar for another drink. Okay, so Welch comes on too strong; she's so eager to impress people with her intelligence she sounds like Pat Robertson on *Meet the Press* (she isn't down-to-earth, like Cher). But who needs to be humiliated at the hands of a Robert Altman? The Reformed Bimbo, that's who. The subtext to Welch's flattery was: "Make me the next Cher." The subtext to Altman's rudeness was: "Forget it, Bimbo." The subtext to Feiffer's cowardice was: "I'm with Bob." The subtext to my horror was: "Thank God I'm not in show business."

Morgan Fairchild

Morgan Fairchild has appeared in so many soap operas she may have bubbles on the brain. In less than ten years, she's either starred or guest-starred on *Dallas, Flamingo Road, Paper Dolls, Falcon Crest,* and *Search for Tomorrow.* But she's less a Soap Star than a Reformed Bimbo because she never found her niche in the sleaziest of all genres.

Morgan Fairchild and Marjoe Gortner in The Seventh Annual Circus of the Stars

In an effort to gain respectability Fairchild starred in the off-Broadway play *Geniuses* shortly after Farrah Fawcett appeared in off-Broadway's *Extremities*. Fawcett, who used the role as a springboard to *The Burning Bed,* had stepped in for the show's original star, Susan Sarandon, a difficult-to-peg actress who gave a marvelous performance in Jonathan Demme's PBS masterwork, *Who Am I This Time?* This hierarchy of Sarandon (a lauded New York thespian), Fawcett (a Bimbo who achieved redemption), and Fairchild (a Bimbo who's still trying) reveals the fine distinctions among TV divas. Fairchild's overwhelming problem is that she lands parts that play to her weaknesses. Her recent role as a schizophrenic attorney on *Falcon Crest* allowed her to pull out all the stops. Child abuse! Memory loss! One-night stands! But Fairchild tackles these traumas with ten tons of eye shadow and three miles of hair. Her acting can't make it through the makeup. At the same time she isn't a convincing glamor queen—her frame is too tiny, her features too pointy, her voice too whiny. Maybe Fairchild should postpone her dreams of being a "serious" actress and take a cue from another Reformed Bimbo, Candice Bergen, who reversed fifteen years of sweaty work by lightening up, poking fun at herself, and developing into a dizzy comedienne. At this point Fairchild has little to lose.

arrah Fawcett

Farrah Fawcett in Murder in Texas

Farrah Fawcett's resurrection didn't take place on a Burning Bed, but on a morgue slab in *Murder in Texas,* a riveting, chilling, mesmerizing, gut-wrenching (add your own superlatives) TV movie about a dashing doctor who dumps his wife by spiking her Tabs and chocolate éclairs with "every known excrement" and then watching her die an excruciatingly slow and painful death. As the ill-fated heiress, Fawcett did two extraordinary things: she swept the hair off her face and gave a performance. She made you love this woman while showing you why a certain kind of man yearned to dominate her, even in death. It was the perfect Farrah role: half glamorous and half stripped-down, part pinup and part hausfrau, poised ever so precariously between submission and self-affirmation—the all-American girl-goddess. But in *The Burning Bed,* Fawcett embraced one side of her personality at the expense of another. She was an about-faced Charlie's Angel, a tattered dishrag, a Total Victim (her masochism charmed audiences because she allowed her looks to be marred). Fawcett's *Burning* face, a twitching mass of skittish stares and tear-stained creases, has become the tragic mask of her career, a searing symbol of

"serious" acting. But her great struggle will be to bring shadings to this undeniably gripping façade. She needs to show flashes of wit and eroticism and grown-up wisdom. In 1986's *Between Two Women* Fawcett slipped in and out of revelation. Her best moments came when she let the little-girl singsong fade from her voice and just talked turkey. Her worst moments came when she behaved like an Aaron Spelling protegée approaching forty. But Farrah's come a long way, baby. She's one of the few TV divas who was born—and born again—on the tube.

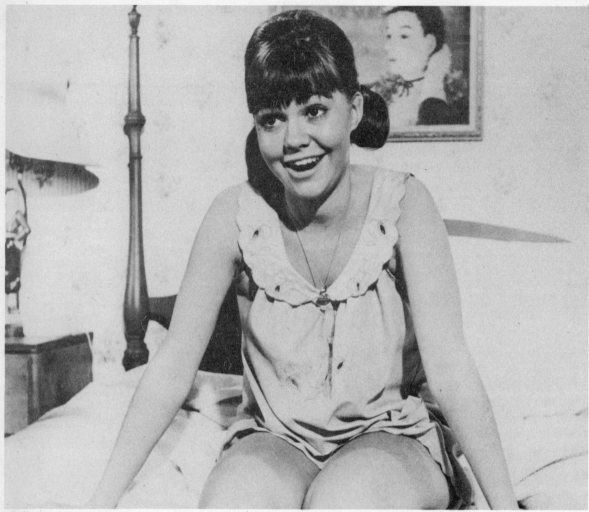

Sally Field in Gidget

Sally Field

Every time I watch *Sybil* (four times so far), I play a little game. I try to pretend that my original reaction to the movie (pity, terror, hysteria, edification, total wipeout) was a fluke, that no prime-time psychodrama, however skillful, could cast such a spell. But twenty minutes into *Sybil* I feel as if I'm seeing it for the first time. Yes, the script and direction are top-notch, but nothing can pre-

pare one for the power of Sally Field's performance. It's a feat of acting that goes way beyond acting—it's more immediate than naked naturalism and more accomplished than technical prowess. I think the key to its impact is when Sybil says, "I don't cry tears like people." Field doesn't act like people either—she physicalizes the monsters inside Sybil and then makes you identify with each of them, pulling you into different states of being, other modes of feeling. Field's achievement came after years of portraying TV's premier Bimbette, a pudgy Valley Girl. She made a charming and intelligent Gidget, full of rapt opinions and screwed-up passion, but her Flying Nun was oddly tense and somehow pathetic. After *Sybil* Field became a Noble Nellie in *Norma Rae* and *Places in the Heart.* If Norma Rae resembled Gidget (an innocent rebel), *Heart*'s frump recalled the Flying Nun (a loner battles the elements). The problem is that Field has filtered her sitcom heroines through her intense Sybil to come up with a surefire Oscar formula: playing nice women who act their heads off. She seems less interested in revelation than respectability ("You like me! You really like me!"). But this is the great tragedy of the Reformed Bimbo: even after she's accepted as an actress, she lives in fear of being hated again.

Kate Jackson

Kate Jackson always seems protected from sex. On *The Rookies* she was a nurse married to a cute cop who spent an inordinate amount of time with the boys. On *Charlie's Angels* she spent all *her* time with the girls when she wasn't chatting up an overweight asexual or listening to John Forsythe on an intercom. In the movie *Making Love* (her one try at big-screen stardom) she played a faithful wife whose husband discovered he was gay. And in her current ode to chastity, *Scarecrow and Mrs. King,* she's a divorced mother who resists the charms of her dashing leading man (she's devoted to her family, ya know). This provocative image of a thin-lipped, raspy-voiced loner surrounded by Freudian basket cases has kept Jackson continuously employed in an industry that thrives on subtextual perversity. Even in her personal life Jackson married and divorced Andrew Stevens, a superfoxy actor who looks punched from the same cookie cutter as Jackson's costars—Bruce Boxleitner, Michael Ontkean, Farrah Fawcett. I think Jackson fits her image. She looks like the kind of woman who'd be more comfortable shooting pool

than changing diapers. But her wardrobe doesn't jibe with how she comes across; her sub–high couture fashions belong on Mary Tyler Moore. After *Scarecrow* Jackson might consider returning to her roots. She began on TV in such creepy cheapies as *Satan's School for Girls, Killer Bees, Death Cruise,* and *Death Scream,* reaching semicult status in the daytime serial *Dark Shadows.* She may be the only Reformed Bimbo who was never presold as a voluptuous babe, and she's still young enough to become the Elsa Lanchester of the twenty-first century. Maybe if she returns to the occult she'll get to play a character who isn't alone when she turns down the lamp.

Cheryl Ladd

Cheryl Ladd is torn between the strained realism of Farrah Fawcett and the embalmed artifice of Jaclyn Smith. While Fawcett boogied through contemporary dramas onscreen and onstage before winding up a respected TV diva (*The Burning Bed*), Smith waltzed into television histories (*Jacqueline Bouvier Kennedy, George Washington*) before becoming the pitchperson for Max Factor. If Fawcett rejects all trappings of old-style Hollywood glamor, Smith doesn't seem to realize that the studio system is dead (in her Max Factor spots, she extols the virtues of Lana Turner and Vivien Leigh as if they were the same actress). Ladd, meanwhile, can't seem to make up her mind whether to make up her face; she drifts in a never-never land between Then and Now. Her role in the deco-drenched miniseries *Crossings* was thoroughly conventional, while her part in the sub–*Murder in Texas* melodrama *A Death in California* stretched credulity. If Ladd's cold-cream smoothness in *Crossings* looked icky next to Lee Horsley's nonchalant naturalism, her honest acting in *California* was betrayed by a script that presented a loathsome leading man and moronic leading lady

Kate Jackson in Scarecrow and Mrs. King

Cheryl Ladd

and then asked us to identify with someone (the only halfway sane character was the mother, smartly played by Alexis Smith). Ladd's best work remains *Grace Kelly,* a too-tame TV movie about an overly revered star. Ladd suggested some of the darker recesses in Kelly's personality by letting the coolness of her face freeze into cracks of bitterness and regret. Maybe this is the direction Ladd's career should take—playing more modern versions of all-American princesses who seem perfect but really aren't. It's something Ladd might understand deep in the pit of her pretty gut.

J ennifer O'Neill

Jennifer O'Neill had to grow up before I could stand to look at her. Her early movie splash as the sumptuous war widow with clean underwear in *Summer of '42* drove me out the theater reeling—not with horniness, but with nausea (if sex were this pure, I wanted no part of it). For the next decade I waited for O'Neill to wrap her gams around meatier parts. Sitting through one bad movie after another, I watched O'Neill struggle with human movement (she walked like a filly at the starting gate), the English language (she talked like a Mary Kay saleswoman), and vocal control (her inflections wavered between schoolgirl squeals and prep-school drawls). Though her two TV series, *Bare Essence* and *Cover-Up,* revealed a more poised and polished leading lady, O'Neill still seemed like a pretty girl playing dress-up. The events surrounding her personal life were anything but pretty: she took a bullet in the stomach in a freak accident at her Connecticut home, and then her *Cover-Up* costar Jon-Erik Hexum unwittingly shot himself in the head with a blank pistol. Yet in between these incidents, almost miraculously, O'Neill delivered a six-minute cameo in the miniseries *A.D.* that began to wipe away, quite literally, fifteen years of awkward acting. As

the scheming Roman wife, O'Neill prowled a tent hatching her plot while removing layers upon layers of makeup (it's the damnedest acting stunt since Jan Sterling's almost identical scene in *The High and the Mighty*). Lowering her voice to a hypnotic register, stretching each syllable to an eerie silence, slowing every body movement to a pantherlike pose, O'Neill showed what a Bimbo can do when a part reforms the pain in her personality.

C ybill Shepherd

Let me go out on a limb: *Moonlighting* is to the '80s what *The Mary Tyler Moore Show* was to the 70's, what *The Beverly Hillbillies* was to the '60s, and what *I Love Lucy* was to the '50s—the series masterpiece of its time. Some might argue for the preeminence of *The Cosby Show,* whose Reagan-retro style revives memories of *The Danny Thomas Show,* but *Moonlighting* reaches all the way back to the studio system that once employed our president. If Bruce Willis's dazzling riffs suggest Michael Keaton impersonating Joel McCrea, Cybill Shepherd's breezy sexiness is like watching Kathleen Turner in *The Carole Lombard Story.* Their quick-witted repartee, which makes mincemeat of Sam and Diane's I-love-you-but-I-can't-make-love-to-you pas de deux on *Cheers,* is heightened by an old-style Hollywood glamor: shadowy photography, tracking cameras, musical underscoring (it makes *Miami Vice* look like a Huey Lewis video). The show's chaotic mix of playfulness and hostility is literally embodied by Shepherd, whose Maddie Hayes swoops through the set like an American eagle outfitted by Calvin Klein. Her hips, her hair, her shoulders—everything's in motion (she gets you high). We've all heard the long, sad story of how Shepherd was cruelly abused by Hollywood before her Big Comeback. Boo-hoo. I don't care if Shepherd had to fight her way back from white

Jennifer O'Neill in Cover-Up

Cybill Shepherd in The Yellow Rose

slavery to get to *Moonlighting*—it's all been worth it. Like Lucy, Granny, and Mary before her, Maddie is defining divahood for a new day. When, in a black-and-white dream world, Shepherd crawls on all fours in a silk slip, bumping butts with Willis to hatch a plot, she's merging movies and TV in a way that's never been done before. She's making fire by rubbing the past and future together.

Suzanne Somers

Suzanne Somers never lost sight of what her career should be, though she sure lost sight of whatever momentum it had. An unrepentant Bimbo, Somers pursued the starlet's dream of Hollywood fame and achieved it briefly as Chrissy, the ditzy blonde on *Three's Company*. Foolishly compared to Marilyn Monroe, Somers was more like Ethel Mertz's granddaughter impersonating Dagmar— a goofy drag joke. Agreeably horse-faced and smothered in platinum-polyester curls, Somers was funniest not as a variation on the dumb blonde, but as slapstick clown. Whenever she did something that corresponded to her exaggerated looks— tripping over rugs, jumping over couches, any kind of shtick—she clicked: you delighted in the silliness of her rambunctiousness (her timing was all physical). But for some strange reason people saw Somers as a sex goddess (when *Playboy* published old nude photos of her, it caused a sensation). Taking this appeal seriously, Somers left *Three's Company* when her demands for more money went unmet—and her career took a nosedive. Playing up the bombshell side of Chrissy, Somers vamped her way through a bad movie, a mediocre nightclub act, and an idiotic miniseries, *Hollywood Wives,* which woefully miscast her as a silver-screen siren who seduces Anthony Hopkins to get a part (the very thought sends chills down the spine). But in 1985 Somers showed the best of herself in a failed pilot, *Goodbye, Charlie,* based on the Debbie Reynolds movie about a tough guy who comes back from the dead in a woman's body. In

one funny sight gag, Somers slips out of a trenchcoat in a single movement, her arms and head disappearing into nowhere. It might not be Chekov, but it's something Somers can do with grace.

Tuesday Weld

Roll all of Tuesday Weld's performance into one and you'd have a definition of "Diva—Junior Class." She's a teen-queen goddess, a splendid actress, a rapturous presence, and a source of inspiration to all Bimbos who seek Reformation. A cutie-pie since birth, Weld was a model before most kids could walk. By puberty she'd suffered a nervous breakdown, a bout with alcoholism, and a suicide attempt. When she played Thalia Menninger in *The Many Loves of Dobie Gillis*—at bittersweet sixteen—Weld had become a bewitching combo of complex bombshell and street nymphet: Marilyn Monroe Meets The Shirelles. Her cult status rests on her snap-crackle-'n'-pop movies—*Lord Love a Duck, Pretty Poison, I Walk the Line*—but her evolution as a TV diva has been all but ignored. Her pivotal performance in the movie *Play It as It Lays* marked her transition from screen siren to tube trembler. Like her spiritual sister, Ann-Margret, Weld works from her instincts, from her emotional understanding of a character. But while Ann-Margret runs her fingers along the contours of a feeling, Weld digs her nails into its edges, exposing tendons, hitting nerves (she can be too raw, even mannered, but she's never a phony). Her Zelda in *F. Scott Fitzgerald in Hollywood* shifted between a radiant seductiveness and a too-true dementia (her beauty very nearly redeemed her cruelty). In *A Question of Guilt* Weld once again pushed image against reality by asking us to indict a system that could railroad a Shady Lady. And in her paramount role, *Madame X,* Weld showed how an actress-proof part can be a stretch for an actress who never condescends to her material. If it's Tuesday, it must be honest.

Tuesday Weld in Madame X

VARIETY PLAYERS & VIDEO ROCKERS

Carol Burnett
Imogene Coca
Judy Garland
Lena Horne
Shirley MacLaine
Madonna & Cyndi Lauper

Liza Minnelli
Dinah Shore
Barbra Streisand
Tina Turner & Aretha Franklin/
Patti LaBelle & Diana Ross

Variety Players & Video Rockers recall James Stewart's famous description of movies as "pieces of time." You never remember a VP/VR for a sustained performance—you remember moments so dazzling they seem like shows in themselves: Judy Garland hitting the last notes of "Ol' Man River," Carol Burnett doing a parody of "Sunset Boulevard," Tina Turner strutting down a Greenwich Village street. A VP/VR is both glorified and imprisoned by random images. She spends her entire career trying to be accepted as something more than what she is. She may want to be a "serious" actress, a cin-ay-mah director, a Carnegie Hall diva. Basically, she wants it all. Bouncing from Broadway to Beverly Hills, from records to TV, from comedy to drama, she seeks a greatness to surpass her lyrical high points. What she doesn't understand is that she's already an aristocrat. While she might get away with playing Lady Macbeth, Judith Anderson couldn't tap-dance her way out of a paper bag. Since her special talents don't always keep her employed, the VP/VR has plenty of time for overreaching. Eternally ambitious and emotionally volatile, she often makes disastrous career choices; her self-image is at odds with reality. At the same time her best work pushes into realms of fantasy. From skit comediennes to pop goddesses, the VP/VR defies the material world. Amazingly, her own world keeps renewing itself. Just as pundits mourned the passing of prime-time variety with the absence of Burnett, along comes MTV to amuse us with lightning-quick spectacles of diva-drenched mayhem. There isn't a world of difference between Burnett's heartfelt send-up of Norma Desmond and Madonna's sex-charged takeoff on Marilyn Monroe. Both re-create moments of intoxication to get new generations drunk with pleasure.

Carol Burnett (left) *and Madeline Kahn in* The Carol Burnett Show

Carol Burnett

In 1963 Carol Burnett told *TV Guide* she'd never do a series. It's hard to imagine what Burnett thought she'd do with her career, but she's never seemed entirely satisfied with her talent. Perhaps by the start of *The Carol Burnett Show,* Burnett knew she was out of her time, a classic clown amid *Laugh-In* and Vietnam. While Martha Raye was very much a part of wartime revues, and Imogene Coca an indispensable icon of the Golden Age of Television, Burnett was the sweetheart of Middle America when she may have wanted to be something else. She held her art together with a satirical affection for showbiz. Her send-ups of old movies were done out of love, but they were also knowing and sometimes hilariously vicious. Her comic anger reached its apex in acid-drenched skits about a typical American family: Ed (Harvey Korman), Eunice (Burnett), and Mama (Vicki Lawrence). More horrifying than *Twilight Zone* reruns, these sketches showed how frustrated Burnett must have felt. It was as if she were saying to her audience, "I fear some of you are as stupid as Ed and Eunice." But her fans never identified with Mama's family—they responded to that part of Burnett they knew was warm and kind, the woman who tugged on her ear to say hello to grandma and invited little boys on stage for a kiss. As soon as her show went off the air, Burnett starred in the antiwar drama *Friendly Fire,* to which she brought even more tight-lipped fury than was necessary. Since then, she's floundered. Torn between an ancient style of comedy and a newer one, between national adoration and social commitment, between the malice and sweetness in her own sensibility, Burnett remains an immensely complex Variety Player—a network Chaplin exiled in Maui.

Sid Caesar and Imogene Coca in Your Show of Shows

Imogene Coca

Without Imogene Coca *Your Show of Shows* would have slipped a gear and landed somewhere in New Jersey. She was the only thing standing between Sid Caesar and the Abyss—a stabilizing force. If Caesar got most of his laughs through an escalating physical lunacy, Coca depended on a concentration so fierce she was transcendently funny. Despite the number of (now) big-name writers on the show—Mel Brooks, Woody Allen, Neil Simon—the skits were surprisingly nonverbal, often repetitive, and almost antisatirical in their meandering nuttiness. The send-up of *From Here to Eternity* ("From Here to Obscurity") has little to do with the movie, while the skewering of *This Is Your Life* takes a single idea—hysterical reunions—and keeps building on it (Howard Morris's Uncle Goopy saves the sketch). Coca's role in this hothouse of high'jinks was to offset excess: she reacted as much as she "acted." She could be crazy, but there was always a part of herself that stayed in control. Her rubber face never moved without a reason. The funniest moments in her movie-theater skit with Caesar aren't when he has his clothes ripped to shreds, it's her repeated instructions to him: "Siddown! Don't let him bully ya!" When *Shows* left the air, neither Coca nor Caesar could quite recapture apart what they had together—they were the Astaire-Rogers of the Golden Age of Television. While Coca's bombed in three sitcoms (*The Imogene Coca Show, Grindl,* and *It's About Time*), Caesar's spent much of his life lecturing on the Meaning of Comedy (they got back together for *Sid Caesar Invites You* but failed). Coca's recent triumph in *National Lampoon's Vacation* suggests her braininess might pay off in a new era: she's one of the few clowns who *knows* what's funny.

J udy Garland

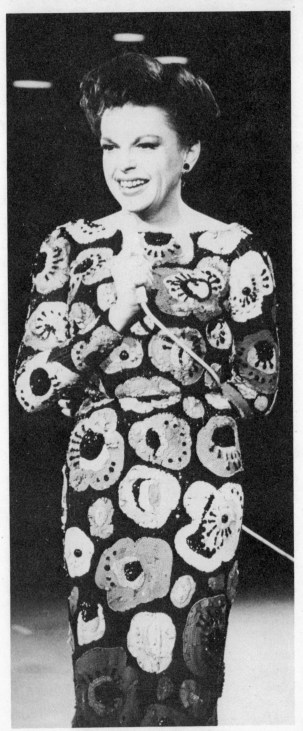

Judy Garland in The Judy Garland Show

The universe of rock video looks like *The Wonderful World of Disney* next to *The Judy Garland Show,* the most intoxicating excursion into lyrical dementia this side of the rainbow. It's impossible to fathom why CBS put a ravaged Garland up against the biggest smash on TV *(Bonanza)* in the heyday of Camelot—it would be like scheduling Billy Idol opposite Bill Cosby. But there was Judy in prime time, wincing at the camera in mug-shot black-and-white and trying to win America's heart. Through sheer naked tenacity Garland pulled off some of the most electrifying moments of her career. Faced with repeated changes in format (the series lasted less than a season) and onstage competition from fresher-faced divas (Streisand, Lena Horne, daughter Liza), Garland exploded in her solo finales on a runway stage whose footlights formed the sign of the cross with a steamer trunk nailed to the center. In the first show filmed (the sixth to be broadcast), Garland sings "Ol' Man River." Shot from discreet angles, she proceeds smoothly until the line, "I get weary/And sick of tryin'," at which point the camera cuts to a graphic, low-angle close-up. Exhausted and trembling, Garland slows her voice to a near dead-halt, regurgitating the next line—"I'm tired of livin'/And scared of dyin' "—before building to a deafening, on-cue climax that makes your body pump with so much adrenaline you think you're on a roller coaster that's just jumped its track. This experience was equaled when Garland closed a show with "The Battle Hymn of the Republic" just days after Kennedy was shot. A devastated audience rose to its feet while perhaps for the only time during the run of this searing folly Nielsen's minions empathized with Garland's exultant anguish.

way in a one-woman tour de force, *The Lady and Her Music,* shown last year on Showtime. Less a concert than a coming-out party, *Lady* revealed a Horne free at last. No longer a precise song stylist, she was a howling mama proudly perspiring through her clothes, fiercely pounding on her stomach, and wryly reminiscing about oppressions. It's as if she were saying, "I'm black, baby—get over it." But I think people were so thrilled by Horne's candor they failed to mourn the lost Lena, the diva who could croon a tune and stomp on your heart without working up a sweat. There was something corny about Horne's public display of self-affirmation—a case of too much too late. Maybe Bill Cosby's planned sitcom for Horne will add a smarter chapter to the legend of Lena. It wouldn't right past wrongs, but it might glorify the present.

Lena Horne

If there's anybody besides Ronald Reagan who still thinks the Hollywood studio system operated on cheery goodwill, consider the case of Lena Horne: a great beauty, phenomenal talent, and obedient contract worker who was just black enough to be denied vehicles to showcase her strengths. Relegated to musical solos that could be edited out when her movies went South, Horne never reached her potential as a dramatic actress. When her ex-employer, MGM, remade *Show Boat,* it cast her good friend, Ava Gardner, as Julie, the mulatto torch singer who passes for white and incurs the wrath of a racist society. Blacklisted by McCarthyites, Horne waited and watched. In the '60s she guested on TV variety shows—Milton Berle's, Judy Garland's. In the '70s she landed her own TV special with Harry Belafonte *(Harry and Lena)* and appeared as herself on *Sanford and Son.* But in the '80s Horne came back to Broad-

Shirley MacLaine

Shirley MacLaine materialized on *Hour Magazine* recently to share with Gary Collins—and mere viewers—her spiritual enlightenment. Crinkling her mouth into creases of certainty, MacLaine explained that if a mugger knocks you over the head, you "created" the experience: you must "examine" why you drew that mugger to yourself. This shining insight, borrowed from est guru Werner Erhard via God knows how many Southern California crackpots, has become a central tenet of Hollywood self-congratulators. When MacLaine accepted her Oscar for *Terms of Endearment,* she boasted how she "deserved" it—not necessarily for a good performance, but because she'd reached a level of consciousness where she attracts only good things to herself. Well, when you're an idolized movie star, it's easy to attract only good things to yourself. But go tell the survivors of Auschwitz that they got what they "deserved," that they should "examine" the experience they "created" for

Shirley MacLaine

themselves. MacLaine's smugness may have helped to resurrect her career but it's killed the spontaneity in her work. As a young movie actress in *Some Came Running* and *The Apartment*, MacLaine gave performances bursting with joy and sorrow and free-flowing eroticism. By the time she did her short-lived sitcom, *Shirley's World*, she was washed up in Hollywood—an old-style star in an *Easy Rider* world. Her recent metamorphosis on the cover of *Time* is indeed miraculous—she looks better than ever. In her one-woman Broadway revue on Showtime MacLaine mixes song-and-dance with pop philosophizing in a surprisingly unobtrusive way. But she does it with such calculation that you don't believe a word she says. She's the only Variety Player who belongs on a Malibu version of *The 700 Club*.

Madonna & Cyndi Lauper

Since a Video Rocker has about as much longevity as Ozzy Osbourne's bat, she must suggest a range of seductiveness beyond her initial image. Madonna and Cyndi Lauper scored definitive hits with "Material Girl" and "Girls Just Want to Have Fun," respectively. If the former was widely misunderstood as a paean to Reaganesque riches, the latter was often overpraised as a hymn to feminist freedom. Both videos succeed at what they set out to do, but while Madonna's is fun to watch, Lauper's is fun to think about watching. This is another way of saying that Madonna has the appeal of a mass-cult star, while Lauper has the earmarks of a high-cult flash in the pan. Her single-minded self-consciousness has led to a series of dead ends: her videos are always "about" something, but her meanings are seldom clear. Is "Time After Time" an old-fashioned love song or a criticism of romance? Is "Money Changes Everything" a celebration of wealth or a lament about it? And what the hell is Hulk Hogan hanging around for? I think

Lauper pretends to ambiguity—she tries so hard to be "different" she resists giving simple pleasure. But originality in rock-and-roll lasts about five seconds, while pleasure is eternal. After she dyes her hair, Lauper has nowhere to go. Madonna changes hair color all the time, but keeps getting better at everything she does. The key to her work is a giddy eroticism—a more potent feminist force than girl-buddy love. She's a girl who wants to have fun, but not at the expense of her sexuality. Widely viewed as a slut, she reserves her soul for the man of her choosing. In "Material Girl" she revels in high-style glamor but winds up with a nice guy in a pickup truck. She has her cake—and eats it, too. Guilt? That's boy stuff.

Liza Minnelli

If Liza Minnelli had been born twenty years earlier, she'd be as legendary as Judy Garland. She never had her mother's wit or liquid-honey voice, but she has the kind of volcanic talent that cries out for what Cole Porter in *Silk Stockings* calls glorious Technicolor, breathtaking Cinemascope, and stereophonic sound. That she won her Oscar for a big splashy musical *(Cabaret)* after the sunset of the studio system is a testament to her star-packed power. But as Hollywood drifted into the hereafter, Minnelli bounced from medium to medium in search of spiritual fulfillment. She had heavenly moments in Martin Scorsese's astringent homage to MGM musicals, *New York, New York*, which recaptured much of the voluptuous masochism and melancholy of mom and dad's (Vincente Minnelli's) masterworks. But inevitably Minnelli got older as showbiz got younger. Her evolution as a TV diva began during her *Cabaret* days in Bob Fosse's superb revue special, "Singer Presents Liza With a 'Z' " (still his best film), and then degenerated into more Academy Award showstoppers than anyone cares to remember.

Cyndi Lauper

Liza Minnelli and Beverly Sills in Gala of Stars 1981

Lately Minnelli has returned to TV with a new vigor following her trip to the Betty Ford Center. Her performance as the steadfast mother of a dying child in *A Time to Live* was surprisingly subdued and even effective. But it's the kind of role almost any Underrated Oddity, from Bonnie Bedelia to Linda Purl, could have done equally well. Don't get me wrong. I'm happy Liza won the Golden Globe for it. I'm delighted she seems to have cleaned up her act. I even kinda like her frosty-blonde hairdo. But watching her go from Garland to Greer Garson by the age of forty is the weirdest case of misplaced gifts since it was Judy's turn to cry in *Judgment at Nuremberg*.

Dinah Shore

Next to Ethel Merman and Mary Martin on *The Ford Fiftieth Anniversary Show*, Dinah Shore is the most enduring musical variety image of the '50s. But unlike M & M, Shore never needed Broadway to be adored by millions—she's a thoroughbred TV diva. Who else but Dinah could have spent six years on a first series (*The Dinah Shore Show*), seven on a second (*The Dinah Shore Chevy Show*), four on a third (*Dinah's Place*), six on a fourth (*Dinah!*), and a summer fill-

Aretha Franklin (left) and Dinah Shore on Dinah!

ing in for Carol Burnett *(Dinah and Her New Best Friends)*? If Shore's appeal rested on a white-bread cheeriness, her longevity depended on qualities only hinted at. Her theme song, "See the U.S.A. in Your Chevrolet," was as redolent of '50s prosperity as her renowned sign-off ("Mmmwwwaaahhh!") was indicative of Eisenhower friendliness. Her image of streamlined capitalism sealed with a kiss presented an edifice smooth on the surface and rocky underneath. Musically, Shore was as pure-pitched as Doris Day, but her heart was located south of the Mason-Dixon line (b. 1917 in Winchester, Tennessee). I remember her singing "Birth of the Blues" on *The Mike Douglas Show* with such full-throttled passion she nearly fell off her stool. Basically, Shore is the original Iron Magnolia. On her talk shows she'd butter up guests with flirtatious flattery only to deliver ladylike zingers when the conversation dragged. Her healthy taste for juicy beefcake, from George Montgomery to Burt Reynolds, complemented her own athletic zeal—she was a jock before Chris Evert was born. My favorite moment in her spots for Holly Farms chicken is when she ogles a tennis hunk's legs while chatting about tender thighs. After all these years Dinah is one TV Diva who still knows the joy of "Mmmwwwaaahhh!"

and his work becomes fixed, processed, remote. If Sinatra's navel-gazing neoconservatism began with the death of Camelot, and Elvis's with his first trip to Vegas, Streisand's slide into Velveeta-land was greased by her rejection of the media that made her—Broadway and TV. Her theatrical triumphs *(I Can Get It for You Wholesale, Funny Girl)* and TV specials *(My Name is Barbra, Color Me Barbra)* preceded her two best movies, *Funny Girl* and *The Way We Were*, released the same year as her last TV special, *Barbra Streisand . . . And Other Musical Instruments*. Since then Streisand has made more synthetic movies, albums, and fashion statements than any myth this side of Elvis. Following the so-so reception of her auteurist oddity *Yentl*, Streisand returned to her "roots" with *The Broadway Album*—a collection of show tunes—and a behind-the-scenes HBO special. Though it put Streisand at the top of the charts, *Broadway* is the coldest thing she's ever done, an exhausting celebration of perfectionism (it's the *Out of Africa* of records). Streisand says she avoids live performing because she doesn't want to disappoint her fans. But that's Bel Air talking—not Brooklyn. Flesh-and-blood art is the only way Streisand can bring her legend back to life.

Barbra Streisand

Barbra Streisand has been embalmed so long it's hard to remember she was once a living legend. What Frank Sinatra was to the '40s, and Elvis Presley was to the '50s, Streisand was to the '60s—a crossover genius who reflected the fantasies of more Americans than any elected official. But such fame carries a price: the Entertainer begins to feel dwarfed by the Myth. Holed up in luxury, shielded by a handpicked handful, the "superstar" evolves into a reclusive icon. Self-consciousness creeps in,

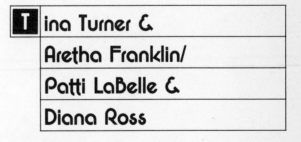

Tina Turner & Aretha Franklin/ Patti LaBelle & Diana Ross

The spectacular comebacks of Tina Turner and Aretha Franklin have underscored the curious strainings of Patti LaBelle and Diana Ross. If LaBelle is a poor man's Turner, Ross remains an ersatz Franklin. The irony is that Turner resurrected her career through compromise while Franklin waited for MTV to come around to her

Tina Turner

Ladylike lilt. And while LaBelle has stayed faithful to gospel-glitz, Ross has compromised her Motown sound ad infinitum. In other words, there's no surefire road to glory. After a certain point it's a matter of soul—not the musical kind, but the spiritual sort. People either warm to you or they don't. Much of Turner's and Franklin's likability rests on their shoot-from-the-hip nonchalance. If Turner makes eye contact and tells us we're all sluts, Franklin lays back, and dares us to be cool (though she was so cool in her concert on Showtime in 1986, she was practically freeze-dried). When Turner inquires, "What's Love Got to Do with It?," or Franklin asks, "Who's Zoomin' Who?," they are saying you can be a bitch about love without being monstrous. LaBelle and Ross, by contrast, croon tunes of joy and triumph without a trace of abandon—they're almost clinically self-conscious in their exultation. LaBelle's TV special in 1985 was like watching Judy Garland if she'd never left Oz. Belting showstoppers from one end of a runway to another, thrusting her spiked nails into throngs of worshipers, LaBelle sang of humanity while her prime concern was clearly herself. Ross, meanwhile, is a virtual automaton of enlightenment. Half Whitney Houston and half est trainer, Ross seems more interested in lecturing the minions than communicating with people. After the disastrous concert in Central Park, recorded by Showtime, fans went on a rampage. Some souls never get the message.

GLAMOROUS STRANGERS

June Allyson
Lauren Bacall
Anne Baxter
Joan Crawford
Yvonne De Carlo

Olivia De Havilland & Joan Fontaine
Sophia Loren
Ginger Rogers
Jane Russell
Lana Turner

The 21 Commandments of the Glamorous Stranger

1. Never drive through the front gate of your old studio thinking Louis B. Mayer is waiting to see you.
2. Never go into shock when your leading man looks like that bald fellow from *The Mary Tyler Moore Show*.
3. Never put arsenic in Angela Lansbury's tea just because you'd like to take her place.
4. Never admit you're doing television because you want to let your grandchildren know who the hell you are.
5. Never appear on a talk show to publicize a guest shot on *Punky Brewster*.
6. Never hold stagehands spellbound with reminiscences of Clark Gable.
7. Never play a scene with James Brolin unless he's ordered to look at you with longing in his eyes.
8. Never brag about owning the store where Bernie Kopell buys all his clothes.
9. Never notice embarrassed stares when you tell Shari Belafonte Harper how much you loved working with Butterfly McQueen.
10. Never assume you're allowed more than two takes per scene.
11. Never ask why your makeup man must also fix the eyeliner of an actress you once vowed to kill.
12. Never share screen time with Dick Van Patten, even if you've spent time with one of his sons.
13. Never boast about remembering a time when ABC didn't exist.
14. Never hurl your cocktail shaker through the television set when you discover billing on *The Love Boat* is alphabetical.
15. Never recall the time you canceled an appointment with William S. Paley to keep a date with William S. Hart.
16. Never look around the set and wonder who the hell everybody is.
17. Never extol the virtues of clean living to the cast of *Airwolf*.

18. Never wince when Connie Selleca mentions she went to kindergarten with your granddaughter.
19. Never inquire if Robert Culp is still appearing on television with that nice black man.
20. Never contend that *Photoplay* outsells *People.*
21. Never weep when your director tells you how much he loved you in *Sunset Boulevard.*

June Allyson

There's really no modern equivalent to June Allyson: Molly Ringwald's too glum, Sandy Duncan's too Broadway, and Marie Osmond's too devout. Surely the girl-next-door isn't extinct, but she no longer represents the ruling culture. If Allyson—sunny, cheerful, wholesome—embodied the spirit of the Eisenhower era, today's symbolic diva would be a cross between Joan Collins and Joan Rivers: '50s health versus '80s wealth. But the '50s, which encouraged James Dean and Elvis Presley to subvert the culture, also yearned to yank Allyson from her house slippers. At the height of her fame, José Ferrer cast her in *The Shrike,* a drab and pretentious melodrama about a shrewish wife who browbeats her intolerably wimpy husband. Allyson seemed to have a good time in the role, but Ferrer, who directed as well as starred, shifted the attention to his character's needs. He usurped Allyson's emotions in the same way Hollywood had for years (she'd been molded as a Heavenly Helpmate to every American hero in town). Even when she hosted her own television series, *The DuPont Show with June Allyson,* she shared screen time with her real-life husband, Dick Powell. I don't mean to make a big case for Allyson as a cruelly oppressed diva, but there's something about her that hasn't been expressed. As recently as a 1986 episode of *Airwolf,* she was playing a variation of *The Shrike*—a vicious ma-triarch stopping at nothing to gain custody of her grandchild. But if her best performance was as a giggly Midwesterner in *A Woman's World,* it's because the darkness in Allyson's soul is less tragic than comedic. I'd love to see her do a mean-spirited farce—maybe a send-up of *The Shrike* opposite Steve Martin.

Lauren Bacall

When Lauren Bacall, Dragon Lady of the Great White Way, gave up the role of Hedda Hopper in *Malice in Wonderland,* she lost her one-way ticket out of the shadowy world of the Glamorous Stranger. I don't think Bacall could have topped Jane Alexander, but she would have finally done something to stake her claim to TV divahood. What's surprising is how much television Bacall has done, and how long ago: a revival of *The Petrified Forest* with Humphrey Bogart, a production of *Blithe Spirit* opposite Noël Coward, and a string of guest shots on classic series. But if Bacall is an all-but-forgotten figure in TV circles, it's because her comeback trail was blazed on Broadway. Her Tony-winning triumphs in *Applause* and *Woman of the Year* made the networks an optional source of income. But with Broadway's skyrocketing expense, especially for musicals, Bacall may be forced to reconsider her videophobia (she can't play the West End forever). Her highly touted TV-movie debut in *Perfect Gentlemen,* a lazy and obvious heist comedy, didn't tell us All About Bacall, but her Emmy-nominated role as an impoverished princess in *The Rockford Files* began to. Playing a down-and-out dame with a raging resourcefulness and a healthy taste for beat-up men, Bacall reworked with James Garner some of the rapport she'd had with Bogie. This is how she scored her theatrical coups—toying with her image as a fire-breathing survivor. If she'd accepted the part in *Malice,* she'd have

Lauren Bacall on NBC Adventure Theatre

bridged what she used to be (a Hollywood clothes-horse harnessed by marriage) and what she's become (a showbiz icon toughened by experience). But we'll have to wait for Bacall to get the grease-paint out of her veins before we see if she has the guts to be a TV diva.

Anne Baxter

For more than forty years cultists have argued furiously whether Anne Baxter is a bad actress, a lucky lady, a gifted diva, a bit of all three, or none of the above. When she suffered a fatal stroke late in 1985 (hailing a taxi on Madison Avenue to take her to the beauty parlor), the debate intensified: Eve Harrington was dead. The irony was that Baxter bowed out before Bette Davis, Margo Channing to Baxter's Eve in *All About Eve*. A further irony was that Baxter stepped in for Davis on *Hotel* when the latter was too ill to continue with the series. And still another irony was that Baxter replaced Lauren Bacall in *Applause,* a Broadway musical based on *Eve* in which Baxter played Margo. This art-reflecting-life/life-reflecting-art scenario would not be believed by even the most devoted fans of *Dynasty*. But it's true: Baxter is basic to the politics of Diva. The round-faced ingenue who worked with Orson Welles (*The Magnificent Ambersons*) and won an Oscar at twenty-two (*The Razor's Edge*) could not have anticipated what was to come. From the beginning Baxter exhibited a striking style—heated, heavy-lidded, hard-breathing. Sometimes she looked on the verge of something only she understood. As Eve, the

Anne Baxter

most vehement character of her career, Baxter molded her mannerisms into an edifice of artifice, a Mount Rushmore of craft. You didn't want to screw around with this girl only because you feared cutting your hands on her face. By the time of *Hotel* Baxter's visage was an awesome sight: a gleeful grin frozen by lip gloss. Playing a nice woman, Baxter suggested a more dicey one underneath. If she never got to show that woman, it's because she knew her place: an understudy to greater divas who watched her every move.

mistakes her for a washerwoman because she's always on her hands and knees scrubbing the floors of her mansion (Crawford to maid in *Mommie Dearest*: "I'm not mad at you—I'm mad at the dirt!"). But her greatest TV performance was as the blind rich bitch who blackmails a surgeon to purchase a poor man's eyes in a classic segment of *Night Gallery*. Written by Rod Serling, post-*Zone*, and directed by Steven Spielberg (at twenty-two!), the episode brought out all the madness and mysticism in Crawford's personality. When the surgeon mumbles something about justice, Crawford snaps, "No one has ever done me justice, beginning with God." The twists and turns of the plot are too complicated to recount, but suffice it to say that Crawford gets her comeuppance. Her portrait of arrogance humbled by mortality teeters between bloodcurdling viciousness and heartbreaking self-delusion. I'd never believed Crawford as a pathetic heroine until this show (I think it's her richest performance, after *Humoresque,* and Spielberg's niftiest picture, next to *The Sugarland Express*). The strength of the production rests on Crawford's admission that self-absorption has its downside. In too many of her vehicles, Crawford suffers from self-sacrifice. But in *Gallery* she acknowledges the enemy in herself; she doesn't blame an evil offspring *(Mildred Pierce)* or a demented sibling *(What Ever Happened to Baby Jane?)*. When she purrs, "My singular preoccupation is myself," she's giving Serling more than he bargained for and Spielberg more than he imagined. Never the greatest of actresses, Crawford defines Diva through the chilling absurdity of her all-consuming narcissism.

Joan Crawford

Joan Crawford's second-best TV role was as herself in an episode of *The Beverly Hillbillies*: Granny

vonne De Carlo

Yvonne De Carlo radiates a strange kind of glamor—a ripe, fruity, B-movie dementia. Her Hollywood credits include *Slave Girl, She Devils,*

Joan Crawford in Route 66

and *Flame of the Islands.* After *Law of the Lawless,* De Carlo settled down to something normal: *The Munsters.* Her vampirish Lily is the sanest character she ever played—a hardworking homemaker with a sweet smile. Okay, so her caftans resemble casket linings and her makeup makes Madonna look like Mother Teresa. But if Lily set up house today, her children's friends would drop by for fashion pointers. The irony is that De Carlo—the most humorless low-camp diva in Hollywood history—has become a high-camp trendsetter in reruns. She never played Lily as a witty cartoon

but approached her with the same workmanlike dedication she used to tackle Salome and Lola Montez. Yes, she lacked the wry delicacy of Carolyn Jones in *The Addams Family,* but she was immensely likable—the Margaret Dumont of the sitcoms. It's De Carlo's straight-faced professionalism that made her such a powerful presence in Stephen Sondheim's Broadway classic *Follies.* Singing "I'm Still Here," De Carlo evoked all the tough-mindedness of showbiz survivors without the Hollywood sentiment Carol Burnett supplied in the *Follies* concert. When she barks, "First you're

Yvonne De Carlo and Fred Gwynne in The Munsters

Joan Fontaine and Gavin MacLeod in The Love Boat

another sloe-eyed vamp/Then someone's mother/ Then you're camp," she's telling truths only the fierce can understand. But her own career is even wilder: she started off as camp, then played a mother who was a sloe-eyed vamp. On a *Murder, She Wrote,* she was holed up in a women's prison with a bomber crew of tenacious pros: Vera Miles, Janet MacLachlan, Barbara Baxley, Adrienne Barbeau, Susan Oliver, Linda Kelsey, and Miss Lansbury herself. They were all still here.

Olivia De Havilland & Joan Fontaine

Olivia De Havilland and Joan Fontaine should end their blood feud and star in a sequel to *Malice in Wonderland.* At the very least they could bury the hatchet in each other's heads. They could also beef up their video résumés, which are skimpy even by Glamorous Stranger standards (yes, they've both played footsie with Gavin MacLeod on *The Love Boat*). The only problem would be who would play which role. I submit that Joan would make a perfect Hedda—thin, cool, freaky—while Olivia could easily embody Louella—plump, earthy, expansive. The casting would even have a chronological symmetry: Joan followed in the footsteps of Olivia in much the same way Hedda chased after Louella. This Big Sister/Little Sister dynamic may be the source of the Olivia/Joan rivalry, but it probably has more to do with two very distinct actresses having the misfortune of sharing the same mother. Still, the question remains: whom does Mom—i.e., History—love best? First, you have to look at how each began. Olivia started as a Warners contract player but fought for meaty roles. Joan got her break as a Hitchcock heroine but slid into silly parts. Right after World War II, they met in the middle: Olivia on her way up, Joan on her way down. Ten years later it was over for both of them. But during their peak period, the high '40s, no two divas sparked a more compelling competition. Surely Joan got the cult directors—Max Ophuls, Fritz Lang, Nicholas Ray—while Olivia got more Oscars (two to one). When all is said and done, I'll take Olivia's full-throttled emotionalism in *To Each His Own* and *North and South* over Joan's stylized histrionics in *Suspicion* and *Crossings*. I say this confidently, and with no *Malice* aforethought.

Sophia Loren

Will the real Sophia Loren please stand up? We've seen the Earthy Sophia, dressed down and full of grief. We've seen the Pretty Sophia, dressed up and full of herself. But where's the Heady Sophia, who gives grit to glitz and sex appeal to kitchen sinks? It's been such a long time that even Vittorio

De Sica wouldn't be able To Tell the Truth. In *Marriage Italian Style* Loren gave a performance that ranks with the greats—a joyous, raucous, blindingly bright explosion of laughter, tears, and bitter invective. It soiled the purity of *Two Women* and exposed the artifice of *Arabesque*. But Loren is the schiziest of goddesses—she embraces the two extremes in her personality. We all know the story of her wretched youth in war-torn Italy, but to hear Loren tell it you'd think she was the only Love Child who ever grew up in a hateful world. She feasts on poverty, just as she hungers for Hollywood-style glamor, spoon-fed to her by an obsessive stage mother. In the telling TV epic, *Sophia Loren—Her Own Story,* Loren plays her own mother opposite a slim, young actress. When the young Sophia grows up, Loren plays herself. By drama's end we have two Sophias, a vacant Movie Star and a ravaged Earth Mother. These are the images Loren has mined all her life, but neither one rings true. They're flip sides of a rusty coin. The Real Sophia, the Sophia who obliterated Gina Lollobrigida and upstaged Anna Magnani, doesn't don a housedress to seek another Oscar *(A Special Day)* or stump for a cosmetics firm looking like an anorexic transvestite. What she does is eroticize drabness and dramatize glamor—*simultaneously*. She's the only diva who's ever done it, but the Pre-Fab Sophia won't allow it anymore.

Ginger Rogers

You can take Virginia McMath out of Missouri, but you can't take Missouri out of Ginger Rogers. For more than fifty years Rogers has been a giddy combo of all-American extremes: bumpkin and bombshell, populist and elitist, hayseed and wisecracker. Even her name is half sweet and half sensible. Her most celebrated work centers on the deceptively frivolous *(Swing Time* & Fred) and the pseudoprofound *(Kitty Foyle* & Oscar). But

Sophia Loren

Ginger Rogers in Zane Grey Theatre

the seductiveness of Rogers is often overlooked (she's a wonderful actress). Her biggest kink is dressing up like a little girl. Her enchanting performance in *The Major and the Minor* waltzed a precarious line between innocence and depravity, while her all-out antics in *Monkey Business* hopscotched from maturity to infantilism. As Rogers reached middle age, her body seemed to change almost overnight from lean and lithe to beefy and square-shouldered. By the time she faced being a TV diva, she could pass for Hulk Hogan's grandmother. So she turned to the stage, scoring triumphs as Dolly Levi (bumpkin/bombshell) and Mame Dennis (populist/elitist). Even so, the little girl inside the large woman couldn't find a voice. She showed some wheedling slyness as a scheming actress on a *Love Boat* cruise, but the show squelched her wilder instincts. Her great TV turn—and her best work in decades—was in a riotous episode of *Glitter.* Playing a long-running soap-opera queen who refuses to be killed off, Rogers let loose with an appallingly funny impersonation of an oversized spoiled brat—she looked like Mae West in *Sextette* impersonating Patty McCormack in *The Bad Seed.* It was a major performance in a minor series, and it glittered like gold.

J ane Russell

Jane Russell has been taken for granted for two very visible reasons. A full-figured gal, she began as a femme scandale in Howard Hughes's *The Outlaw* and wound up a pitchwoman for Cross Your Heart bras. In between, she shaped up as the third-most underrated actress of the '50s, after Ava Gardner and Doris Day. Actually, Russell was sort of a cross between the two, combining Gardner's earthy insolence with Day's brainy self-effacement. What all three had in common was a touching tenderness beneath gestures of capability and independence. But if Gardner's warmth came

from a down-to-earth humor, and Day's from a willingness to reach a common ground, Russell's belonged to the wide-open spaces—a prairie decency. Even amid the glamorous surroundings of *The French Line* or the exotic shenanigans of *Macao,* Russell embodied James Cagney's famous definition of acting: plant your feet, look the other fella in the eye, and tell the truth. If she's most fondly remembered for *Gentlemen Prefer Blondes,* it's because she had a lot of truth to tell Marilyn Monroe (they're transcendent together). It's no surprise that Russell eventually left Hollywood and settled in Arizona. You can just see her in a checkered blouse, suede skirt, and cowgirl pumps. So could the producers of *The Yellow Rose,* a perfectly cast western soap that left the air in 1984. As Rose Hollister, Russell looked like the long-lost mother of rough-hewn Sam Elliott. But she had little to do at a time when the series was struggling to survive. Maybe she could have taken a cue from Elliott's coltish costar, Cybill Shepherd, and kept coming back to television until Hollywood was ready to appreciate her.

L ana Turner

A friend of mine says that if you visualize MGM's reigning queens of the '40s and '50s—Ava Gardner, Elizabeth Taylor, and Lana Turner—you can see Gardner reading a book, Taylor reading a magazine, and Turner not reading at all. This may be why I've always stopped short of loving Turner. I don't expect divas to be rocket scientists, but I get queasy thinking of them as space cadets. There's a thickness, a humorlessness, a mechanical quality about Turner that drives me straight to the liquor cabinet. Her image as a well-behaved zombie is all part of the MGM ethos, which groomed goddesses to be Spencer Tracy's daughter (Taylor in *Father of the Bride*) or James Mason's mistress (Gardner in *East Side, West Side*), but never both

Jane Russell in The Yellow Rose

Lana Turner in Falcon Crest

at once. Still, if Taylor subverted studio policy with a zesty humor, and Gardner made Leo the lion cower with an earthy intelligence, Turner played the game like a good little girl. Her private life often told a different story. This brings us to another grating Turnerism—hypocrisy. I don't believe Turner as the high-minded matrons of *Peyton Place* and *Imitation of Life*. I *do* believe her as the pathetically deluded drunk in *Madame X,* stepping out of her shower to find Burgess Mer-

edith and hoarsely barking, "What the *hell* are you doing here?" (Her hangover scene is one of the best I've ever seen.) Her recent lunge at TV stardom, excepting the obligatory stint on *The Love Boat,* put her head-to-head with *Falcon Crest*'s Jane Wyman, who happily called her a "bitch." Shortly thereafter, she was shot to death and dumped from the show. If she'd been more honest with herself these past forty years, she might have been allowed to turn the tables.

WILY WITS

Stockard Channing
Selma Diamond
Betty Furness
Ruth Gordon
Bette Midler

Sally Jessy Raphael
Joan Rivers
Liz Smith
Lily Tomlin
Barbara Walters

A Wily Wit is known less for the variety of her roles than the quality of her mind. She may be a News Hound (Barbara Walters, Betty Furness, Jane Pauley), a Talky Tina (Virginia Graham, Oprah Winfrey, Sally Jessy Raphael), a Gabby Gossip (Liz Smith, Rona Barrett, Marilyn Beck), a Critical Curmudgeon (Judith Crist, Linda Ellerbee, Pia Lindstrom), a Canny Comedienne (Lily Tomlin, Whoopi Goldberg, Joan Rivers), a Doting Doctor (Joyce Brothers, Ruth Westheimer, Sonya Friedman), a Variety Vamp (Hermione Gingold, Dody Goodman, Madeline Kahn), or an Autobiographical Actress (Ruth Gordon, Stockard Channing, Arlene Francis). Sometimes, the categories overlap. Rivers is both a Talky Tina and a Canny Comedienne, while Bette Midler seems a combo of all eight. But the common denominator is a conspicuous exercise of brainpower, whether electrifying or not. A WW is hard to peg. Her talents are often overvalued (Walters, Ellerbee, Rivers), underappreciated (Furness, Pauley, Francis), or just not ready for prime time (Tomlin, Midler, Kahn). She spends a lifetime trying to find her niche. She may start out as a Hollywood ingenue and wind up a consumer reporter. She may work the Continental Baths one day and be up for an Oscar the next. She may bounce from a Vegas lounge to the cover of *People*. Even when she finds her place in the sun, it's often shaded. If she's a News Hound, she's in a subordinate position to men. If she's a Canny Comedienne, she can't find a wide audience. If she's an Autobiographical Actress, she upstages her characters. But a WW is far from a tragic figure. She may pay a price for using her brains instead of her looks, but she has fewer apologies to make for her career. Working from her own personality, she's either loved for who she is or just left out in the cold.

Stockard Channing in Silent Victory: The Kitty O'Neil Story

tockard Channing

Stockard Channing has had more shots at stardom than Captain Kirk. Following her disastrous movie debut as the put-upon heiress in Mike Nichols's *The Fortune,* she fizzled in back-to-back CBS sitcoms. What Nichols and the networks failed to understand about Channing is that she's neither a contemporary Martha Raye nor a conventional comedienne. She's a witty soul who triumphs over physical deformity. Her recent resurrection as the sharp-tongued mother of a spastic child in Broadway's *Joe Egg,* for which she received a Tony, recalls her paramount TV performances as the deaf stuntwoman in *Silent Victory: The Kitty O'Neil Story* and the vengeful ugly duckling in *The Girl Most Likely to . . .* (she was disgraced by the smarmy antidrug melodrama *Not My Kid*). In these roles Channing undercuts the humiliation of her characters with a penetrating sarcasm that's neither self-pitying nor self-congratulatory. Even her looks are a battle between the beautiful and the bizarre: glacial smoothness offset by lopsided features, vocal power undermined by grating inflections, cool assurance betrayed by emotional seizures. When, in *Girl,* she cracks wise in grotesque disguise, she makes the homeliness of her character seem superfluous. The harshness of Channing's feelings and the ambiguity of her presence have always kept her from mass-cult stardom. When she tries to be a sitcom cutie, she looks repellent; but when she's free to shatter the restraint of her roles, she earns every tear she squeezes out of you. She's less an Underrated Oddity than a Wily Wit because the acidity of her characters comes from the wit in her own sensibility. Too wily for most media, she's a unique TV presence.

Selma Diamond

Selma Diamond

When Selma Diamond, on an episode of *Night Court,* was told by a male colleague not to intrude on "guy talk," she cracked, "So sorry. Let me go hang myself in the toilet." A TV comedy writer for Sid Caesar, Milton Berle, and Groucho Marx in the '50s—no Golden Age for witty women—Diamond paid the price for (almost) being one of the guys. Tough-talking, chain-smoking, gravelly voiced, she showed us how an outsider who deserves to be an insider can celebrate her exclusion. As *Night Court*'s Selma Hacker, a part written especially for her, Diamond reveled in sarcasm even as she revealed her vulnerability. When she quipped that she removed the blood-pressure monitor from her exercise bike to "make room for the ashtray," you wanted to hug her even as you withered from the darkness of the gag. Yes, she died (at sixty-four) of lung cancer—a horrible jest Diamond would have been the first to appreciate. That she left "no known survivors" is a testament to her uncompromisingly solitary art.

Betty Furness

If Betty Furness had been born a man, she'd be sitting in Dan Rather's chair today. A Hollywood ingenue in the '30s (she was Fred Astaire's round-faced fiancée in *Swing Time*), Furness turned to television almost at its inception, becoming the legendary pitchperson for Westinghouse products on *Studio One* (contrary to myth, she was not the woman whose refrigerator door refused to open). At the same time Furness hosted a number of shows, including *Byline,* renamed from *News Gal.*

Ever since then, Furness has been an exemplary news gal. But unlike Mike Wallace, who parlayed his shameless hucksterism into a spot on *60 Minutes,* Furness was left to fight for Barbara Walters's vacated job on *The Today Show,* which went to her spiritual daughter, Jane Pauley. A victim of ageism as well as sexism, Furness remained undaunted: she became a consumer reporter be-

fore David Horowitz knew how to spell "seat belt." Whether exposing the deficiencies of fitted bed sheets or showing us her lifetime collection of hats, Furness expresses an attention to detail almost unparalleled among News Hounds. With her sprayed-back mane, firmly set jaw, and breathless delivery, she whizzes through facts with an exactitude that creates its own kind of wit. Unlike

Betty Furness and daughter at the Democratic and Republican National Conventions, 1960

Wallace or Rather or Brokaw, who fancy themselves world-class intellectuals, Furness knows that every story is a collection of minute observations. But her feminine self-effacement has always kept her from rising in the network ranks. Like Pauley, who still makes less money than her male counterpart on *Today,* Furness is a sweetly intelligent and deceptively smart reporter. She's a News Hound with more wit than wiles.

R uth Gordon

For a woman who spent the better part of a century trying to be a Great Dramatic Actress, Ruth Gordon did all right for herself—she turned her personality into her art. Jaunty, wisecracking, hilariously self-centered, she became a showbiz symbol of irrepressible wit. Her scripts with husband Garson Kanin for the Tracy-Hepburn vehicles *Adam's Rib* and *Pat and Mike* and the TV movie *Hardhat and Legs* are models of sophisticated comedy. She echoed Hepburn's assertion that men and women shouldn't live together— they should live next door and visit often. Her rapturous appreciations of actresses from Greta Garbo to Meryl Streep were based on envy: no matter which role she played, she was always Ruth Gordon. Even as a supporting player in the '40s (she had appeared on stage and screen since 1915), Gordon seemed incapable of becoming another person. As she got older she sharpened her brain and let the dumber beauties win acclaim. She also wrote plays about her early years, followed by full-scale autobiographies. She was smart enough to know that her life story was the only production of which she could be the sole star. When she took this extravaganza on the talk-show circuit she was a riot. When asked by Tom Snyder if the casting couch existed, Gordon not only admitted it, but defended an actress's right to use it: "What's she savin' it for?" Gordon's personality dwarfed her

work. Her Oscar-winning performance in *Rosemary's Baby* was almost identical to her Emmy-winning work in *Taxi.* Until her death in 1985 at eighty-eight, Gordon never stopped. Her motto was summed up in her Oscar acceptance speech after fifty years in show business: "You don't know how encouragin' a thing like this is."

B ette Midler

A unique sensibility attuned to no single medium, Bette Midler is her own Barnum and Bailey Circus. Her stage act, an ever-changing spectacle, is the bedrock of her career: she's the Bruce Springsteen of Wily Wits. But her gifts are too explosive to be contained by a mere proscenium—her Sophie Tucker jokes alone are enough to close down Radio City Music Hall. In a sense she's overqualified for every job she seeks and underqualified to be a normal human being. Her big-screen successes in *Down and Out in Beverly Hills* and *Ruthless People* tapped only part of her talents. The wickedness of her wit can also be seen in her Emmy-winning TV special, "Ol' Red Hair Is Back," and her stints as an awards-show hostess at the Oscars, Emmys, and Grammys, mocking selected nominees (". . . the endless *Endless Love*") and going-for-the-gold greediness. But the wealth of emotion behind her wisecracks has been left unmined (*The Rose* was mostly fool's gold.) Unlike Mae West, who happily lived the naughty ironies of her work, Midler keeps reaching for a passion that might give "meaning" to her jokes. She's snuck some of this weightiness into her stage act, dancing to ah-sweet-mystery-of-life ballets, but it's usually come across as pretentious. Perhaps Midler isn't the person to do justice to herself. Maybe she needs someone to fashion a project that combines the force of rock-and-roll, the zing of stand-up routines, the bawdiness of vaudeville, the charge of musical theater, and the allure of

Bette Midler

movie divahood. If there's a soul in showbiz to carry it off, Bette's the best bet.

⑤ally Jessy Raphael

This St. Louis talk show host is like a spunky Phil Donahue camped out in Mary Hartman's kitchen. A gleeful dynamo with bleached-blonde hair, red-rimmed glasses, and aggressively tailored outfits, Raphael earns her spot as the most consistently enjoyable interviewer on television. Unlike the self-conscious Sonya (Friedman) or the self-promoting Oprah (Winfrey), Sally is never afraid to be vulgar or tell a stupid joke. She just barrels along, coaxing confessions from her Midwestern minions and grilling guests ("Gosh, that sounds wrong!") with a jolly grin on her face. Sometimes, her brazen yakety-yak is so ridiculously self-reflexive it overpowers her guests. But Sally is far from the rabble-rousing hucksterism of a Joe Pyne or a Les Crane—she just wants to get her ego out there with the least amount of damage (deep down, she's scared). Her palpable anxiety is often reflected in her guests: from "redeemed" homosexuals to hysterical psychics, Sally's subjects seem like refugees from Tom Snyder's green room. But whether emceeing a particularly graphic male beauty contest or devoting an entire show to the merry bitching of her predominantly female audience, Sally exercises brainpower without ever being a solemn bore.

Ⓙoan Rivers

Joan Rivers is a new breed of '80s comedian—the Phyllis Diller of the MTV generation. She exudes a showbiz slickness and a compulsive urge to brutality, often aimed at the very minorities Lily Tomlin and others championed in the '70s. To Rivers, Eleanor Roosevelt is a "dyke," Yoko Ono is a "dog," Vanessa Williams is a "tramp," Princess Caroline is a "slut," and Boy George is paired with the ruler of the British Empire as "a queen who can't dress." These barbs are offset by her cloying adulation of her daughter Melissa (no slut jokes for this princess), the Republican Party (no Nancy Reagan digs), and Jerry Falwell ("very smart," she told *Interview*). As Tomlin once told Rivers on *Tonight,* "You've been sucking up to Nancy and Ronnie too long." Her borscht-belt gags and Vegas shtick, innocuous on the surface, mask a comedy rooted in a malicious self-loathing. She yearns to be accepted by Polite Society but fears she isn't worth it. Earlier in her career Rivers concentrated on jokes about her own appearance ("My body's falling so fast my gynecologist wears a hard hat"). But through a series of physical transformations, including face-lifts, and a career boost from hosting *Tonight,* Rivers turned her self-hatred outward—to "dykes," "tubbos," "sluts," "tramps," "pigs," "dogs," "queens," "scum." Her targets are now almost exclusively other women and gay men (she downplays her Jewishness) because these are the images with which she most identifies. Indeed, at first glance, Rivers looks like a manic transvestite "doing" Tallulah, Bette, and Joan—aping excessive mannerisms and slaying imaginary phantoms. But Rivers's targets aren't imaginary—they're real people with families, families that Rivers and Falwell ennoble with sanctimonious speeches. After all, the survivors of Karen Carpenter and Princess Grace don't need to hear locker-room gags about their dead relatives on television. Except, of course, their circumstances have rendered them vulnerable, and Rivers finds vulnerability—weakness or powerlessness of any kind—irresistible. As for the slut jokes, there's barely a female guest of a Rivers show left unscathed. If she's living with a man, like Susan Anton, she's asked when she's going to "get a ring." If she's married, like Valerie Bertinelli, she's quizzed on her husband's extramarital activities. And if she has done "lesbian porno," like Vanessa Williams, she won't even get on the show ("I don't like society making heroines out of porno stars," she explained to *Interview*). All these women, in Rivers's view, are somehow unclean, unlike, say, our First Lady. And God forbid anybody should sling mud at Melissa. Forget Sean Lennon. Melissa has feelings. The true insight into Rivers's career is a marvelous 1973 TV movie entitled *The Girl Most Likely to . . .* Rivers wrote the script, and it's the most bitterly self-revelatory work by a comedian since Chaplin's *Monsieur Verdoux*. In it, a grotesquely ugly college student (Stockard Channing, much disguised), tormented by her peers, undergoes extensive plastic surgery following a car accident and returns to campus, a dazzling swan, to murder her persecutors. This is, of course, *The Joan Rivers Story*. Rivers's recent metamorphosis as comedic megastar has allowed her to get even with all those sluts and queens and tramps who made her feel ashamed of being ugly and unwanted and unsuccessful. Unlike Johnny Carson, who genially pokes fun at everybody, Rivers seem to harbor her own private enemies list. She's the only TV diva who wreaks revenge on other TV divas.

L iz Smith

A Gabby Gossip with a conscience, Liz Smith launched an assault in 1985 on critic John Simon for calling a play about eight heterosexual women "faggot nonsense" and being overheard to joke that all homosexuals in the theater should die of AIDS. Within weeks Simon penned a retraction, his boss publicly chastised him, and his colleagues signed a letter of condemnation. If Smith was so successful in her campaign, it may be because she's one of the few gossip columnists whose ego is smaller than her circulation; she doesn't use her power to pander to petty prejudices on a grand scale. Unlike Marilyn Beck, who whipped up Hol-

lywood hysteria over AIDS on *Nightline,* or Rona Barrett, who outweeps Barbara Walters in nationally televised interviews, Smith has remained a sensible Manhattan celebrity despite her syndicated status. Her regular stint on *Live at Five,* a news/talk show on NBC's station in New York (a.k.a. *Jive at Five*), adds to the allure of the most spectacular collection of News Hounds, Gabby Gossips, and Critical Curmudgeons ever assembled in one place: Betty Furness, Fred Astaire's sweetie before Ginger Rogers in *Swing Time,* as consumer reporter; Pia Lindstrom, Ingrid Bergman's daughter by the doctor before moving in with Roberto Rossellini, as entertainment critic; Sue Simmons, David Letterman's frequent target, as co-anchor. It's the only assemblage of Wily Wits that could be called a divafest. As its down-to-earth Gabby Gossip, Liz Smith is right at home.

L ily Tomlin

On *Rowan & Martin's Laugh-In,* the show that launched her career, Lily Tomlin was an anomaly. Her acid portrait of the vengeful telephone operator made sock-it-to-me girls and here-come-da-judge guest stars seem tame. There was a frightening maliciousness to Ernestine. When she phoned Gore Vidal, referring to him as "Mr. VEE-dle" and upbraiding him for the rape scene in *Myra Breckinridge,* Tomlin showed the leering voyeur inside the petty bureaucrat—she was turned on by her anger over being titillated. When *Laugh-In* left the air, most of the cast dispersed to game shows and celebrity roasts, but Tomlin kept growing as an artist. Her attention to characterizational detail led to key roles in major movies and a series of Emmy-winning specials. The great strength of Tomlin is that she's less concerned with the punch line than with the comedy of human behavior. Her collection of grotesques are not so much Felliniesque as instantly identifiable—we enter the heads

Lily Tomlin in Rowan & Martin's Laugh-In

of her bag ladies, barflies, and Bible Belt preachers. Her respect for the eccentricities of character makes us see the world from a minority viewpoint; she's the least elitist of all Canny Comediennes. But her latest one-woman show on Broadway, *The Search for Signs of Intelligent Life in the Universe*, began to cement that viewpoint into an elitism of its own—a *Ms.* magazine certitude about the appropriate attitude to take on "life." Though the show wasn't as mawkish as Whoopi Goldberg's, it was a bit too pat and finally exhausting. But like Bette Midler, Tomlin will always have trouble finding her niche. She's a Wily Wit touched by genius.

B arbara Walters

This roving-eyed muse of psychobabble—a.k.a. Ba Ba Wawa—bounced from *Today* to a riveting exercise in showbiz exhibitionism called *The Barbara Walters Specials*. Ever since she drowned in a flood of negative publicity for signing a multi-million-dollar contract with ABC, Walters has sacrificed her journalistic objectivity by identifying with similarly persecuted personalities, from the Shah of Iran to Bernhard Goetz. She prefigured the '80s obsession with wealth and power

(*Lifestyles of the Rich and Famous*) and the rise of the broadcast newsperson as glamorous megastar (Dan Rather). The conjunction of the two—voyeurism and egomania—has created an indispensable form of celebrity interrogation. At the very least Walters has gained the kind of access Dorothy Kilgallen would have killed for. Who else but Barbara could shmooze with the Reagans in prime time and then amend their observations of Lady Di ("even prettier in person")? Whether taking us on a tour of Barbra Streisand's bedroom or eliciting a terrifying childhood memory from Richard Pryor, Walters accents the horror of international fame by exceeding the smarminess of her most shameless guests.

20

CLASS CLOWN

Lucille Ball

Late in 1985 Lucille Ball glided into a roomful of reporters at the Four Seasons to promote *Stone Pillow,* her TV movie about a Manhattan bag lady. Flanked by hubby Gary Morton and director George Schaefer, Lucy was decked out in a black velvet suit, a white ruffled blouse, and a comically oversized pair of diamond cluster rings. Witnessing this spectacle, an eager-beaver reporter suggested that Lucy would be the last citizen of Beverly Hills to understand the plight of the homeless. But at this point in her career, Lucy could play Mother Teresa and make it a reflection of her own life.

Stone Pillow is totally expressive of its TV diva—it's *The Lucille Ball Story* in bag-lady drag. Every line, every inflection, every plot twist mirrors a woman who's been pounding showbiz pavements for more than half a century with a Philip Morris in one hand and a margarita in the other.

Lucy plays a character Schaefer described as "independent, selfish, eccentric, gabby, and cocky." Her husband and son left her years before. She takes under her wing a young, black-haired woman whom she mistakes for a runaway, endlessly barking advice: "You gotta know how to protect yourself. First of all, you gotta make 'em think you're *crazy!* And you gotta kick 'em anywhere, everywhere! And you gotta bite 'em, scratch their eyes out! Remember, you're fightin' for your life!"

For twenty-five years—from the days of Prohibition to the dawn of McCarthyism—Lucille Ball fought for her life. She struggled as a model, a salesgirl, and a waitress; as a bit player, a Goldwyn Girl, and a "Technicolor Tessie"; as a straight man, a radio clown, and an unlucky leading lady. By the time *I Love Lucy* hit the air in 1951, she was forty years old, had appeared in nearly seventy films, and had been married to Desi Arnaz for a decade. She had matched Ginger Rogers and Eve Arden in *Stage Door,* upstaged Spencer Tracy and Katharine Hepburn in *Without Love,* and exhibited great gifts in Dorothy Arzner's *Dance, Girl, Dance.* But none of that gave Lucy what she wanted. She was not a star.

On TV she got what she could never get in movies—control. Lucy and Desi called the shots

Lucille Ball

with a business savvy that's become part of the Desilu legend: how she insisted Desi star with her; how he pioneered shooting for TV on film with three cameras, thereby insuring the preservation of the show; how both retained all rights to the show in exchange for a tiny pay cut. In a few years Desilu was a giant, owning even the RKO lot where Lucy and Desi were once contract players. After their divorce in 1960, Desi sold his share to Lucy, who sold it all to Gulf + Western.

Brilliantly unbridled as she was in her prime, by the time of *Here's Lucy* (1968–74) she was a too-thin baritone squeezed into form-fitting suits with alarmingly high collars. Heavily made-up and teased to the max, Lucy had become a mesmerizing parody of herself, reworking old plots without a change in attitude and continually being referred to as "girl." In one late episode—a horrifying excursion into surrealism—Lucy plays herself as a dignified TV personality in a black fright wig and gold brocade muumuu. She holds a Lucille Ball lookalike contest, which the red-headed Lucy and her daughter, Lucie, enter. Dressed in matching wigs and muumuus, mother and daughter compete on TV. Mommie wins.

During the filming of *Stone Pillow* near Grand Central Terminal, I was dining at the Oyster Bar. Halfway through the red snapper, I dropped my fork: Lucy, in full bag-lady drag, traipsed by with an entourage of five. Plopping down at a table, she ordered a margarita. A waiter, a waitress, a maitre d', and two busboys scurried in all directions. Lucy sent back her drink—once, twice, three times. "She's crazy!" cried one worker, racing past my table in a sweat. When I asked if I should go over and tell Lucy how much I love her, another worker gasped, "I wouldn't if I were you."

At the *Pillow* press conference Lucy was on her best behavior—she is, after all, seventy-five. Smoking nonfiltered Philip Morris (an early sponsor) and fielding some inexplicably hostile questions, she wavered between riotous wit (her imitation of Katharine Hepburn is a scream) and moody confusion. Several times she asked Morton, her husband of twenty-five years and apparent protector in all matters, to help her respond to particularly perplexing questions. But when asked if she saw any parallels between the character's life in *Stone Pillow* and her own, Lucy delivered a beautifully timed double take that brought down the house. "No!" she shrieked. But Schaefer chose to contradict his star, insisting on how she'd kept detailed notes on her character and understood this woman better than anyone could.

Lucille Ball is not so much at the end of the line as in a catch-22: she can't exactly do her style of comedy anymore and can't really do drama (she was "scared to death" of *Pillow*). What she can do—and what she does to riveting effect in this film—is tell us all about the legend of Lucy. It's a legend built on very little—perhaps four years out of sixty—but it dwarfs any other to come out of TV. As she got up from her chair at the Four Seasons, the Legend still seemed capable of collaring a waiter and intoning a speech from *Pillow*: "I'm not crazy. I'm smart. I'm still here. And I know how to protect myself."